Library of
Davidson College

ARMS and INDEPENDENCE
The Military Character of the American Revolution

UNITED STATES CAPITOL HISTORICAL SOCIETY
Fred Schwengel, President

PERSPECTIVES ON THE AMERICAN REVOLUTION
Ronald Hoffman and Peter J. Albert, Editors

Diplomacy and Revolution: The Franco-American Alliance of 1778

Sovereign States in an Age of Uncertainty

Slavery and Freedom in the Age of the American Revolution

Arms and Independence: The Military Character of the American Revolutio

Arms and Independence

The Military Character of the American Revolution

Edited by RONALD HOFFMAN
and PETER J. ALBERT

Published for the
UNITED STATES CAPITOL HISTORICAL SOCIETY
BY THE UNIVERSITY PRESS OF VIRGINIA
Charlottesville

THE UNIVERSITY PRESS OF VIRGINIA
Copyright © 1984 by the Rector and Visitors
of the University of Virginia

First Published 1984

Library of Congress Cataloging in Publication Data
Main entry under title:

Arms and independence.

(Perspectives on the American Revolution)
Includes index.
1. United States—History—Revolution, 1775–1783—Influence—Addresses, essays, lectures. 2. United States—History—Revolution, 1775–1783—Campaigns—Addresses, essays, lectures. 3. United States—History—Revolution, 1775–1783—Social aspects—Addresses, essays, lectures. 4. United States—Armed Forces—History—Revolution, 1775–1783—Addresses, essays, lectures. 5. United States—History, Military—To 1900—Addresses, essays, lectures. I. Hoffman, Ronald, 1941–   . II. Albert, Peter J. III. United States Capitol Historical Society. IV. Series.
E209.A75 1984   973.3′4   83-14599
ISBN 0-8139-1007-2

Printed in the United States of America

Contents

Preface   vii

DON HIGGINBOTHAM   1
Reflections on the War of Independence, Modern Guerrilla Warfare, and the War in Vietnam

CHARLES ROYSTER   25
Founding a Nation in Blood: Military Conflict and American Nationality

ROBERT K. WRIGHT, JR.   50
"Nor Is Their Standing Army to Be Despised": The Emergence of the Continental Army as a Military Institution

STEVEN ROSSWURM   75
The Philadelphia Militia, 1775–1783: Active Duty and Active Radicalism

JAMES KIRBY MARTIN   119
A "Most Undisciplined, Profligate Crew": Protest and Defiance in the Continental Ranks, 1776–1783

RICHARD BUEL, JR.   141
Samson Shorn: The Impact of the Revolutionary War on Estimates of the Republic's Strength

IRA D. GRUBER   166
George III Chooses a Commander in Chief

PIERS MACKESY   191
What the British Army Learned

CONTENTS

THEODORE ROPP   216
The General Military Significance of the American Revolution

Contributors   233

Index   237

Preface

THERE IS A PECULIAR IRONY in studying the military character of the American Revolution. The subject itself constitutes one of the most celebrated and patriotic myths in our history. The martial spirit of 1776 and the heroic suffering exemplified by Valley Forge are perennially advanced by spokesmen of various political persuasions as indisputable reminders of the need for courage and sacrifice in behalf of an ideal. Contemporary calls for a renewal of our national spirit through a rededication to the values and commitments of the Founding Fathers are but the latest rhetorical flourish in a tradition that stretches back to the age of Jackson and before. The myth invoked in such remarks is clear: united in the quest of an ideological ideal, a young nation managed—despite enormous adversity—to defeat a tyrannical power and create a model republic fashioned on the principles of freedom and equality. Thus, the generation of Washington, Adams, and Jefferson demonstrated that men of honor, tenacity, and virtue can triumph, no matter how severe the challenge, if they remain steadfast in the face of deprivation and hardship.

As with all stereotypes, there is an undeniable element of truth in this description, but there is also substantial misrepresentation and wishful thinking. As the study of the military experience of the years 1775–83 makes abundantly clear, the valor and courage of the Revolution coexisted with other less laudable realities—dissension, chaos, mutiny, murder, insurrection, anarchy, and violence. The recognition of these equally characteristic dimensions of America's Revolution has compelled historians to reevaluate that society's commitment to the war and the cause it embodied and, from that perspective, to reexamine the traditional assumptions about the nature of the War for Independence. The resulting scholarship has both clarified and enlarged our understanding of the American Revolution because it has forced attention to the

PREFACE

most basic of questions—who was going to fight the war and for what? Although the query is a patently obvious one, the research undertaken to answer it has exposed the popular mythology of the Revolution by confronting us with evidence of an ambivalent citizenry and a people of divided and shifting loyalties. Similarly, the manuscript sources present us with a reluctant soldiery often more reliably motivated by the payment of bonuses or the sanction of punishment than by libertarian rhetoric.

Parenthetically, the examination of the military experience also reveals the enormity of the task faced by the Revolutionary elites as they sought to defeat a formidable adversary while simultaneously struggling to create a viable nation amidst an angry and often violently disaffected people. Although an explicit focus on elites is not considered as fashionable by the newer social historians as an approach that directs attention to the common people, emphasis on the leadership provides another important corrective to the myth of the American Revolution. At issue here is a matter of perceptions. The generals knew one war while the political leaders, ensconced in the relative safety of Philadelphia, New York, and the state capitals, knew another. To be sure, they all shared a similar framework of concern, uncertainty, and fear, but, unlike the Continental army's commanders, few political leaders were forced to deal directly with the very real possibility that the Revolution might collapse into an orgy of bloodshed and indiscriminate violence. Conversely, few citizens experienced the full impact of a divided people engaged in a brutal war as immediately as did the poorly maintained and ill-clad troops—those whom Nathanael Greene called "my ragged and starving continentals."

Don Higginbotham opens the volume with a study of parallels between the American Revolution and twentieth-century wars of national liberation, particularly the Vietnam War. He underscores the fact that while both the British and Americans had considerable experience in irregular warfare during the eighteenth century, they preferred to use more orthodox tactics during the Revolution, the British primarily because of their military traditions, and the Americans be-

Preface

cause of their close ties with the mother country and their desire to avoid the localism that a guerrilla war would entail. Moreover, the general moderation of British actions and the relative weakness of the British army tended to discourage the evolution of the conflict into a guerrilla war. Nevertheless, there were irregular aspects to the war, engendered by the factors of space and numbers—that is, small armies operating in a vast territory increasingly led to civilian participation in military activities. Higginbotham concludes his essay with an examination of the war in the South, a principal theater of irregular warfare during the Revolution.

In the following essay Charles Royster examines an aspect of the mythologizing of the Revolution—the exploitation of the shared violence of the conflict to create an important bond of American nationhood. In this sense, he argues, the nation was founded not only on the rational basis of commonly held political principles but also on the passions of bloodshed, and he traces the utilization of this image—the communal experience of violence—from the Revolutionary era through the War of 1812.

The next three essays in the volume study aspects of the military man in the Revolution, from the creation and development of a fighting force to its growing radicalization. Robert K. Wright, Jr., explores the development of the Continental army as a blending of the colonial military heritage with European military theory and practice. Americans entered the Revolution with the belief that the militia was the short-term military institution appropriate to a republic, to be supplemented by provincial units of semiregulars organized on the colonial model that could fight for a longer period. The 1776 campaign, however, led to the perception of a need for a large, regular army, and gave rise to changes in the army's organization and the development of new types of units, such as engineers, surveyors, and a partisan corps. Further reorganizations followed in 1778 and 1780. European influences made themselves felt both through military texts that circulated in America and through European advisors who served in the Continental army.

Then, in an essay that integrates military with social history, Steven Rosswurm studies the Philadelphia militia, which

PREFACE

was composed to an important degree of men from Philadelphia's "lower sort." The radicalization of the Philadelphia militia began in 1775 as it and the "resistance movement" in general came into conflict with the Pennsylvania assembly and the moderates; in 1776, led by the Committee of Privates—a group composed of representatives from each militia company—the Philadelphia militia played an important role in the overthrow of the proprietary government and the establishment of Pennsylvania's democratic constitution. The militia's active duty experience in 1776–77 intensified its sense of its own identity and its feeling of being exploited, perceptions that led, in part, to the events of 1779. In that year, the "high point of popular insurgency" in Philadelphia, the city's militia played a major role in the popular movement's attempt to punish tories, lower prices, and defend the state's constitution. The "Fort Wilson Riot" of October 4, 1779, however, was a defeat for the militia and the popular movement and had the long-term effect of splitting the radicals and demoralizing the city's lower classes. As a result, the militia responded poorly to the war's final call-up and offered no effective resistance to Robert Morris's political-economic program.

Finally, James Kirby Martin examines patterns of protest and defiance among Continental soldiers during the Revolution. After 1775, he maintains, the Continental army evolved from a militialike force composed of short-term enlistees, often men of some property, into a long-term, disciplined force of regulars. Drawn increasingly from the poorer and more repressed elements in American society, this new breed of fighting man hoped for upward mobility through military service. At the same time this change was occurring, the institutions of civil government were failing more and more frequently to honor their promises of bounties for enlistment and such other incentives as food and the like. As the war continued, the soldiers developed a unit cohesion that dramatically altered the ways in which they protested their treatment. Instead of relying on purely individual expressions of dissatisfaction—swearing, drinking, assaulting officers, deserting, and bounty jumping—the men shifted to the

Preface

collective, controlled action exemplified by the mutinies of the Pennsylvania and New Jersey lines in 1781.

In the following essay Richard Buel, Jr., argues that the Revolution revealed "a far more complex range of American vulnerabilities than historians have generally acknowledged." He examines two of these—one military, the other economic—and demonstrates how the war led to a revision of unrealistic American assumptions about their capabilities—assumptions that had been based in part on the belief that the republican nature of their society would give them a distinct advantage over Great Britain. Militarily, the American conviction that free citizens with a stake in their society (the militia) would have more incentive to fight than soldiers procured with money or compulsion (British regulars) gave way before the growing perception of a need for a permanent, professional army. Similarly, the war exposed a critical weakness in the American economy as the disruption of the colonial pattern of exchange led to a shortage of imported goods—commodities that were critical to the creation of domestically produced surpluses.

The next two essays examine aspects of the American War from a British perspective. Ira D. Gruber evaluates George III's decisions in 1775 to retain Gage as commander in chief in North America and to appoint Howe, Clinton, and Burgoyne to assist that officer in maintaining royal authority. The king had initially preferred to replace Gage with Amherst, but when the latter declined, he decided to keep Gage and "send the best Generals that can be thought of to his assistance." Soon after, he selected Howe, Clinton, and Burgoyne. Gruber demonstrates the soundness of these decisions by reviewing in detail the qualifications of the other officers who were available for service. Piers Mackesy explores the question, What military lessons did the British army learn from the American Revolution? He concludes that the war's greatest significance to the British army lay in the opportunities it presented for large units to function together (Great Britain lacked training areas that could accommodate sizable groups), the experience it provided the army in *la petite guerre*—"the war of posts and ambushes," the enthusiasm for the use of

PREFACE

light infantry it generated among officers who served in America, and the parallels it provided with the military problem in Ireland. By contrast, he argues that most of the lessons the Revolution offered in strategy, tactics, and logistics were of little use to the British army in the wars of the Napoleonic era.

Theodore Ropp concludes the volume with an analysis of both the long-term military significance of the American Revolution—its "lessons," he argues, were primarily colonial and naval—and the factors that have prevented scholars from perceiving the war's significance. Among these factors, he maintains, are the mythologizing of the Revolution, over-narrow concepts of military significance, and the fact that the war has been considered marginal to "mainstream" (that is, western European) military thought except in the two decades after 1775 and again in the years after 1960.

DON HIGGINBOTHAM

Reflections on the War of Independence, Modern Guerrilla Warfare, and the War in Vietnam

IT IS ALWAYS tempting to become preoccupied with parallels between the past and the present, and for historians there is a particular incentive for doing so. If we advance some innovative and provocative ideas, there is scarcely a quicker way for us to inflate our scholarly reputations. After all, it may take years to prove that our originality was actually eccentricity, to take what we heralded as seminal and consign it to the junk heap of historical ideas. We are sometimes reluctant to acknowledge the complexity of history to the extent that Carl Becker did in a question he put to his seminars at Cornell: "Should we finally insist that while the world may change, it changes slowly—or that while the world may change slowly, it does change?"

The immediacy of any momentous occurrence seems to generate historical parallels that literally leap out at us. In the aftermath of World War II, for example, the Munich syndrome instilled in us a fear of repeating the appeasement of the 1930s and led us in the direction of becoming the world's policeman. Recent decades have witnessed new efforts to examine the American Revolution in the framework of comparative history. Its nonmilitary aspects have long been the subject of historical comparisons that were often made to enhance the reputation of this nation and to show how other revolutionary movements were either good or bad depending upon whether they followed the Spirit of '76. But it is only in the last quarter century or so that there have been major efforts to measure our Revolution's military aspects against the warfare conducted by insurrectionists elsewhere. Such undertakings invariably lead to an examination of guerrilla fighting, with comparisons between our War of Independence and the wars of national liberation in our own era, especially with our own involvement in the Vietnam War.

These concerns with irregular conflict are no more surprising than our earlier preoccupation with Munich and appeasement. Several years ago when I was a visiting professor at the United States Military Academy at West Point, I found that the most popular elective taught by the history department was devoted to revolutionary guerrilla warfare. But initial forays into comparative history—be it Munich or the War of Independence—usually result in overkill, in exaggerating the similarities. For example, some historians and journalists found the origins of modern guerrilla strife in the American wilderness, in the combat methods of the English colonists, whose militia was their primary organization for defense and whose early military experiences supposedly determined the nature of our Revolutionary War. By their employment of skirmishers and small units, by their hit-and-run tactics, ambuscades, and the like, the Americans are said to have displayed New World methods entirely foreign to those practiced in Europe at the time.

There is assuredly grist for this interpretive mill in the events of April 19, 1775, which generated a bushwhacking battle if there ever was one. But within a few days the rebels turned to a form of orthodox warfare when they laid siege to Boston, highlighted by Henry Knox's dramatic arrival over snow-covered trails with cannon from Fort Ticonderoga. And in a real sense the war in America ended with another siege—at Yorktown in 1781.

I confess that in the 1960s I overstated the case for the uniqueness of early American warfare. I was influenced not only by the Vietnam War but also by having written a biography of Gen. Daniel Morgan, a frontiersman and Indian fighter.[1] We have now put some distance between us and the first wars of national liberation in the Third World. Moreover, the passionate divisions that ravaged this country in the sixties are behind us, and historians are now taking over from the generals, politicians, and journalists in analyzing for us what our Vietnam years were all about. Perhaps we are also better equipped at this juncture to reassess our own experiences with guerrilla warfare more than two centuries ago and to reevaluate comparisons between insurgency in the eighteenth and twentieth centuries.

When we place the fighting forces of America and Britain in their proper eighteenth-century historical environment, we find that both sides had considerable experience with guerrilla warfare. European military men had used such words as *guerrilla, irregular,* and *partisan* to describe fighting carried out by small units, usually composed of nonprofessional soldiers who devised their own combat techniques. They are found, for example, in accounts of the 1740s struggle between Austria and Prussia over Silesia. Austria's Empress Maria Theresa acquired aid from Balkan nobles who had long recruited hardy Slavic mountaineers to repel the Turks and their Asiatic auxiliaries, contests marked by their savagery and brutality. In the service of Austria these Balkan irregulars so bedeviled and bloodied the invading Prussians that they earned from them the epithets *banditti, barbarians,* and *savages.* Later, when Maria's struggle widened into the War of the Austrian Succession, involving much of Europe, both British and French commanders in the Low Countries encouraged irregular forces to attack enemy outposts and to ambush columns and patrols. The decade of the 1740s also witnessed the Scottish rebellion of '45 in which the forces of both the British and the Pretender, Prince Charles, resorted

---

[1] Don Higginbotham, *Daniel Morgan: Revolutionary Rifleman* (Chapel Hill, N.C., 1961) and "Daniel Morgan: Guerrilla Fighter," in George A. Billias, ed., *George Washington's Generals* (New York, 1964), pp. 291–316. More recently I have examined some of the problems in making historical comparisons. See "The Uses and Abuses of Comparative History," *Latin American Research Review* 13 (1978):238–45.

to native auxiliaries who maneuvered on the fringes of the opposing armies, disrupting communications and picking off stragglers and small parties.

Although we may conclude that British and American experiences in irregular war reveal similarities, they were largely unrelated before the mid-eighteenth century, with the former derived from Europe and the latter from the colonial wilderness. A mating of these two irregular military traditions occurred in the 1750s when for the first time Britain dispatched thousands of regulars to the thirteen colonies for the North American phase of the Seven Years' War. In that final, climactic imperial confrontation, British commanders in the provinces, even Braddock of Monongahela infamy, experimented with operational methods tailored to the peculiar problems of campaigning in the American forests; Generals Wolfe, Forbes, and Amherst were particularly successful in these endeavors. In doing so, they drew upon their European service in the 1740s, their reading of military treatises on the little wars by Humphrey Bland, the comte de Saxe, and others, and their exposure to Col. Robert Rogers and other veteran colonial Indian fighters.[2]

From all that has been said thus far, one could conclude that the American War of Independence might well have been a guerrilla confrontation. The rugged nature of the countryside obviously presented innumerable hazards to formal campaigning, making for stubborn defenses and snail-like advances. A century and a half of encounters with French and Indian adversaries had taught the Americans the tactics

---

[2] The previous two paragraphs are based in part on Peter E. Russell, "Redcoats in the Wilderness: British Officers and Irregular Warfare in Europe and America, 1740 to 1760," *William and Mary Quarterly*, 3d ser. 35 (1978):629–52. Early American warfare is most accurately placed within the context of military developments in the western world in two essays by Peter Paret: "Colonial Experience and European Military Reform at the End of the Eighteenth Century," *Bulletin of the Institute of Historical Research* 37 (1964):49–56, and "The Relationship between the Revolutionary War and European Military Thought and Practice in the Second Half of the Eighteenth Century," in Don Higginbotham, ed., *Reconsiderations on the Revolutionary War: Selected Essays* (Westport, Conn., 1978), pp. 144–57.

of the "bush."³ And the British were hardly without experience in combatting partisan activities and had at times actually turned to them offensively, in both the Old World and the New.

Nevertheless, both sides preferred orthodox warfare, with guerrillas seen only as auxiliaries, supplementing but not replacing standard armies. Why this was so for Britain is fairly obvious. Though we have alluded to alterations in European military thought and practice, they were occurring at a slow pace. Here the conservative part of Carl Becker's question is applicable: "While the world may change, it changes slowly." Even the French and Indian War, especially the last campaigns, was "a European conflict in a New World setting," declares Lawrence H. Gipson, who goes on to describe the British use of siege operations and linear formations in reducing Louisbourg, Quebec, and other French citadels.⁴ And, indeed, the time-honored canons of military science prevailed in European armies until the Napoleonic era, when units proficient in raids and patrols gradually fused with the heavy infantry of the line. Thereafter, beginning with the French and Prussian armies, the same men were trained to engage in line fire, form assault columns, and skirmish.

The brutality and savagery that inevitably would have been a major part of a guerrilla war of independence had no appeal for the Americans in 1775. Already before Lexington and Concord Americans were accustomed to the use of restraint in opposing the mother country. They displayed it in resisting British taxation and imperial reorganization from 1765 to 1775, from the Stamp Act to the Coercive Acts. This subject is fully described in Pauline Maier's *From Resistance to*

---

³For frontier forms of warfare, see—among the most recent literature—John K. Mahon, "Anglo-American Methods of Indian Warfare, 1676–1794," *Mississippi Valley Historical Review* 45 (1958):254–75; Daniel Boorstin, *The Americans: The Colonial Experience* (New York, 1958), pp. 345–72; John E. Ferling, *A Wilderness of Miseries: War and Warriors in Early America* (Westport, Conn., 1980).

⁴*The British Empire before the American Revolution*, 15 vols. (Caldwell, Idaho, and New York, 1936–70), 7:x.

Revolution. "Colonial leaders," she writes, "quickly learned that unrestrained popular violence was counter-productive. They organized resistance in part to contain disorder." When violence and physical intimidation occurred, they were usually confined to specific targets and achieved without bloodshed.[5]

Compared to contemporary revolutionary preconditions, it may seem amazing that no stamp collector or customs official was assassinated, no redcoat sentry picked off by a sniper, no wealthy ministerial sympathizer kidnapped. The commonly given explanation for this restraint is that it was typical of the eighteenth century in America and Europe. On both continents political murders were almost unknown, and political mobs were usually intent only on the redress of specific grievances, not mindless destruction or bloodshed. The Age of Reason—or so the argument runs—so notably short on fanaticism, collapsed in the hysteria and passion unleashed by the French Revolution.[6]

In any case, Maier is correct when she states that "the need to reconcile the impulse toward resistance with the injunc-

---

[5] *From Resistance to Revolution: Colonial Radicals and the Development of American Opposition to Britain, 1765–1776* (New York, 1972), p. xv.

[6] American studies of crowd or mob behavior owe much to the work of George Rudé and other European historians. Only a sampling of the American literature on the subject can be mentioned here. Gordon S. Wood, "A Note on Mobs in the American Revolution," *William and Mary Quarterly*, 3d ser. 23 (1966):635–42; Jesse Lemisch, "Jack Tar in the Streets: Merchant Seamen in the Politics of Revolutionary America," ibid. 25 (1968):371–407; Pauline Maier, "Popular Uprisings and Civil Authority in Eighteenth-Century America," ibid. 27 (1970):3–35; John P. Reid, *In a Defiant Stance: The Conditions of Law in Massachusetts Bay, the Irish Comparison, and the Coming of the American Revolution* (University Park, Pa., 1977). A most thoughtful conceptual statement is from the distinguished British scholar E. P. Thompson, "The Moral Economy of the Crowd in the Eighteenth Century," *Past and Present* 50 (1971):76–136. I am indebted to Franklin L. Ford for a copy of his highly suggestive essay "Assassination in the Eighteenth Century: The Dog That Did Not Bark in the Night," which appeared in the *Harvard Magazine* 78 (1976):50–53. Such restraint, of course, had not been true of the sixteenth and seventeenth centuries, which were characterized by a general atmosphere of cruelty, even barbarism. The point is well stated in André Corvisier, *Armies and Societies in Europe, 1494–1789*, trans. Abigail T. Siddall (Bloomington, Ind., 1979), ch. 1.

tion to restraint became, in fact, one of the central intellectual and practical problems of the American revolutionary movement."[7] Organized resistance carried out with restraint continued to be a goal of the Revolutionists after the outbreak of hostilities, one that could be accomplished best by a central army under the control of the Continental Congress.

What other factors lay behind this restraint, enabling the colonists to turn from the skirmishing, partisan kind of warfare that they knew best? First, there were other military responses available to them. Their options were increasingly more varied than they could have been a hundred or even fifty years before. The explanation is that theirs was a society rapidly growing in maturity, sophistication, and material affluence. Historians have informed us that the middle years of the eighteenth century were a time in which provincial culture was becoming more like that of the mother country.[8] If we keep in mind this rapid and pervasive Anglicization and with it the rejection of customary patterns that had denoted life in the opening period of settlement, then we can appreciate one of the sharpest differences between the American War of Independence and the wars of national liberation in our own era. None of these post-1945 conflicts has involved colonies as intimately linked to the imperial nation

---

[7] *From Resistance to Revolution*, pp. 53, 61.

[8] For studies dealing directly or indirectly with the Anglicization of colonial life and culture, see John M. Murrin, "The Legal Transformation: The Bench and Bar of Eighteenth-Century Massachusetts," in Stanley N. Katz, ed., *Colonial America: Essays in Politics and Social Development* (Boston, 1971), pp. 415–49; Jack P. Greene, "Search for Identity: An Interpretation of the Meaning of Selected Patterns of Social Response in Eighteenth-Century America," *Journal of Social History* 3 (1970):180–220; idem, "An Uneasy Connection: An Analysis of the Preconditions of the American Revolution," in Stephen G. Kurtz and James H. Hutson, eds., *Essays on the American Revolution* (Chapel Hill, N.C., 1973), pp. 32–80; Rowland Bertoff and John M. Murrin, "Feudalism, Communalism, and the Yeoman Freeholder: The American Revolution Considered as a Social Accident," ibid., pp. 256–88; Robert M. Weir, "Who Shall Rule at Home: The American Revolution as a Crisis of Legitimacy for the Colonial Elite," *Journal of Interdisciplinary History* 6 (1976):679–700.

by culture, language, and direct descent as were the thirteen British provinces.[9]

It was because of the very closeness of those ties that the Americans were reluctant revolutionaries, still deeply appreciative of their British heritage—a people driven to rebellion against their wishes, as Jefferson explained in the Declaration of Independence. Jefferson himself was quite content to kill the king symbolically in 1776. Had the Revolutionists been able to put their hands on the royal Hanoverian they probably would not have known what to do with him, although we can be confident his would not have been the fate of Charles I or Louis XVI.

Consequently, it is impossible to imagine the Americans as terrorists in the modern sense, for terrorists hate their opponents and all they stand for. Terrorism spawns guerrilla warfare, which in turn produces more terrorism; terrorism rips apart the vitals of the community. If in 1776 Americans turned to independence, they did not wish to risk the destruction of their social and institutional fabric in winning it. With our perspective after two centuries, having viewed countless liberation struggles, we can see that "have-not" societies are more prone to chance all-out pervasive conflicts than "have" societies. And surely the American people in the Revolutionary era had one of the highest standards of living of any society in the world.

From all this we can conclude that the Americans opted for conventional military responses in the Revolution because of their British background and because of the nature of their society. Once hostilities erupted and independence became the final goal, there was still another reason. A martial approach that stressed guerrilla methods would inevitably tilt the Revolution in the wrong direction—toward localism and provincialism, with each colony-state devising

---

[9] Thoughtful comparisons—though at times exaggerated—between the American Revolution and the revolutions in the Third World are found in Richard B. Morris, *The Emerging Nations and the American Revolution* (New York, 1970); Thomas C. Barrow, "The American Revolution as a Colonial War of Independence," *William and Mary Quarterly*, 3d ser. 25 (1968):452–64.

its own ways of striking at the enemy. Thus, among other things, Washington's army—appropriately called the Continental army—was a nationalizing factor in American life.

For the most part that army functioned in a traditional manner, not too differently from its British counterpart. Its commander in chief, George Washington, had long admired British regimentals; as a young militia officer he had pulled out all the stops in his failing effort to obtain a royal commission. American generals Gates, Lee, Montgomery, and St. Clair were former redcoat officers. The British articles of war served as a partial model for the military code that Congress drafted for the Continental army. Respect for European military conventions is also reflected in the recruitment of foreign officers for the American service. The American artillery corps, itself a sign of military legitimacy, "formed in parade, in the foreign manner," reported the marquis de Chastellux, who further stated that "each brigade" of the Pennsylvania Line "had a band of music." Thus a sympathetic William Pitt, earl of Chatham, could assure the House of Lords in 1777 that the rebel soldiers were not "wild and lawless benditti."[10]

Yet things might have turned out quite differently, with terrorism and eventually the wholesale guerrilla warfare that the American leadership clearly did not want. We need to pause before we give all the credit to our forefathers for their good judgment and their ability to see the conflict in its relation to the totality of American life and the forthcoming years of peace and nationhood.

There has been enough violence in our history to demonstrate that we Americans are not immune from destructive behavior. In the last decade some researchers have laid great stress upon this turbulent past, not only in the colonial period but in the Revolution as well.[11] While they have likely

[10] *Travels in North America, in the Years 1780, 1781, and 1782*, ed. Howard C. Rice, Jr., 2 vols. (Chapel Hill, N.C., 1963), 1:107; [John Almon] *Anecdotes of the Life of William Pitt, Earl of Chatham . . .*, 3 vols. (London, 1797), 3:351.

[11] The articles, monographs, and edited volumes of Richard M. Brown, the most prolific author on the subject of American violence, are the best starting point. See especially his "Violence and the American Revolution," in Kurtz and Hutson, eds., *Essays on the American Revolution*, pp. 81–120,

exaggerated this aspect of the American record—for the Revolutionary era at any rate—it can hardly be ignored; and it indicates that a struggle of sizable guerrilla dimensions was not an impossibility.

Let us speculate on how such a conflict might have come about by playing a little counterfactual history. Assume that the Stamp Act rioters had been imprisoned; that Patrick Henry, Samuel Adams, and his cousin John had been convicted of treason in England under that infamous statute from the reign of Henry VIII; that British troops had been quartered in homes in major provincial cities, where magistrates displayed no hesitancy to call them out to crush civil disorders. Assume, moreover, that the Stamp and Townshend acts had not been repealed but were vigorously enforced with the assistance of General Gage's scarlet regiments.

The point of the counterfactual scenario is to suggest that had Britain pursued a really vigorous program of imperial reordering, the restraint that Maier sees as so deeply rooted in the Anglo-American past might have melted in the heat of colonial anger. Just as it would doubtless have triggered violent reactions from solid whigs up and down the Atlantic seaboard, so it would have increased the likelihood of a war of national liberation as brutal as those in our time in Algeria, Angola, and elsewhere.

Fortunately, this version of history did not occur in America, but something like it or worse did happen in British-ruled Ireland in the eighteenth and nineteenth centuries: trials for sedition and treason, houses broken into in the dead of night, secret arrests and internments without trial, and tenants ruthlessly evicted from ancestral lands. To be sure, Ireland and America were not the same. The British had long exploited nearby Ireland, whose people embraced the despised Catholic faith and who had fewer political and constitutional rights than the inhabitants of Massachusetts or Virginia.

"Historical Patterns of Violence in America," in Hugh D. Graham and Ted R. Gurr, eds., *The History of Violence in America* (New York, 1969), pp. 45–83, "The American Vigilante Tradition," ibid., pp. 154–226, "Legal and Behavioral Perspectives on American Vigilantism," *Perspectives in American History* 5 (1971):93–144, *Strain of Violence* (New York, 1975), and idem, ed., *American Violence* (Englewood Cliffs, N.J., 1970).

As John P. Reid has said, the Irish were more violent because they had more to be violent about. Violence begot violence; the Irish fought fire with fire. In contrast, Americans, never treated so harshly, had primarily constitutional complaints that they replied to with legal arguments in their speeches, pamphlets, and petitions. Had their grievances been social—as Hannah Arendt reminds us—intolerable tensions would have generated virulent animosities followed by atrocities.[12]

One reason, though not necessarily the only one, that explains the absence of British suppression and American vengeance is obvious. Britain's physical hold on America was weak, and not only because America was separated from the mother country by a greater distance than the Irish Sea. Through their legal and political institutions, their courts at all levels and their representative assemblies, the colonists were able to do a great deal to cripple the London government's ambitious schemes for more effective management of the empire. So while Maier is correct about the colonial chieftains' consciously rejecting a campaign of violence, the strength of their own structures and the weakness of British administrative and military institutions also cast light on why between 1765 and 1775 there failed to emerge conditions making for a war of savage retaliation after Lexington and Concord.[13]

One can point to yet another way in which the War of Independence might have taken a more destructive turn. For-

---

[12] *In a Defiant Stance*, especially ch. 13; Hannah Arendt, *On Revolution* (New York, 1965), ch. 2. Arendt writes: "The whole record of past revolutions demonstrates beyond doubt that every attempt to solve the social question with political means leads into terror, and that it is terror which sends revolutions to their doom" (p. 108).

[13] Reid, *In a Defiant Stance*, stresses particularly the legal and judicial restraints upon British efforts to bring America to heel. Reid's study, as well as R. B. McDowell's *Ireland in the Age of Imperialism and Revolution, 1760–1801* (New York, 1979), contains valuable comparative information on America and Ireland. Reid has also written a more recent study emphasizing Britain's inability to use military force before Lexington and Concord. See his *In Defiance of the Law: The Standing-Army Controversy, the Two Constitutions, and the Coming of the American Revolution* (Chapel Hill, N.C., 1981).

ARMS AND INDEPENDENCE

tunately for the Continental army, it dueled British regulars in the eighteenth century rather than in the nineteenth or twentieth. Had the king's generals possessed massive superiority in firepower and other technological advantages over the rebel forces, Washington could not have opposed them as he did in standard, positional combat. A conflict of small flexible units which were local in their concerns and objectives, which were dedicated to partisan activity and to making the countryside uninhabitable to the enemy, and which resorted to fear and intimidation to hold the civilian population in line—all this might have characterized the American military response had our Revolution erupted in a later day. Instead, our independence struggle took place in a technologically primitive age compared to future wars; and it was also a time when there was little innovation in tactics and strategy. The result was that in these respects eighteenth-century Americans were at no great disadvantage in a land war, or it might be more accurate to say that they could carry on despite their disadvantages and in some instances overcome them.

Certainly the Continental army had enough problems as it was. The army received poor support from its own countrymen. Richard Kohn and Charles Royster have demonstrated how Americans saw their own forces—particularly the officer corps—as a threat to the ideals and goals of the Revolution.[14] The soldiers suffered from shortages of pay, provisions, equipment, and of everything else because of the war's disastrous effect on the domestic economy of the states. Had the British destroyed the Continental army or had it collapsed from internal causes—and the latter may have been a stronger possibility—then irregular military operations would have become the paramount method of continuing the conflict.

What then can we say, given the preferences for regular armies on both sides and given the absence of these counter-

---

[14] Richard H. Kohn, *Eagle and Sword: The Beginnings of the Military Establishment in America* (New York, 1975), pp. 1–16; idem, "American Generals of the Revolution: Subordination and Restraint," in Higginbotham, ed., *Reconsiderations on the Revolutionary War*, pp. 104–23; Charles Royster, *A Revolutionary People at War: The Continental Army and American Character, 1775–1783* (Chapel Hill, N.C., 1979).

factual circumstances, about parallels between the War of Independence and the Vietnam War? Most of those parallels, as Piers Mackesy has stated, are on the British side.[15] Britain in 1775, like America in the early 1960s, suffered from a superpower mentality, from the conviction that she could not lose a war. But eventually Britain, as was true of the United States two centuries afterward, faced the question of whether to risk a full-fledged confrontation with her traditional enemies in order to cut off their assistance to the rebels. It was no inconsequential matter in either century. As for our own time, Geoffrey Fairbairn has remarked that no national liberation movement "in recent years has actually prevailed without large-scale infusions of outside aid and arms."[16] The Johnson administration escalated the Vietnam War, but not to the extent that some of its military critics wished and not to the degree that it brought the direct intervention of the major communist states. Britain, on the other hand, did confront her inveterate adversaries, and the entry of France and Spain profoundly influenced subsequent military operations.

The war for America sparked internal dissension in Britain though not to the degree that our Vietnam involvement bred acrimony at home. But in America much of the widespread opposition was voicing moral objections, whereas in the island kingdom the cleavage was either mainly political or based on the conviction, particularly after Yorktown, that Britain could not win or, at any rate, could not prevail without sacrifices that eighteenth-century European monarchies were unwilling to make. The Johnson government and to some extent the king and the North administration persisted in the face of dissent as long as they did largely because they believed in the domino theory—for Britain this meant the loss of the colonies would lead to secessionist movements in Ireland, the West Indies, and elsewhere; for the Johnson team, "the best and the brightest," it meant the fall to communism, one by one, of most Southeast Asian states.

[15] "The Redcoat Revived," in William M. Fowler, Jr., and Wallace Coyle, eds., *The American Revolution: Changing Perspectives* (Boston, 1979), p. 175.

[16] *Revolutionary Guerrilla Warfare: The Countryside Version* (Baltimore, 1974), p. 19.

ARMS AND INDEPENDENCE

Britain's military venture in America—three thousand miles from her own shores—was logistically arduous almost beyond our comprehension. Perhaps because of modern instantaneous communication and rapid transportation we have overdrawn the similarities between Britain's obstacles in 1776 and America's problems in fighting at an even greater distance in Vietnam. Still, in neither conflict was it an uncomplicated task to engage in combat in a remote part of the globe, each with its own heavy foliage and rugged terrain. Much of the time in both wars the superpowers and their local foes were in a classic standoff, with the foreign army occupying the cities and the insurgents dominating the countryside, with the former using the roads by day and the latter making them unsafe by night. Even before the United States' adventure in Vietnam, Eric Robson, a young British scholar, saw several of these same parallels between France's war for Indochina and Britain's war for America; but Robson was never required reading in the Pentagon or the White House.[17]

So far as comparisons between the forms of insurgency are concerned, between the American rebels and the Vietcong and their allies, one needs to proceed more cautiously. Most important of all, America intruded in a Vietnamese civil war. Of course our War of Independence was in part a civil war, with whigs and tories opposing each other, but it only became an American civil war after fighting broke out between British regulars and American whigs. Only then did the crown's supporters in the colonies have to choose sides. Whatever the follies of George III's ministers in their desire to crack the American rebellion, there was more logic to Britain's effort to retain control of *her* colonies than there was justification for America's intervention in Vietnam.

In national liberation movements of the Third World—certainly in Vietnam but also in Cuba, Algeria, and elsewhere—the principal task of the revolutionary vanguard was to win the allegiance of at least a part of the civilian population and to erect an underground political organization. In America, however, the militia and its parent local govern-

---

[17] *The American Revolution in Its Political and Military Aspects* (1955; reprint ed., New York, 1966), chs. 5–6.

ments, the provincial congresses, provided the rebels with a valuable revolutionary infrastructure from the very outset of hostilities. Even so, the patriot militia was usually ill-disciplined and poorly trained, hardly as tightly controlled and furiously effective as the Vietcong cadres. Moreover, the latter sometimes resorted to sanctuaries and staging areas beyond the borders of South Vietnam, a strategy that was hardly possible or even necessary for the American revolutionary forces. Finally, the Vietcong and their allies deliberately chose to wage what was, in the early years at least, a guerrilla war, and they did so along Marxist-Leninist concepts of revolutionary conflict as interpreted and updated by Gen. Vo Nguyen Giap and the other leaders of North Vietnam. Our Revolution, in contrast, is noted for its political literature, not its military treatises, of which there were few. The one we best remember, Baron von Steuben's *Regulations*, the so-called Blue Book, is scarcely a clarion call for guerrilla activity.[18]

Even so, there was more to the war than military conservatism. It had irregular aspects as well that, for various reasons, could hardly be avoided. In this essay we will discuss only one, but it may well have been the most important: the factor of space and numbers. Peter Paret has reminded us that the wars of mid-eighteenth-century Europe were fought on a small fraction of land compared to the area that was the battleground of the American War of Independence. For instance, the War of the Bavarian Succession of 1778 saw Prussian and Austrian armies, each composed on about 160,000 men, contesting in a region of Bohemia and Moravia that measured about 220 miles by 60 miles. But if the space was limited, the armies were huge.[19]

In America the theater of action was vast, and the armies were tiny compared to those of the Prussians and Austrians. Howe's British army at New York in 1776 numbered 34,000, several times bigger than Burgoyne's army that descended

---

[18] *A Revolutionary People*, ch. 5; Alvin R. Sunseri, "Frederick Wilhelm von Steuben and the Re-education of the American Army: A Lesson in Practicality," Armor 74 (1965):40–47.

[19] "The Relationship between the Revolutionary War and European Military Thought," pp. 154–55.

from Canada in 1777, and twice the size of Clinton's army at Charleston in 1780. As for the American armies, they were usually numerically inferior to their opponents. Americans seemed more independent-minded than they were independence-minded; they looked askance at the discipline and regimentation of formal military life, although it is doubtful that Washington could have accommodated hordes of Continental regulars. Americans had not developed an adequate system of marketing and distribution to provision and equip massive forces.

A war of large space and small numbers meant the armies on both sides needed help. The likelihood of civilian assistance appeared promising in a country teeming with people who owned firearms. It was the Revolutionists, not the British, who first turned to the citizenry for military support. Thousands of militiamen served in the war, far more than joined the Continental army. But most of them performed for brief periods, and they did not always try partisan tactics. When there was guerrilla activity, the militia were usually involved after the British had settled into an urban center and endeavored to spread their tentacles outward into the countryside, as they did after capturing New York and Philadelphia, or after they had penetrated deep into the interior during Burgoyne's campaign in the North and during Cornwallis's operation in the South.[20] Local people will not infrequently fight fiercely, by whatever methods are available to them, to defend their own soil from an invader, whether it be Bulgarians against the Turks or Pennsylvanians against the troops of Sir William Howe, especially if the invader is heavy-handed with the civilian populace; and there were times when Howe's regulars—particularly his German mercenar-

---

[20] Don Higginbotham, "The American Militia: A Traditional Institution with Revolutionary Responsibilities," in Higginbotham, ed., *Reconsiderations on the Revolutionary War*, pp. 83–103; Clyde R. Ferguson, "Functions of the Partisan-Militia in the South during the American Revolution: An Interpretation," in Robert W. Higgins, ed., *The Revolutionary War in the South: Power, Conflict, and Leadership* (Durham, N.C., 1979), pp. 239–58; idem, "Carolina and Georgia Patriot and Loyalist Militia in Action, 1778–1783," in Jeffrey J. Crow and Larry E. Tise, eds., *The Southern Experience in the American Revolution* (Chapel Hill, N.C., 1978), pp. 174–202.

ies—got out of control, most notably when they looted and pillaged their way across New Jersey in 1776.

Incidents such as the murder of Jane McCrea by Burgoyne's Indians may have done more to turn out the countryfolk with their flintlocks than all the appeals from the American northern army. Burgoyne had routed the northern army at Ticonderoga and appeared to have an open path ahead of him to Albany and the lower Hudson. But that was before American militiamen cut his supply lines and harassed his flanks, and before other American partisans rose up and checkmated his detached columns in the Mohawk Valley and near Bennington, Vermont. Although the struggle for the north country had turned into a guerrilla campaign, Burgoyne was ultimately defeated and captured by the American army, which had been given precious weeks to revive thanks to the guerrillas. As General Giap of North Vietnam reminds us, a guerrilla campaign can only evolve into a full-scale confrontation after the enemy is worn down by a thousand and one small strokes.[21]

The British, in contrast to their opponents, did not give serious thought to relying heavily upon loyal colonists until 1778 when, in effect, they acknowledged the complaint of one of their German generals, Friedrich von Lossberg, who saw the problem of space and numbers. Or as he phrased it, the land was "too large, and there are too many people."[22] They did so by gradually retrenching in the North and focusing on the hitherto neglected South, alleged to be a hotbed of crown support. The result, as events would soon show, was that royal officials set off a guerrilla war of their own making, although that had never been their intention.

After failures elsewhere, it appeared reasonable to turn to a region that offered new opportunities for military manpower, and at the very time when French intervention resulted in a depletion of British forces in North America. The capture of Georgia in December of 1778 by only three thou-

---

[21] Vo Nguyen Giap, *People's War, People's Army* (New York, 1962), pp. 101–10.

[22] Ernest Kipping, ed., *The Hessian View of America* (Monmouth Beach, N.J., 1971), p. 34.

sand redcoats underscored the wisdom of fresh strategic initiatives, but the British southern offensive did not reach high gear until a year later when Sir Henry Clinton landed below Charleston and then proceeded in short order to capture that city and the entire five thousand-man American southern army. Soon South Carolina as well as Georgia *appeared* to be a crown colony once again.

What then? How would the king's regulars be employed, and what would be the loyalists' assignment? Here at last the British thought they had a solution to the problem of space and numbers (actually, it was first proposed seriously in March 1778 when Lord George Germain began to advocate a southern strategy): the loyalists were to police the "liberated" territories so that the army could move on to free other areas still in rebel hands.[23]

Germain, however, was scarcely a critical military analyst, never one to examine methodically all angles of a question; rather, he was impulsive, and an eternal optimist to boot. We now know that the British grossly exaggerated the extent of loyalism in the South. Even so, could the southern strategy have worked? Could the king's friends have effectively maintained control without the presence of substantial British muscle to back them up? In retrospect, we cannot be certain, although probably the new approach would have succeeded only if the former rebels were shown real leniency and a better life under British rule.

In comparative terms, we are in a broad sense concerned with what the Johnson administration called pacification and Vietnamization. As the so-called Komer Report of 1966 described the objective, the focus was to be on "eliminating terror and intimidation, and producing radical and constructive changes in the lives of the people. Its aim is to dry up the source of VC local support and build a strong and progressive society from the hamlet up." Security in those regions previously or still open to Vietcong infiltration or attack was

---

[23] Lord George Germain to Sir Henry Clinton, Mar. 8, 1778, Historical Manuscripts Commission, *Report on the Manuscripts of Mrs. Stopford-Sackville* . . ., 2 vols. (London, 1904–10), 2:94–99.

to be entrusted to South Vietnamese units such as the Regional and Popular Forces and the National Police Force.[24] Authorities differ as to why this program of pacification failed, although a number of factors were involved, including the strength of the Vietcong infrastructure, the ineptness of South Vietnamese officials, and the failure of the United States to press vigorously for its implementation.

As for the War of Independence in the South, John Shy, conscious of historical parallels, suggests that pacification and Americanization are concepts applicable to Britain's southern aims.[25] But in America, as in Vietnam, there were problems and difficulties of implementation. Pacification for Germain, Clinton, and company was at best a hazy notion, with little serious thought given to methods of permanently winning southern hearts and minds. Their inability to do so is not hard to understand. British authorities, after all, had an eighteenth-century mindset, which included an inbred attitude of condescension toward colonial peoples—even, as Paul Smith has demonstrated, toward their loyalist allies.[26] Assuredly, royal officials were incapable of what Guenter Lewy, in writing of Vietnam, describes as "the complex task of achieving a politically and economically viable society within the framework of an effective government which enjoyed the support of the people."[27]

Moreover, British attempts at Americanization com-

---

[24] *Revolutionary Guerrilla Warfare*, p. 240.

[25] "British Strategy for Pacifying the Southern Colonies, 1778–1781," in Crow and Tise, eds., *Southern Experience in the American Revolution*, pp. 159–60.

[26] *Loyalists and Redcoats: A Study in British Revolutionary Policy* (Chapel Hill, N.C., 1964), ch. 5. An earlier student of loyalism stated the matter briefly but succinctly: "There can be not the slightest doubt that the haughty arrogant demeanor of the British 'regulars' toward the 'provincials,' combined with ill-treatment of Loyalists by the army, lost to the royal cause thousands upon thousands of friends and well-wishers in all the colonies" (W. O. Raymond, "Loyalists in Arms," New Brunswick Historical Society *Collections* 5 [1904]:190).

[27] *America in Vietnam* (New York, 1978), p. 52.

pounded the problem of pacification, for the American loyalists acted as though they could care less about winning hearts and minds. They were for the most part angry, bitter men and, to be sure, those who tried earlier to assist the mother country had been roughly handled. Despite pleas from Washington and other Continental leaders for restraint, the potential for extreme violence was always present, as is invariably the case in revolutionary wars. "The Revolution itself," observes Richard M. Brown, "with its emergent concept of popular sovereignty furnished a powerful justification for the violent abuse of alleged enemies of the public good."[28]

Or as John Locke, whose ideas were embedded in the Declaration of Independence, might have expressed it: Those who joined the social contract in 1776 felt a need to protect themselves from persons hostile to the new order and determined to remain outside it. Consequently, we can better understand why the king's friends in the South favored anything but pacification as that word is currently used. Instead they wanted a course of harsh retribution, and their views were shared by some of Clinton's subordinates, especially those most exposed to tory opinions such as Banastre Tarleton, Patrick Ferguson, and Lord Rawdon.[29]

Clinton himself soon returned to New York City, now the only important British foothold outside the South. Before leaving he took a step that was intended to mollify the hardened loyalists without giving in totally to their cries for vengeance. On June 3, 1780, he announced that prisoners currently on parole—except those taken at Charleston—were to be released from their paroles and restored to full citizenship in return for which they had to take an oath of allegiance and go to arms against their former whig comrades if summoned. Too generous to please the tories, too harsh for the former patriots, the proclamation was a disaster. The terrorist-minded loyalists mainly ignored its moderate features as they cracked down on their old enemies, who in turn—

---

[28] "Violence and the American Revolution," p. 108.

[29] Shy, "British Strategy for Pacifying the Southern Colonies," pp. 166–69; idem, "American Society and Its War for Independence," in Higginbotham, ed., *Reconsiderations on the Revolutionary War*, pp. 80–81.

when pushed—chose renewed rebellion rather than being coerced to bear arms by insolent loyalists.[30]

From the summer of 1780 onward, the southern backcountry shook from the impact of a full-scale civil war as the loyalists fought fire with fire: that is, treated the patriots, reformed or not, with the kind of bitter medicine they had been compelled to swallow before Britain had gained the upper hand in South Carolina. This is hardly the place to chronicle the myriad skirmishes and battles that ensued,[31] although we should stress that the three patriot guerrilla officers who were most effective were driven into open defiance by bloodthirsty loyalists: the now-legendary trio of Francis Marion, Andrew Pickens, and Thomas Sumter.

And they, too, fought fire with fire. Indeed, sober, reasonable leaders in both the British and American camps were appalled. Ferguson's loyalist militia, causing havoc in western South Carolina, were almost completely annihilated at the Battle of King's Mountain, and Tarleton's Legion was destroyed at the Battle of Cowpens where only the quick intervention of American officers kept scores of surrendering legionnaires from being cut down, the fate which befell dozens of Ferguson's men.

There appeared to be very little that either side could do to put a stop to the atrocities and massacres—neither Lord Cornwallis, who succeeded Clinton as commander in the South, nor Gen. Nathanael Greene of the Continental army, whom Washington and Congress had sent to the Southern Department to revive American fortunes.[32] Cornwallis did,

---

[30] There were in fact several proclamations issued by Clinton between the fall of Charleston on May 12, 1780, and the final one of June 3, 1780, which blew the lid off the very fragile peace in South Carolina. See Smith, *Loyalists and Redcoats*, pp. 130–33; Franklin and Mary Wickwire, *Cornwallis: The American Adventure* (Boston, 1970), pp. 182–83.

[31] They have been conveniently listed, along with known casualty figures, in Howard H. Peckham, ed., *The Toll of Independence: Engagements and Battle Casualties of the American Revolution* (Chicago, 1974).

[32] The severity of the backcountry civil war, together with an analysis of its underlying causes, is well described in Ronald Hoffman, "The 'Disaffected' in the Revolutionary South," in Alfred F. Young, ed., *The American*

however, have a curious theory about how to smother the flames of sedition in South Carolina: he proposed to invade North Carolina. In possession of that province, he would then have the South Carolina partisans isolated and cut off from supply lines to the north. Of course as soon as Cornwallis moved his army into North Carolina, he found the rebels anything but hospitable and the loyalists mostly unwilling to come forth and identify themselves. Those who did were as vindictive as their South Carolina counterparts. The most fiercely effective of them was hardly more than "a hired gun" as one historian has described him. He was David Fanning, a crude, boisterous man, grotesque in physical appearance, suffering from a visible skin disease that had left him bald. Fanning, whom contemporaries said reeked of an unusually strong body odor, had a penchant for teenage girls; he married a sixteen-year-old and later was tried for raping a fourteen-year-old.[33]

Just as Cornwallis had earlier argued that to snuff out insurgency in South Carolina he must occupy North Carolina, so now, failing in North Carolina, he claimed that he must overrun Virginia to complete the subjugation of both Carolinas. All of these meanderings, wearing on his army and dangerously extending his command over three provinces, led him in time to Yorktown, where he succumbed not to guerrillas but to ancient and honorable siege tactics, carried on in the classical manner by Washington's army and French expeditionary forces.[34]

Revolution: Explorations in the History of American Radicalism (DeKalb, Ill., 1976), pp. 275–316.

[33] I am indebted to Richard Buel, Jr., for his characterization of Fanning as a hired gun. For Fanning's own story, see *The Narrative of Colonel David Fanning (a Tory in the Revolutionary War with Great Britain), Giving an Account of His Adventures in North Carolina from 1775 to 1783* (Richmond, Va., 1861). See also Lindley S. Butler, "David Fanning," William S. Powell, ed., *Dictionary of North Carolina Biography* (forthcoming).

[34] My interpretation of Cornwallis's strategy is obviously critical. It follows that of William B. Willcox, "The British Road to Yorktown: A Study in Divided Command," *American Historical Review* 52 (1946):1–35; idem, *Portrait of a General: Sir Henry Clinton in the War of Independence* (New York, 1964), chs. 9–10. A more sympathetic treatment of His Lordship in the

Reflections on the War of Independence

There is one other aspect to guerrilla war in the Revolution; it concerns the only American army commander who deliberately assumed the part of a guerrilla, and that was Cornwallis's antagonist Nathanael Greene, who took command of an American military department that existed mostly on paper, after the surrender at Charleston and after the crushing of a second and smaller American army under Horatio Gates at Camden in August 1780. Greene, with fewer than two thousand men, decided to work with the South Carolina partisans, who had learned to live off the land they knew so well, with its forests, swamps, and other hideaways. He successfully encouraged them to coordinate their operations with his, and he divided his tiny army to throw Cornwallis off balance; that in turn led Cornwallis to divide his own forces, one of which was smashed at the Cowpens by Gen. Daniel Morgan, a Continental officer with a fine reputation as a partisan fighter. In this case Greene's guerrilla strategy inverted one of the main precepts of orthodox war, the principle of concentration; but Greene, with only a remnant of Continentals, had no choice and the outcome could scarcely have produced better results.

After Cowpens, Greene withdrew into North Carolina, joined Morgan, and then moved into Virginia. If, as Mao Tse-tung has said, the willingness to run away is required of the guerrilla, then Greene had learned his role quite well.[35] Yet another characteristic of guerrilla war—one that allows parallels to be drawn with Mao's war with the Chinese Nationalists and Giap's struggle with the French in Indochina—is this: sooner or later, after debilitating the enemy, the irregulars themselves may concentrate their forces and come out into the open in a more orthodox manner of fighting. And so it was with Greene, who fleshed out his army with new recruits and fresh militia units and who knew that Cornwallis was bruised and battered by King's Mountain, Cowpens, and

---

South appears in the Wickwires' *Cornwallis*, chs. 12–16. For a recent overview of the years 1778–81, see Ira D. Gruber, "Britain's Southern Strategy," in Higgins, ed., *The Revolutionary War in the South*, pp. 206–38.

[35] *Basic Tactics*, trans. Stuart R. Schram (New York, 1966), pp. 62, 83, 97–98.

his long, arduous chase through North Carolina. Greene flung down the challenge to positional combat at Guilford Courthouse, and Cornwallis accepted. The outcome of the battle was indecisive, but Cornwallis's casualties were twice those of Greene. His lordship limped away to Wilmington and then to Virginia, exposing his posts in South Carolina to Greene who, with the partisans, picked them off one by one, leaving the British with only toeholds at Charleston and Savannah in the lower South.[36]

Now for a few concluding comments. First, why have the guerrilla aspects of the War of Independence taken such a hold on the public mind? Probably in part because the final year and a half or more of actual struggle was a guerrilla conflict in many ways, and what comes last is usually remembered best. Then, too, our own current preoccupation with irregular war has also played a part in how we have seen the Revolutionary War. That calls to mind another question: Is the present the product of the past, or is the past the product of the present? Those who see our Revolution mainly as an exercise in backwoods tactics have fallen victim of the latter notion. A second point: to the extent that the Revolution was a guerrilla conflict, this developed out of problems of space and numbers that afflicted both sides, most notably in the South. Had the war dragged on, it would have become even more of a civil war, with irregulars playing a larger role and with severely damaging results to American institutions and to hopes for creating a unified nation. Or as the earl of Chatham once warned, if America were destroyed, there would be no winners, only losers, for who would want a burned-out empire?

---

[36] The definitive study of Greene in the South remains to be written. The most useful accounts at present are Theodore Thayer, *Nathanael Greene: Strategist of the American Revolution* (New York, 1960); M. F. Treacy, *The Southern Campaign of Nathanael Greene, 1780–1781* (Chapel Hill, N.C., 1963); and Russell F. Weigley, *The Partisan War: The Southern Campaign* (Columbia, S.C., 1970).

CHARLES ROYSTER

Founding a Nation in Blood:
Military Conflict and American Nationality

*There is no sure foundation set on blood,
No certain life achieved by others' death.*
                               King John

DURING THE AMERICAN REVOLUTION and for at least two generations afterwards, politicians and public speakers often tried to define the nation that the Revolution had created. The United States seemed anomalous because Americans lacked many of the usual bonds of a people. The country had no monarch, no hereditary social order, no nationally established church or single religion, no ethnic uniformity or timeless customs of living together as one people.[1] Yet if the United States wanted to avoid foreign subjugation and internal fragmentation, its citizens would need a strong dedication to their new nationality as Americans. Explaining and celebrating this dedication became a prominent theme in public discourse.

[1] For theoretical discussions of the bases of nationality, see especially Frederick Hertz, *Nationality in History and Politics: A Psychology and Sociology of National Sentiment and Nationalism* (London, 1944), pp. 7–24; Anthony D. Smith, *Theories of Nationalism* (New York, 1971), esp. ch. 9. The distinctiveness of an American definition of nationality is discussed in Yehoshua Arieli, *Individualism and Nationalism in American Ideology* (Cambridge, Mass., 1964), pp. 22–32.

ARMS AND INDEPENDENCE

Defining American nationality proved complex. Even its perpetuity remained open to debate until conclusively established by the Civil War. The public discussions during the years between the Revolutionary War and the War of 1812 first broached the main themes in the process of definition. I have sampled this political and religious discourse in order to analyze one of the crucial bases of nationality: military conflict.

Why isolate this theme? First, because of the frequency and fervor with which it recurs in the literature. Second, because it seemed to influence Americans of the early republic with an emotional power that differed from other explanations of the distinctiveness of the United States. To identify the elements of America's distinctiveness and to inspire dedication to it were the main purposes of the first celebrators of nationality. The memory of military conflict held a central place in their efforts. And it founded America not just on principles but also on the passions of bloodshed.

One of the most famous later evocations of the Revolution's military conflict as an element of American nationality comes at the end of Abraham Lincoln's first inaugural address, in which he sought to deter the seceding Southerners by reminding them of their national heritage in the Union. He prophesied, "The mystic chords of memory, stretching from every battle-field, and patriot grave, to every living heart and hearthstone, all over this broad land, will yet swell the chorus of the Union, when again touched, as surely they will be, by the better angels of our nature."[2] Lincoln assumed that every American had a tie to the battlefields of the past and that sharing this connection helped make Americans one people. Moreover, Lincoln's metaphor—the harmony of music—suggested that this connection took its strength from feeling more than from political doctrine. The national memory emerged in "mystic chords"—sympathetic resonances with the past. Finally, Lincoln also assumed that this mystic memory of battlefields should unify Americans by its

---

[2] Roy P. Basler, ed., *The Collected Works of Abraham Lincoln*, 8 vols. (New Brunswick, N.J., 1953), 4:271. Some of this wording was suggested to Lincoln by William Henry Seward (ibid., pp. 261–62, n. 99).

harmony with their "better angels." Remembering the military conflicts that patriots now in their graves had fought should awaken sympathetic emotions of nationality.

One can find evidence, in the first forty years of America's independence, that the founding generation left a legacy which Lincoln's generation inherited. True, scholars have shown how the era of sectional conflict preceding the Civil War gave rise to a new, abstract ideal of the Union that had a transcendental existence and a perpetuity unknown to most Americans of the Revolutionary era.[3] Thus, Lincoln and his contemporaries did not rely solely on the founding generation for their understanding of American unity but also created their own. Even so, the attempt to evoke nationality by appealing to the experience of battles was as old as the republic. From the country's first two wars and from the political controversies that filled the intervening years came the legacy which Lincoln's inaugural address recalled. That legacy relied heavily, as did Lincoln's eloquence, on Americans' emotional ties to their nation. However, as we shall see, the emotions that originally shaped the nation were not always responding to Americans' "better angels."

Spokesmen for the Revolutionary generation, although they dwelt on the passions aroused by military conflict, did not want to establish their country on mystical or irrational bases. The United States was founded by a revolution, and this origin formed the central basis of its founders' explanation of the new country. By *revolution* they meant primarily the act of establishing republican political principles embodied in their new governmental institutions, the citizens' virtuous sacrifice of self-interest to maintain these principles, and the vision of a happy national future that such a citizenry could attain. Revolution established its primacy through the voluntary al-

---

[3] For discussion of the nineteenth-century concept of union, see Kenneth M. Stampp, "The Concept of a Perpetual Union," *Journal of American History* 65 (1978):5–33; Paul C. Nagel, *One Nation Indivisible: The Union in American Thought* (New York, 1964); Garry Wills, *Inventing America: Jefferson's Declaration of Independence* (Garden City, N.Y., 1978), prologue; George B. Forgie, *Patricide in the House Divided: A Psychological Interpretation of Lincoln and His Age* (New York, 1979), esp. ch. 1.

legiance of Americans who understood the threat of permanent enslavement by Britain if they failed to resist.[4] Voluntarism—free choice—was supposed to create a republican nation.

By placing so much emphasis on voluntarism, the founding generation set itself a demanding standard—a standard that neither the Revolutionaries nor their descendants could fully sustain. The original ideal demanded of Americans a continuous, reasoned choice to remain Americans and to help preserve their republic. Yet even while invoking this ideal, Revolutionary rhetoric also resorted to another American claim to solidarity: the communal experience of violence. By contrasting the doctrine of voluntarism with the appeal to bloodshed, we can see the ways in which Americans, though aspiring to create a unique republic, nevertheless portrayed themselves in one of the oldest national guises—a people at war.

The first generation frequently called the United States a "nation" and sought to define a "national character" for themselves. But "nation" and "national" did not usually mean for them that their Revolution had guaranteed perpetuity for itself. Instead, nationality depended on Americans' continual willingness to remain one people governed by common consent.[5] This popular commitment to the new republican form of government justified the separation from Great Britain. Explaining the French Revolution, James Madison later argued that "every nation has a right to abolish an old government and establish a new one. This principle ... is the only lawful tenure by which the United States hold their existence as a nation."[6] By this reasoning the political ideas of the Revolution constituted American nationality.[7]

Orators could celebrate their country's distinctiveness be-

---

[4] On voluntarism and Americanness, see James H. Kettner, *The Development of American Citizenship, 1608–1870* (Chapel Hill, N.C., 1978), ch. 7.

[5] Arieli, *Individualism and Nationalism*, pp. 34–35.

[6] *Letters of Helvidius* . . . (Philadelphia, 1796), p. 26.

[7] Reginald C. Stuart emphasizes this theme in his article "The Origins of American Nationalism to 1783: An Historiographical Survey," *Canadian Review of Studies in Nationalism* 6 (1979):145–46.

cause the United States was founded not on conquest, tyranny, and superstition, as other countries were, but on ideals and the voluntary consent of citizens. "Americans, you stand alone," a Fourth of July speaker said in 1792. "You rise an exception to the general tendency of mankind. You shew, that government is founded in the reason, and not in the destruction of man."[8] Part of America's distinctiveness lay in the moral superiority of this voluntaristic origin. Any return to the ancient, discredited engines of empire might sabotage American nationality by violating the righteous institutions on which the country was founded. A Jeffersonian orator celebrating American independence reminded his audience that "the altars of a *Republic* can never rise or stand secure on a basis of blood."[9]

The customary national bonds, which Americans lacked and repudiated—monarch, church, antiquity—were what Lincoln might have called "mystic." They did not so much appeal to a people's reason as incorporate a people emotionally through forms of solidarity almost beyond one's conscious power to accept or reject. Although such solidarity might also enjoy widespread voluntary support, one of its strengths lay in the unquestioned assumption that it was perpetual and all-inclusive. Leading American Revolutionaries treated most of these forces as, at best, superstition and, at worst, instruments of tyranny. The United States was "not an empire, which sets monarchs and tyrants on the throne, but the rational empire of human liberty and equality, founded upon the natural rights of mankind and sovereignty of the people."[10] The new nation would consist of citizens who chose to be patriots. In 1788, looking back on the Revolutionary War, an army veteran said, "all was the result of reason."[11]

---

[8] John Mercer, *An Oration Delivered on the 4th of July 1792* . . . (Richmond, Va., [1792]), p. 16.

[9] Benjamin Gleason, *An Oration, Pronounced . . . July 4, 1805* (Boston, 1805), p. 7.

[10] Benjamin Wadsworth, *America Invoked to Praise the Lord* . . . (Salem, Mass., 1795), pp. 18–19.

[11] William Pierce, *An Oration, Delivered at Christ Church, Savannah, on the 4th of July, 1788* . . . (Savannah, 1788), p. 8.

ARMS AND INDEPENDENCE

Americans' creating a nation through revolution meant that their country owed its existence to war. Military conflict became, in the conduct and in the memory of the first generation, a fundamental component of American nationality. Reliance on war to establish the country did not necessarily repudiate the principle of voluntarism. The Revolutionaries used that principle as an inspiration for people to join the army and to provide supplies. But the Revolutionary War and the ways in which Americans later celebrated it demanded unity and victory above all—with or without voluntarism. War's demands did not always wait on principle and choice. War's demands were not always reasonable. Yet the arbitrariness, fears, hostility, and violence of war also became characteristic components of nationality, components that made fighting itself a test of Americanness. We can trace this process in the early political and religious definitions of the Revolution and its national legacy. These definitions are the memories that Lincoln hoped a later generation would revive. They showed that American nationality rested partly on bloodshed. Having sent friends to their deaths and having killed enemies left a permanent, inescapable heritage that shaped Americans' understanding of their country in ways not completely dependent on political principle and rational choice.[12]

After former colonies had asserted their new nationality by separating from Britain, belligerence toward Britain became a recurring preoccupation for many Americans. Wishing to kill British soldiers and hating their masters in England united Revolutionaries while sharply differentiating them from their former fellow subjects. Orators sometimes lamented the special sadness of a war between people of the same blood. Yet the war itself went far to break the bond by the lasting emotional legacy of killing and cruelty. Early in the war Samuel Adams and other advocates of independence welcomed bloodshed because it would move Americans toward permanent separation more effectively than did the rational explanations of the long-term threat of British tyranny. Adams wrote that "mankind are governed more by feelings than by

---

[12] Arieli, *Individualism and Nationalism*, p. 87.

reason. Events which excite those feelings will produce wonderful Effects. . . . one Battle would do more towards a Declaration of Independency than a long chain of conclusive Arguments."[13] Adams seemed to assume that feelings and reason would ultimately coincide in their results, even though the former worked more persuasively. A declaration of independence evoked by combat would come sooner but would hardly differ from one inspired by political discourse. However, the effects of fighting might not always validate Adams's assumption. Resorting to battle as a form of political persuasion ran the risk of making combat self-justifying, whether or not it conformed to principled arguments. What then would be the nation's fundamental charter: the declaration or the killing that preceded it and implemented it?

During the war Revolutionary leaders sometimes hoped that violence would arouse greater public effort on behalf of independence when political virtue seemed to have failed. The violence might be either a great wished-for American victory or a great British victory, such as Camden and Charleston in 1780. Though Revolutionaries of course preferred the former, they counted on the animating effect of either. Most important was the shock—inspiring or frightening—of bloodshed. This shock was a formative experience for Americans. During the war Samuel West said of the first fight at Lexington, "A nation was born at once: for we were then immediately severed from Great-Britain, and obliged to consider ourselves as a distinct people from them."[14] Thus, as early as 1777 combat rather than political processes of common consent seemed like the beginnings of America's distinctiveness. West's statement does not accurately describe the initial effect of hostilities in 1775, but it does summarize one of the legacies that Americans would take from the war after independence had become an accomplished fact. Fighting, as well as political reasoning, helped to originate the United States. In his *History of the Revolution of South-Carolina*,

---

[13] To Samuel Cooper, Apr. 30, 1776, Harry Alonzo Cushing, ed., *The Writings of Samuel Adams*, 4 vols. (New York, 1904–8), 3:284–85.

[14] *An Anniversary Sermon, Preached at Plymouth, December 22d, 1777* (Boston, [1778]), pp. 40–41.

David Ramsay recalled, "All statutes of allegiance were considered as repealed on the plains of Lexington, and the laws of self-preservation left to operate in full force."[15] War reduced Americans to elemental emotions, and from those emotions they constructed a national identity. This emphasis on Lexington retrospectively distilled the whole war's meaning into its first battle.

After the Revolutionary War the record of British wartime cruelty—starting with the unprovoked attack at Lexington and running through eight years of murders and atrocities—remained a favorite theme of orators who were celebrating American independence. Before recommending that his listeners support the movement for a new United States Constitution in 1787, David Daggett reminded people in New Haven of their sufferings at the hands of the British. "Here one of your neighbors was in a moment struck dead!—and yonder you saw one, whom you had long known, weltering in his blood, till his agonizing struggles had stretched him a breathless corps!—Such scenes we have beheld, and such have been realized in many other towns." Americans' ability to defeat such "hellish malice" showed that their country was "the peculiar favorite of heaven."[16]

As the postwar relations of the United States with Britain and France became domestic political issues in America in the 1790s, Republicans sought votes and support by perpetuating the memory of violence. Opposing John Jay's treaty with Great Britain, Robert R. Livingston asked, "What first raised the American character? . . . Was it tame submission to the injuries of Britain? . . . No, my fellow citizens, it was a bold resistance."[17] Continuing the Revolutionary resistance, Republicans would remind their countrymen of British malice. In 1808 one of America's most conspicuous patriot

---

[15] *The History of the Revolution of South-Carolina from a British Province to an Independent State*, 2 vols. (Trenton, 1785), 1:30.

[16] *An Oration, Pronounced in . . . New-Haven, on the Fourth of July, A.D. 1787* (New Haven, [1787]), p. 18.

[17] *Examination of the Treaty . . . between the United States and Great-Britain* (New York, 1795), p. 59.

graves—New York harbor's tidal mud flats littered with the bones of American prisoners of war who had died on British prison ships—received the special attention of New York Republicans. They organized the burial of some of the bones that had long lain visible and neglected. The ceremony combined honor to the dead with defense of America's national dignity, hatred of the wartime enemy, and support of President Jefferson's embargo. The memory of bloodshed that had occurred thirty years earlier was supposed to establish for Americans how greatly they differed from their cruel attackers in interests, character, and policy. The message on the front of "The Grand National Pedestal" in the burial procession was clear: "AMERICANS! REMEMBER THE BRITISH."[18] Those American politicians most vigilant against Britain in this election year would of course be the most reliable defenders of independence.

The popularity of appeals like these seems to have arisen from the assumption that America had become a nation partly *because* blood had been shed. The violence helped make former colonists a distinct people, at the expense of Anglo-American ties of language, ancestry, commerce, political forms, tradition, or other inducements to see themselves still as British subjects. First on Revolutionary battlefields and then in decades of belligerent oratory—recalling war, predicting war, threatening war, and in 1812 declaring war—Americans of the early republic knew that they had a common identity that could not be British, which came in part from killing Britons and from blaming Britons for having killed Americans.[19]

To celebrate the successful union of the states, Americans often said that soldiers' blood had "cemented" the states together. Potentially divided by their diversity, the states needed reasons to believe that they could trust each other to perse-

---

[18] *An Account of the Interment of the Remains of 11,500 American Seamen, Soldiers and Citizens* . . . (New York, 1808), pp. 67–68.

[19] The importance of the war years in fostering a sense of American distinctness from Britain is stressed in Max Savelle, "Nationalism and Other Loyalties in the American Revolution," *American Historical Review* 67 (1962):901–23, esp. p. 923.

ARMS AND INDEPENDENCE

vere in a new national unity. One of the most cogent reasons came from their shared experience. Political collaboration was one such experience, through which representatives of the states found that they could accommodate differences of interest. Another bond—one that enabled Americans not just to negotiate their unity but also to feel it—originated in the shared experience of combat. The states had sent men to kill and to die on their common behalf. Americans would remember this joint loss and revere the union that had enabled them to save one another from slavery. In 1793 a former president of the Continental Congress told his July 4 audience that those "who have fought side by side—who have mingled their blood together, as it were in one rich stream ... must surely be more than brethren—it is a union cemented by blood."[20]

This cement consisted primarily of feeling and memory—more "mystic" than written constitutional arrangements could afford to be and yet not less powerful. A Republican congressman defending the policy of commercial coercion directed against Britain in 1808 explained it by saying that "the same spirit of slaughter which roused the Americans at the battle of Lexington now looks you in the teeth, and demands of you submission.... The cause is a common cause." It had been made so by the Revolution. During the war, he recalled, "the enthusiasm of liberty was general, and men, women, and children joined in its execution. The Union is one and indivisible."[21] This categorical assertion of national consolidation relied not on analysis of the Constitution but on the precedent of having shared the fight against Britain. And the sacrifices in that fight derived even greater emotional appeal from victory: Americans were united by their losses; moreover, they had successfully joined in destroying their enemies. A Republican orator in 1809 celebrated the Battle of Bunker Hill because, by killing so many British soldiers, "the

[20] Elias Boudinot, *An Oration Delivered ... on the Fourth of July, 1793* ... (Elizabethtown, N.J., 1793), p. 16.

[21] U.S., Congress, House, *Annals of Congress*, 10th Cong., 2d sess., 1808, p. 590.

bravery of the Americans . . . wrote in characters of blood, their determination to be free."[22] Political partisans might subsequently bicker over who had done the most, but they had all been part of the killing. Their unity partook of horror.

This fact may help us to understand why orations and patriotic verse dwelt with such extended, lurid detail on the bloody deaths of patriots or enemies. A Massachusetts minister's sermon at the end of the Revolutionary War typifies the treatment of this theme. He recreated "the frightful scenes—of bloody fields and burning towns, of bleeding brothers—of mangled and expiring friends . . . with the groans of the wounded . . . with the shrieks of ravished virgins—the moans of bereaved widows—and the piercing cries of helpless orphans, wailing round a butchered father's bloody corse."[23] Thirty years later, during the war of 1812, a poet commemorated the Revolutionaries' attempt to conquer Canada in 1775 and used similar images:

> *His gallant troops rush on to meet the foe,*
> *And carnage swells the catalogue of wo.*
> *In rivers glides the purple tide away,*
> *When killed and wounded on the rampart lay . . .*
> *The bloody scene spreads far and wide, around;*
> *In heaps the killed and wounded strew the ground.*[24]

Such sentimental effects were of course standard devices for a writer trying to move his audience to see the importance of his subject and the skill of his art. Still, the celebrator of American nationality had more than stylistic reasons for striving to make his audience feel the violence of the Revolution. Vicariously joining the bloodshed in a thrill of emotion—as victim or victor or both—reawoke one of the first memories shared by Americans and reminded them of the

---

[22] Elbert Herring, *An Oration on the Anniversary of the Battle of Lexington* . . . (New York, 1809), p. 9.

[23] John Murray, *Jerubbaal, or Tyranny's Grove Destroyed* . . . (Newburyport, Mass., 1784), pp. 6–7.

[24] Alexander Coffin, Jr., *The Death of General Montgomery, or, the Storming of Quebec, a Poem* (New York, 1814), pp. 37, 40.

lethal consequences of their resistance to Britain. The purple rhetoric carried this experience to many who would never know military conflict at first hand; the rhetoric then further perpetuated the memory of the experience for those born after the Revolution. Later generations, by recalling the formative struggle, would share complicity in the bloodshed, and this sharing would help them to know that they were Americans. The price of independence, in losses and in the shock of killing, also made it seem more valuable. Four years after the war one orator recalled, "We waded thro' seas of blood to establish ourselves in that peace, and independence."[25] Horror, then, was one of the elemental experiences making Americans one people. To revive it by making it poetic was to transmute it from butchery to ritual. But the quaint figures of speech could only sentimentalize, not efface, the violence out of which nationality had arisen. A college-student speaker said in 1792, "The crimson car of desolation has marked thy country."[26]

Having declared its independence, the United States seemed to need a justification. Many nations glorified their own strength, but Americans' boasting contained a special preoccupation with defending the nation's right to exist. Although the political doctrine of the Revolution left no reasonable doubt of this right, political doctrine was not enough. Almost every nation or group looked back to its heroes in a mythical past. The nation existed because those heroes had won its right to exist through their larger-than-life strength and pain.

Such a claim did not explain itself through rigorous reasoning. The American orators who celebrated the voluntary, principled, well-documented beginnings of the United States scorned the fables and tyrants that clouded the origins of less enlightened nations. Yet Americans, too, found their mythic antecedents. They sometimes mentioned the founders of the first colonies who had wrested the land from the Indians.[27]

[25] Daggett, *Oration in New-Haven*, p. 17.

[26] Mercer, *Oration on the 4th of July 1792*, p. 8.

[27] The significance of the early colonists to later generations is analyzed in Wesley Frank Craven, *The Legend of the Founding Fathers* (New York,

But America's nationhood took its heroic beginnings primarily from the sacrifices of the Revolutionary dead. A former Continental army chaplain promised in 1791, "We will teach our *sons' sons* how early and how nobly WARREN fell. MONTGOMERY, that high-sounding name . . . shall swell the tale. To show the price of liberty, we will uncover MERCER's bleeding wounds, and traverse all the fields of death."[28] These battlefield losses had been purposeful, as a member of Congress explained in advocating resistance to British commercial restrictions after Independence, "a Warren, a McClary, a Montgomery, a Mercer, and a host of heroes, fought, and bled, and died—for what? For the rights, the liberties, the freedom, and independence of our country."[29] The frequent, almost rote incantations of names were less an argument than a prayer—surely so many heroes could not have gone to such gruesome deaths in a cause that was unjust or doomed.

The grander the men and the more awful their dying, the less one dared doubt that their purpose—the creation of the United States—had an inevitability even greater than the survival of other nations from remote antiquity. "No Period of the History of Man, is more interesting than that in which we have lived," wrote the artist John Trumbull in offering for sale engravings of his paintings, *The Death of Major General Warren, at the Battle of Bunker's Hill* and *The Death of General Montgomery, in the Attack on Quebec, Canada*. Americans should welcome the depiction of heroes' deaths in battle because these were "Scenes, in which were laid the Foundations of that free Government, which secures our national and individual Happiness."[30] America's perpetuity mystically proceeded from

---

1956). The effect on American character of the conflict between whites and Indians is explored in Richard Slotkin, *Regeneration through Violence: The Mythology of the American Frontier, 1600–1860* (Middletown, Conn., 1973).

[28] William Linn, *The Blessings of America: A Sermon Preached . . . on the Fourth July, 1791* . . . (New York, 1791), p. 28.

[29] U.S., Congress, House, *Annals of Congress*, 9th Cong., 1st sess., 1806, p. 788.

[30] *Proposals by John Trumbull, for Publishing by Subscription, Two Prints* . . . (New York, 1790), p. 2.

the battlefields of the Revolution.³¹ To preserve the nation, its later defenders would have to emulate the founding heroes. As a poet of the War of 1812 said about America, "Her sons imbibe warrior blood from her breast."³²

In the years between the Revolutionary War and the War of 1812, political partisans brought the Revolutionary War into politics. They did so by using it as a defining analogy with which to understand partisan controversy. Republicans accused Federalists of attachment to Britain and of striding rapidly toward monarchy. Federalists accused Republicans of subservience to France and of proclivity toward the French revolutionary radicalism that would lead to anarchy and the destruction of republican government. Thus, a partisan cause seemed to its adherents not just a position on issues of official policy but a struggle for the nation's continued existence, like the Revolutionary War. A satirist wrote in 1808, "We have been told repeatedly by these patriots, on both sides, that if such a person was not elected, our independence was no more than a name."³³

In the political contest, the memory of the War for Independence became a device used by candidates to exemplify their dedication to the nation, while discrediting the claims of their opponents. Such debates, enlivened by rhetorical excommunication of rivals from the ranks of true patriots, might seem to make this partisan reenactment of the Revolutionary War a source of division among Americans. However, despite the belligerent warnings against internal enemies, the political analog of the war served both parties as an assertion of nationality. By reviving the emotions and outlook of wartime, as by appealing to the United States Constitution, partisans—even when disagreeing with each other—turned to a

---

[31] Benjamin T. Spencer discusses the literary commemoration of Revolutionary heroes in *The Quest for Nationality: An American Literary Campaign* (Syracuse, N.Y., 1957), esp. pp. 14–15, 40–44.

[32] *The American Star: Being a Choice Collection of the Most Approved Patriotic and Other Songs* . . . (Richmond, Va., 1814), p. 50.

[33] *Here Is a Looking Glass, for Our Party* . . . (New Bedford, Mass., 1808), p. 5.

shared basis for America's national existence: the struggle for independence. The memory of military conflict buttressed nationality not through the elimination of political parties but through an underlying agreement on the fundamental experience of being American—the fight for liberty.

In the analogy between political conflict and the Revolutionary War, there could be only one patriotic side, the American side. A supporter of Jefferson's commercial coercion of Britain invoked "the spirit of '76" in Congress: "I wish it would appear and purge the body politic of tories and British influence. I wish the line of demarcation to be drawn, that we may ascertain who is for his country, and who is against his country."[34] This outlook made the partisan hero defending republicanism like the heroes who won the war against the British monarch. In 1794 the Republican John Taylor wanted to preserve the word "party" to describe only the Federalists. Their opponents should not be considered partisans but should be called "a band of patriots."[35] During the Quasi War with France and in support of the Alien and Sedition Acts, Federalists made similar claims. They even created an army to embody their patriotism. After Jefferson's election to the presidency, one of his supporters explained with a Revolutionary War metaphor how the Republicans had raised their own army, too, for the presidential canvass: "A comparison was drawn between the principles which actuated our resistance to tyranny in 1775, and the principles of the Hamiltonian school of anglo-federalism. The result of this investigation, was one blaze and burst of indignation. The drum of republicanism beat to arms, and THOMAS JEFFERSON was seated, with acclamation, in the chair of state."[36] Eventually, Federalists became, in the eyes of their opponents, "anti-

---

[34] U.S., Congress, House, *Annals of Congress*, 10th Cong., 2d sess., 1808, p. 660.

[35] [John Taylor], *An Enquiry into the Principles and Tendency of Certain Public Measures* (Philadelphia, 1794), p. 85.

[36] [John Mason Williams], *The Hamiltoniad: Or, an Extinguisher for the Royal Faction of New-England* . . . (Boston, [1804]), p. 9n.

American."³⁷ Permanent partisan rivalry did not yet enjoy legitimacy as a patriotic activity. Legitimacy came from conclusive victory. The inspiration of the Revolutionary War gave political controversy the clarity of absolute division in combat: one side defended independence; the other side sought to destroy it. One side could be trusted as custodians of the republic after the war; the other could not. But the metaphors of both sides returned to a shared image of battle.

Republicans called the election of Jefferson to the presidency the "Revolution of 1800." By driving the Federalist leaders out of office, they were rewinning the American Revolution through the defeat of those whom they called tories and monarchists. But during the administrations of Jefferson and Madison the Republicans found that the republic was not yet safe. Besides winning a domestic political revolution, they decided that they would have to win another military conflict—a "second war of Independence"—with Great Britain.³⁸ Both Britain and France had repeatedly interfered with America's neutral commerce and violated the rights of national sovereignty claimed by the United States. However, the Republicans saw in British conduct a special malevolence, a design to reverse the outcome of the American revolution, to resubjugate Americans into a colonial status in fact if not in name. The Republicans decided that America must fight. As one writer in Washington, D.C., defined the issue in 1809, "Americans are hailed by the genius of 76 to step forth and defend the rights of that country made free by the blood of their fathers." Only through war could America become and remain "a people to ourselves, a nation unconnected with all others; a *republic.*"³⁹ Federalists who denied the need for a

---

³⁷ Zabdiel Sampson, *Republican Celebration of American Independence: An Oration, Pronounced . . . July 4, 1808* (Boston, 1808), p. 9; U.S., Congress, House, *Annals of Congress*, 12th Cong., 2d sess., 1813, 2, p. 825.

³⁸ O. C. Merrill, *An Oration, Delivered . . . in Bennington, Vermont . . .* (Bennington, 1815), p. 26.

³⁹ Mathew Clay, *Washington City, February 27th, 1809, Fellow Citizen . . .* (N.p., [1809]), p. 1.

second war were accused of "apostacy" and treason.[40] They were "the same murky and cankering opposition" that the tories had been earlier.[41] Republicans, in combat, would establish their primacy as patriots by bloodshed as they already had by votes. John Randolph, with his customary pithy sarcasm, penetrated to one of the motives for the American declaration of war: "It had been pronounced that this was to be a second war for independence—in order (he supposed) to enable the patriots aforesaid to enrol their illustrious names among those of the heroes of the Revolution No. 2."[42]

The War of 1812 was less clearly necessary and less successful than the War of Independence. Americans suffered ignominious military defeats and won none of the concessions to their claims of sovereignty for which they had fought. Consequently, public glorifications of the War of 1812 had to rely heavily on the symbolic, or "mystic," in Americans' memory of military conflict in order to demonstrate that the second war had reproduced the successes of the Revolution. Not all Americans joined in the glorification. Those who did so, primarily Republicans, had to work harder to demonstrate the importance of the war for the nation's greatness. Those who did not, primarily Federalists, fell into increasing political disrepute. The war became, in retrospect, a critical measurement of America's ability to survive as a republic. Later, both parties in the second party system, Democrats and Whigs, turned to heroes of the War of 1812 for candidates to win the presidency. Those Americans who argued during and after the war that they had rewon their country's independence further identified American nationality with military conflict. This identification operated more through the emotive power of bloodshed than through rigorous analysis of the formal justifications for the second war.

[40] U.S., Congress, House, *Annals of Congress*, 13th Cong., 1st sess., 1814, p. 1035.

[41] James T. Austin, *An Oration, Pronounced at Lexington, Mass.* . . . (Boston, 1815), p. 6.

[42] U.S., Congress, House, *Annals of Congress*, 12th Cong., 1st sess., 1812, 2, p. 1400.

ARMS AND INDEPENDENCE

The war songs and orations of 1812–15 emphasized a symbol that had been much less prominent during the Revolutionary War: the American flag. As long as the ship or the fort still flew the flag, American nationality remained intact, unsubdued by Britain, and this nationality was most effectively proved—the flag most effectively served—by combat. In a "victory" oration to the Tammany Society, Samuel Berrian claimed that in the War of 1812 "victory followed victory; achievement succeeded achievement: the pulse of national valor beat high, and the British flag that was so oft raised in exultation, was as oft lowered in dishonor; whilst our own waved triumphant in all the winds of heaven."[43] Appropriately, the war song that later became the national anthem of the United States was written about the American flag during the War of 1812. The star-spangled banner waving in triumph symbolized a country with a dual identity: it was not only "the land of the free," defined by voluntary allegiance to republican principles, it was also "the home of the brave," defined by victory in battle.

Francis Scott Key's verses praised heaven as "the power that hath made and preserved us a nation." The proof of that preservation lay in the expulsion of the British: "Their blood has wash'd out their foul foot-steps' pollution."[44] In the end, British blood, not British concessions in a peace treaty, made the War of 1812 seem a victory for the Americans who celebrated it. The Battle of New Orleans, fought after the peace treaty had been signed, was an overwhelming American victory. More than two thousand British soldiers were shot down by entrenched Americans, who lost only thirteen men. This destruction became for orators a demonstration of America's secure sovereignty and the war's justness, a demonstration far more satisfying than comparing the treaty to the manifestos with which the war had been declared. A reasoned assessment of the war's course and outcome—of the important

---

[43] *An Oration, Delivered before the Tammany Society* . . . (New York, 1815), p. 12.

[44] *National Songster; or, a Collection of the Most Admired Patriotic Songs, on the Brilliant Victories, Achieved by the Naval and Military Heroes of the United States of America* . . . (Hagerstown, Md., 1814), pp. 30–31.

differences between the War of 1812 and the Revolutionary War—held less appeal than the mystic images of blood washing out the British threat and consecrating national greatness. Even before he knew the terms of the treaty, one member of Congress said that "the victory at Orleans has rendered them glorious and honorable, be what they may.... Who does not rejoice that he is not an European! Who is not proud to feel himself an American—our wrongs revenged—our rights recognised! ... The catastrophe at Orleans has fixed an impress, has sealed, has consecrated the compact beyond the powers of parchment and diplomacy."[45]

A Fourth of July oration in 1815 defined the relationship between America's first two wars: "The war of the Revolution gave existence to the American nation, and enabled the increasing millions of your country to enjoy the blessings of self-government.—The War of 1812 has drawn into notice the republican virtue of the American people, and established the foundations of your national character."[46] The Revolutionary War, its reenactments in partisan politics, and the second War of Independence had not settled all defintions of nationality; however, they had established a pattern by which such definitions could be made final. And that pattern made war an ultimate recourse for a legitimate claim to Americanness. Praising the victories of the War of 1812, one orator anticipated Lincoln's assessment of the role of combat in America's beginnings: "It is argument like this, which binds and endears Americans to their country, and teaches them a sense of their personal dignity. It is this mysterious chain that makes us proud; that, we also are Americans!"[47]

---

[45] U.S., Congress, House, *Annals of Congress*, 13th Cong., 3d sess., 1815, pp. 1159, 1161.

[46] Austin, *Oration at Lexington*, p. 6.

[47] John B. White, *An Oration, Delivered in . . . Charleston, South-Carolina* . . . (Charleston, 1815), p. 18. The importance of the War of 1812 in confirming American nationality is discussed in John F. Berens, "The Sanctification of American Nationalism, 1789–1812: Prelude to Civil Religion in America," *Canadian Review of Studies in Nationalism* 3 (1976):183, and Paul C. Nagel, *This Sacred Trust: American Nationality, 1798–1898* (New York, 1971), p. 11.

ARMS AND INDEPENDENCE

Defining American nationality through war had important consequences for Americans' understanding of the Revolution that founded their country. War and revolution went together, so that anyone speaking of "the American Revolution" usually meant both. War need not be only the calculated defense of national interests; it could also look like the virtuous pursuit of Revolutionary ideals. But those who linked ideals with war always ran the risk that ideals might be submerged in the passions of bloodshed, that the weapon might turn its wielder, and violence overwhelm reason. During the War for Independence the civil conflict between loyalists and Revolutionaries often grew so bitter that bloodshed seemed to have become an end in itself. One postwar orator recalled that "the progress of freedom thro' the war was sometimes wild and irregular; her sacred purity was often stained with murder and depredation."[48] This was especially true of the vicious vendettas in the South. One South Carolinian reported that the war had excited an "inveterate hatred & spirit of vengeance. . . . The very females talk as familiarly of shedding blood & destroying the Tories as the men do."[49] Similarly, a contemporary historian, recalling wartime Georgia, wrote, "Retaliation on both sides became the order of the day; and the war for freedom and independence, became a war of extermination."[50]

Military conflict sometimes overrode principle. This excess did not lessen the importance of war in founding the nation. In fact, it provided Americans with a solidarity derived from their complicity in such violence. Killing, unlike reasoned choice of principle and allegiance, could not be reversed. It had a finality greater than any commitment to ideals. A nationality based on rational choice could last no longer than its adherents chose to reason in its favor. Minds changed. But

---

[48] Theodore Dwight, *An Oration Spoken . . . on the 4th of July, 1792* (Hartford, 1792), p. 7.

[49] Aedanus Burke to Arthur Middleton, Jan. 26–Feb. 5, 1782, "Correspondence of Hon. Arthur Middleton, Signer of the Declaration of Independence," *South Carolina Historical and Genealogical Magazine* 26 (1925):192.

[50] Hugh McCall, *The History of Georgia*, 2 vols. in 1 (1811–16; reprint ed., Atlanta, 1909), 2:458.

dead men—casualties of creating a nation—would not come back to life. The connection between the killing of men and the victory of principles might not always be logically explicable, might even be forgotten in the passion of violence. But the connection between violence and its result, the nation, would be a lasting one, originating in those "mystic" or "mysterious" resonances of killing that had the permanence of an inescapable memory. Paul C. Nagel, tracing the link between war and nationality that was consummated in the Civil War, concludes: "This intimate bond between bloodshed and uneasy virtue in America's history and thought is probably the most important revelation of the difficulty in being American. It discloses how indistinct is the line between the rational and irrational in the minds of men called to prove righteousness and progress."[51] Ultimately, American nationality did not depend on the distinctness of that line. Americans could found their nation on blood as readily as on reason.

By 1861 the Revolution's rational legacy of principle had become even more debatable, ambiguous, and flexible than it had been earlier. In the Civil War both sides claimed to be fighting in defense of the ideals of the American Revolution. Should liberty confine and eventually end human slavery, or should liberty protect the property rights of slaveholders? Did the preservation of self-government depend on the permanence of the union or on the political autonomy of the states? In contrast with this ambiguity of Revolutionary doctrine, the Revolution's sanction of ideological war had become clear to both sections, even as they disputed the interpretation of ideals. Americans in 1861 could agree on one thing: they must shed blood. The mystic music of remembered battles might encourage rather than discourage violence in those who heard it. In nothing were both sides more American than in killing for the sake of ideals.

And yet military conflict was also a characteristic of most other peoples. In this obvious fact lay a difficult problem for the early definers of the American Revolution. By resorting to war to establish its claim to uniqueness, the United States had

[51] *This Sacred Trust*, p. 130.

lost part of that claim, had implicated itself in the irrational origins and bloody crimes common to other nations. American orators emphasized the distinctively enlightened, voluntary, and principled character of their nation's founding. Could they reconcile this pride with the alarms and belligerence of the republic's early years? A recurring theme in the postwar celebrations of the American Revolution insisted that Britain, not America, bore responsibility for the war. Orators stressed the colonists' prolonged disposition toward peace and the repeated American petitions to the king. We might expect that, on occasions of rejoicing for the benefits of independence, Americans would not thus exaggerate the extent to which the colonists had tried to remain part of the British Empire. By including such passages, orators did not mean to censure their ancestors for fighting Britain; the orators wanted to exonerate the Revolutionaries from all responsibility for seeking violence. They perpetuated the judgment of a Connecticut minister who said soon after the Revolutionary War began, "All the blood shed, horrors felt, and distresses endured, must be laid at the doors of the aggressors."[52]

The new nation, its creators wanted to believe, was founded on liberty, not on belligerent haste to attack British rule. For if the latter were the case, the loyalist James Chalmers might have been justified in blaming "turbulent ambition" for having led Americans "to anticipate an event which the fulness of time would probably produce without bloodshed."[53] Americans thus would have killed and died unnecessarily, and the memory of military conflict would invite recrimination instead of national pride. To spare the country this fate, the war must be correctly interpreted, and one of the sermons celebrating peace in 1783 summarized the interpretation that thereafter predominated: "A widely extended desolation has been made, innumerable calamities produced, and many, many thousands of lives sacrificed in the late contest: Their blood still *crieth from the ground*. That it doth not cry against our

---

[52] Nathan Perkins, *A Sermon, Preached to the Soldiers* . . . (Hartford, [1775]), pp. 7–8.

[53] [James Chalmers], *Additions to Plain Truth* . . . (Philadelphia, 1776), p. 105.

country, is surely a most pleasing reflection, a circumstance which greatly heightens the joy of the present occasion."[54]

This theme grew even more pressing during the War of 1812. Federalist opponents of the war publicly blamed it on the American leaders, not the British. Republicans would have to bear the guilt for the bloodshed in an unnecessary war. Perhaps partly for this reason, Republicans called their accusers "tories." The second War of Independence was no less essential and no less the fault of Britain than the first. In 1813 Benjamin Gleason compiled a list of British atrocities from the Revolution to the War of 1812 and contrasted them with America's innocence: "How do these deep hues and direful shades in the escutcheon of *England's* glory, brighten the *Stripes and Stars* of our American Republic!—Look at HER *victorious* colors; they are untarnished with a single *blood-speck* of inhumanity."[55] Anyone who questioned the Americans' guiltlessness in the second war implied similar doubts about the first and was, therefore, like the tories, no true American. If the Federalists were right—if the United States had in fact sought conflict—it might thereby have revealed a similarity to the tyrannical and bloodthirsty nations from whom Americans sought to differentiate themselves. This was Congressman Brigham's warning when he denied the Americans' right to invade Canada: "There is no right but a Napoleon right, and that right is power, and not that which reason approves."[56] Such a resemblance between America and other countries could be fatal to a republic founded on voluntarism, since it might lead to wars of conquest, standing armies, domestic corruption, and a tyrant.

These attempts to preserve the uniqueness of America's nationality helped shape the memory of the Revolution. From the start Americans often remembered selectively. They glorified the Revolution through pride in victory or declarations of principle. Perhaps equally important, they strove to re-

[54] David Osgood, *Reflections on the Goodness of God* . . . (Boston, 1784), p. 14.

[55] *An Oration, Pronounced . . . July 5, 1813* (Boston, 1813), p. 7.

[56] U.S., Congress, House, *Annals of Congress*, 12th Cong., 2d sess., 1813, p. 514.

member the war as humane and reasonable. Recalling the War of Independence while praising the War of 1812, Samuel Berrian said, "Other revolutions have been conducted with sanguinary violence; ours with a spirit of dignified moderation, worthy of the cause, and characteristic of the nation. The patriots of the revolution were as humane as they were brave.... Here, war is the act of the people who fight. It emanates from a source that cannot guide it wrong."[57] War seemed more palatable, even honorable, as part of the country's founding if the war had been reasonable and decent. This version of the Revolution glorified military conflict by trying to prove its conformity with the rational, voluntaristic definition of America. Lincoln relied on this version in the closing of his first inaugural address. He assumed that the memory of the battlefields of the Revolution would appeal to "the better angels of our nature." Surely the Revolutionary War had established a moderate, humane national character in which Northerners and Southerners could unite.

But perhaps Lincoln was wrong. Reviving the memory of battles might have other consequences. The "mystic chords" emanating from the Revolution might reawaken the memory of violence that had not been completely subordinated to principles, even by eighty-five years of orations. Only another and far bloodier war, not a romanticized recollection of the Revolutionary War, could define the political legacy of the American Revolution. The Civil War established by force that the Revolution had made America a nation.[58] To appeal to the lesson of the Revolution, as Lincoln did, was to appeal to bloodshed as well as ideals. And this bloodshed had not always seemed as inspirational as the ideals said that it should be. Recalling, late in life, his "horror and sickness of heart" at the suffering he saw after one of the Revolutionary War

[57] *Oration before the Tammany Society*, pp. 6, 27.

[58] The relationship between the military conflict and American nationality in the Civil War is thoughtfully treated in David M. Potter, "The Historian's Use of Nationalism and Vice Versa," *The South and the Sectional Conflict* (Baton Rouge, 1968), pp. 34–83; James H. Moorhead, *American Apocalypse: Yankee Protestants and the Civil War, 1860–1869* (New Haven, 1978); Robert Penn Warren, *The Legacy of the Civil War: Meditations on the Centennial* (New York, 1961).

battles, at Saratoga, John P. Becker said, "The remembrance cannot be effaced." He drew from the battlefield a legacy no less "mystic" than Lincoln's. But the chords of memory to which he responded in his old age were not touched solely by better angels. He asked, "And is public happiness then bought at the price of individual wretchedness? Must blood and tears and sorrow be the result of even the most just and righteous controversies? The human heart, 'a tangled yarn,' brings a curse on its own plans. Even its virtues are allied to the demons of its fallen nature."[59] The citizens of a nation founded and united through military conflict would return to a legacy of war when they sought to know themselves as a people. It was a legacy that their principles could never fully sanctify nor their memory ever completely escape. And their nationality would partake as much of the violence they remembered as of the principles they avowed.

[59] *The Sexagenary: Or, Reminiscences of the American Revolution*, ed. Simeon DeWitt Bloodgood (Albany, 1866), p. 96.

ROBERT K. WRIGHT, JR.

"Nor Is Their Standing Army to Be Despised":
The Emergence of the Continental Army as a Military Institution

HISTORIANS OF EARLY AMERICA have frequently traced the evolution of European institutions as they adjusted to New World conditions. Military historians have recognized the validity of this theme and have employed it in their study of the colonial militia. We must remember, however, that evolution was a process that continued into the era of the American Revolution. It played an important part in the creation of the Continental army as a force of regular troops distinct from the militias and other units of the several states. The American achievement was the development of this new military institution—the Continental army—by blending contemporary European theory and practice with a colonial military heritage.

By the end of the seventeenth century the flintlock musket and the socket bayonet had supplanted the more cumbersome matchlock firearm and long pike as the dominant infantry weapons in both hemispheres. Western armies devoted the eighteenth century to the search for tactics and a system of unit organization that would effectively employ these weapons as well as other technological advances. The search for a rational and efficient use of limited resources led to

The opinions expressed in this paper are the author's and do not necessarily represent the views of either the United States Army or its Center of Military History.

major innovations and transformed battles from relatively ponderous collisions into fluid events.

Europeans and Americans began the century with regiments and companies as basic military units. Subtle changes resulted from the tactical impact of the new weapons. The pike and, to a lesser extent, the bayonet are weapons of shock action; they gain value from the impact made by men grouped in dense, deep formations. The musket is a weapon of fire. Units equipped with it are most effective when the maximum numbers of soldiers are able to shoot at the same time at the same target. In the eighteenth century, muskets were extremely inaccurate, and Europeans preferred firing at an area rather than an individual target, counting on the cumulative impact of a volley to shake the opposition.

The deployment Europeans arrived at to maximize the effectiveness of the new weaponry was one that placed the musketmen in long lines three men deep. The platoon became the basic element of fire, representing the largest body of men that could be controlled by a handful of officers. A battalion served as the basic element of maneuver, coordinating the movements of eight platoons. During the course of the century most armies simplified organization by deploying a regiment in one or two battalions, and a company in one or two platoons; brigades and divisions were developed as echelons to handle groups of battalions. Other improvements included the cadenced march step, unified systems of drill, and fixed maneuvers, all of which advanced battlefield mobility and flexibility. Military theorists such as the comte de Saxe and the comte de Guibert started to articulate written systems to deal with these changes and the emergence of true field artillery, particularly after 1750. During the course of the century European nations were frequently at war; as a result, they maintained relatively large permanent, or standing, armies that fought in open areas where transportation systems could support movement by large bodies. Men made the military a career and naturally devoted more attention to resolving organizational problems than did their American counterparts.[1]

[1] The best general discussions of military change in the eighteenth century are David G. Chandler, *The Art of Warfare in the Age of Marlborough*

ARMS AND INDEPENDENCE

Unique conditions of the colonial environment, particularly the absence of a significant European threat, led the mainland colonies down a different path of development. They did not need to maintain a permanent military establishment and relied instead on the militia. Virtually the entire adult male population of a colony was grouped according to geographical patterns of settlement into companies and regiments, required to maintain arms, and placed under some form of obligatory periodic training. While this system could mobilize large forces in local defense, it could not deal with problems involving service over distances or long periods. A separate institution emerged—semiregular provincial units enlisted for the duration of a single campaign. These forces relieved the militia from the burden of offensive combat. The absence of a permanent regular force lessened the need of the colonists to develop a military literature or to adopt many of the other refinements appearing in Europe. They did, however, place heavy emphasis on firepower rather than shock.[2]

American political leaders during the decade before the Revolution condemned the regular British regiments stationed in North America after the Seven Years' War. They perceived them to be a standing army placed in their midst by a corrupt ministry to enforce unpopular laws and subvert colonial lib-

---

(New York, 1976); Robert S. Quimby, *The Background of Napoleonic Warfare: The Theory of Military Tactics in Eighteenth-Century France* (New York, 1957); and Richard Glover, *Peninsular Preparation: The Reform of the British Army, 1795–1809* (Cambridge, 1963). J. F. C. Fuller, *British Light Infantry in the Eighteenth Century* (London, 1925) should be used with some caution.

[2] See especially Louis Morton, "The Origins of American Military Policy," *Military Affairs* 22 (1958):75–82; John Shy, "A New Look at Colonial Militia," *William and Mary Quarterly*, 3d ser. 20 (1963):175–85; Darrett B. Rutman, "A Militant New World, 1607–1640: America's First Generation, Its Martial Spirit, Its Tradition of Arms, Its Militia Organization, Its Wars," Ph.D. diss., University of Virginia, 1959; Patrick Mitchell Malone, "Indian and English Military Systems in New England in the Seventeenth Century," Ph.D. diss., Brown University, 1971; and Douglas E. Leach, *Arms for Empire: A Military History of the British Colonies in North America, 1607–1763* (New York, 1973).

erties. Especially after 1770 American leaders emphasized the traditional role of the militia as the military institution of a virtuous citizenry. They believed that a vigorous militia proved that honest American yeomen deserved the rights of Englishmen and eliminated the ministry's justification for stationing regulars in the colonies.[3]

The Continental army of 1775 followed a precedent set in the French and Indian wars. In the aftermath of Lexington each New England colony raised an army patterned after the provincials. The regiments composing these armies enlisted to serve for the remainder of the year and stood outside the militia system. This decision made economic sense, but it also had ideological appeal. The regiments did not constitute a permanent or standing army; they were raised by the people through revolutionary governments and thus were subordinate to American civilian authority in a way that British regulars had not been. Politicians also assumed that citizens would voluntarily take turns serving in them. On June 14, 1775, the Continental Congress adopted these existing troops and started raising others as "the American continental army," a national force. Subsequent legislation appointed George Washington as commander in chief and created general officers, a staff system, two major territorial commands, and Articles of War.[4]

In 1776 Congress continued raising regiments for a single year but enlarged the army to include units from every state

---

[3] John Todd White, "Standing Armies in Time of War: Republican Theory and Military Practice during the American Revolution," Ph.D. diss., George Washington University, 1978, pp. 1–74; Lawrence Delbert Cress, "The Standing Army, the Militia, and the New Republic: Changing Attitudes toward the Military in American Society, 1768 to 1820," Ph.D. diss., University of Virginia, 1976, pp. 1–126.

[4] Worthington C. Ford, ed., *Journals of the Continental Congress, 1774–1789*, 34 vols. (Washington, D.C., 1904–37), 2:49–67, 73–74, 89–106, 111–22, 194; Paul H. Smith et al., eds., *Letters of Delegates to Congress, 1774–1789*, 8 vols. to date (Washington, D.C., 1976–), 1:351–548. Full discussion and documentation for many of the themes in this paper are found in Robert K. Wright, Jr., "Organization and Doctrine in the Continental Army, 1774 to 1784," Ph.D. diss., College of William and Mary, 1980.

and Canada. In addition, it expanded the staff and the system of dividing field command into territorial departments. It also formed a standing committee, the Board of War and Ordnance, to supervise military affairs. Army leaders organized some regiments from the veterans of 1775; others entered as new formations raised by the individual states. The latter included both existing units transferred from state control and organizations recruited at Congress's request. The army of 1776, like its predecessor, contained infantry regiments under a number of different organizational structures and supported by units of riflemen and artillerists.

Washington, Congress, and the Continental army's leaders developed a standard infantry regiment as an ideal in 1776. Unlike the British army, which emphasized the European tradition of shock action through bayonet charges, the Continentals stressed colonial experience in the value of aimed musket fire. The ideal Continental regiment contained 728 officers and men in eight companies that deployed 640 musketmen in two ranks as a battalion of eight platoons. A typical British regiment had a dozen companies with an aggregate strength of 809. This figure is highly misleading, however, for two of the companies were recruiting depots in the home islands and two (the grenadier and light infantry companies) normally served in special composite battalions instead of with the regiment. The remaining eight companies fought in a single battalion with a maximum strength of 448 muskets. The Continental unit was a simpler organization which placed all 640 musketmen in a formation for effective volley fire and which retained a high ratio of officers and sergeants for control. The British practice of deploying in three ranks (changed in 1778 to two ranks) reduced its power to only 300 effective shots per volley since the fire of the third rank was sacrificed to achieve depth for bayonet action.[5]

[5] Ford, ed., *Journals of Congress*, 3:321–25, 399. John C. Fitzpatrick, ed., *The Writings of George Washington* . . ., 39 vols. (Washington, D.C., 1931–44), 4:213–14. British organization can be traced in the Headquarters Papers of the British Army in America, Colonial Williamsburg Foundation, Williamsburg, Va. (photostats of documents presented to the Queen in 1957 and currently Class 30/55 in the Public Record Office).

By the summer of 1776 British pressure on New York and Fort Ticonderoga outstripped Continental army resources. Congress asked the states to mobilize almost thirty thousand militiamen. Delegates hoped that militia units would reach the field fairly rapidly, but their action had ideological roots as well. Many political leaders believed that the Continental army should remain relatively small and rely in a crisis on popular commitment expressed in the form of militia service. The fall of New York convinced a majority of army officers that militia reinforcements could not take the place of regulars. Washington summarized this view when he told Congress, "I am persuaded and as fully convinced, as I am of any one fact that has happened, that our liberties must of necessity be greatly hazarded, If not entirely lost, If their defence is left to any but a permanent standing Army, I mean one to exist during the War."[6]

On September 16, 1776, Congress agreed with this argument and reversed its earlier policies: it authorized 88 regiments under the 1776 structure to be enlisted for the duration of the war. Congress expected this force to eliminate most militia responsibility for direct battlefield combat. Longer enlistments allowed the army to improve training and discipline and employ revised Articles of War.[7] Further reverses and Washington's requests augmented the force by the end of December to 110 regiments of infantry, 5 of artillery, 4 of light dragoons, and a small group of specialized support troops.[8]

[6] Fitzpatrick, ed., *Writings of Washington*, 6:5. Also see Russell W. Knight, ed., "General John Glover's Letterbook," *Essex Institute Historical Collections* 112 (1976):3–6.

[7] Ford, ed., *Journals of Congress*, 5:729, 762–63, 788–807, 853–56; Smith, ed., *Letters of Delegates*, 3:294–96; 4:291–93, 649–50; 5:62–63, 117–18, 128–29, 162–64, 228–31. On September 15 Francis Lightfoot Lee captured the spirit of Congress: "We find from experience that regulars can only effectually be opposed to the British troops ... we shall not have recourse to the militia, but upon extraordinary occasions" (Smith, ed., *Letters of Delegates*, 5:173–74).

[8] Ford, ed., *Journals of Congress*, 6:963, 981, 995, 1025, 1040, 1043–46; 7:7, 178–79; Peter Force, ed., *American Archives*, 5th ser., 3 vols. (Washing-

ARMS AND INDEPENDENCE

A number of specific changes increased the effectiveness of the regulars in 1777. Systematic innoculation of recruits brought smallpox under control.[9] Imported arms, including over one hundred thousand French muskets of the 1763 model, magnified the organizational strength of the infantry. The "Charleville" musket's range, accuracy, and durability suited the Continental army's preference for aimed fire rather than bayonet charges and justified the deployment in two rather than three ranks.[10]

The most important development of 1777 came with the organization of tactical brigades and divisions, with the former emerging as the basic element of maneuver. In January, based on experience in the Trenton campaign, Washington planned to have three full infantry regiments and a company of artillery in each brigade, and three brigades in a division. Four months later he established the first permanent brigades in the main army. Each called for about two thousand men in four or five understrength regiments and an artillery company. Two brigades formed a more transitory division. The brigade staff included the general's personal aide, a brigade major (administrative specialist), a quartermaster, and a chaplain. The division staff included two aides, a quartermaster, and a conductor of military stores who prepared the ammunition and repaired small arms. Similar arrangements occurred in the other major field armies. Washington frequently used brigades in a cordon formation, expecting each in turn to delay an enemy advance while the rest of the army

---

ton, D.C., 1848–53), 3:1314; Fitzpatrick, ed., *Writings of Washington*, 6:280–82, 332–33, 350–51, 379–84, 400–409, 474; 7:18–23, 83.

[9] Hugh Thursfield, "Smallpox in the American War of Independence," *Annals of Medical History*, 3d ser. 2 (1940):316–17.

[10] Richard K. Showman et al., eds., *The Papers of General Nathanael Greene*, 2 vols. to date (Chapel Hill, 1976–), 2:46–48; Smith, ed., *Letters of Delegates*, 3:211, 320–23; 4:103–5, 126–28; 5:20, 144–45; Charles J. Stille, *Major-General Anthony Wayne and the Pennsylvania Line in the Continental Army* (Philadelphia, 1893), pp. 64–65; Neil L. York, "Clandestine Aid and the American Revolutionary War Effort: A Re-Examination," *Military Affairs* 43 (1979):26–30; Arcadi Gluckman, *United States Muskets, Rifles and Carbines* (Harrisburg, Pa., 1959), pp. 55–61.

concentrated. In battle a double line of brigades furnished depth to absorb shock; light dragoons, militia, and small units served as skirmishers and flank guards.[11]

Artillery organization complemented the infantry. Henry Knox and Washington continued the practice, initiated at Trenton, of assigning an intact company to each brigade. It normally used two 3- to 6-pound fieldpieces, but adjusted armament to suit a specific mission. Other companies remained in a reserve (artillery park) or defended forts. Knox had his gunners concentrate their fire on enemy infantry, a practice that reinforced aimed musketry. The British preferred counterbattery fire. This facilitated bayonet charges by focusing efforts on eliminating cannon that could inflict prohibitive casualties on advancing infantry. American artillerists relied on John Muller's *Treatise of Artillery* when they cast tubes or constructed carriages. This book was used as a text at the Royal Military Academy at Woolwich although the Royal Artillery did not formally endorse the Muller system.[12]

Congress created a large standing army in 1777. It ap-

[11] Fitzpatrick, ed., *Writings of Washington*, 7:49–51, 236, 278, 396–97, 447–48, 451–52; 8:40–41, 49–50, 62–64, 88–89, 97–101, 170–72, 203–4, 337; 9:103–4, 149; 10:94–95, 138–39; Otis G. Hammond, ed., *Letters and Papers of Major-General John Sullivan, Continental Army*, 3 vols. (Concord, N.H., 1930–39), 1:352; Ford, ed., *Journals of Congress*, 8:390, 609; Showman, ed., *Papers of Greene*, 2:212–13; Weekly Return, Main Army, May 21, 1777, Record Group 93, National Archives. Note the similarity in this usage and Napoleon's use of a corps as described in Steven T. Ross, "The Development of the Combat Division in Eighteenth-Century French Armies," *French Historical Studies* 4 (1965):84–94.

[12] Fitzpatrick, ed., *Writings of Washington*, 6:364, 454; 8:100–101, 175, 235, 396–99, 457–58; 9:290; Showman, ed., *Papers of Greene*, 2:64–65; Smith, ed., *Letters of Delegates*, 4:109–10; Eleazer Oswald to John Lamb, June 17 and 25, July 23 and 25, Aug. 14, 1777, Robert Walker to Lamb, July 21, 1777, Andrew Moodie to Lamb, May 9, 1777, Henry Knox to Lamb, Dec. 2, 1777, and Aug. 30, 1780, Lamb Papers, New-York Historical Society, New York City; Sebastian Bauman to Lamb, June 25, 1779, Samuel Shaw to Bauman, Feb. 17, 1777, Bauman Papers, N.-Y. Hist. Soc.; John Muller, *A Treatise of Artillery*, 3d ed. (1780; reprint ed. with intro. by Harold L. Peterson, Ottawa, 1965), pp. v-xxv. Muller was first published in 1757 and was reprinted in 1779 in Philadelphia expressly for the Continental army's artillery officers.

proved virtually every suggestion made by the military leaders but expected results on the battlefield. During that year Ticonderoga and the forts on the Hudson River above New York fell to the British, and William Howe took Philadelphia. On the other hand, Horatio Gates's Northern Department regulars captured Burgoyne with the assistance of militia reinforcements. In each case, Continentals carried out the major burden of fighting. On January 18, 1778, Capt. Johann Heinrichs of the Hesse-Cassel Jäger reported to his government, "Nor is their standing army to be despised . . . [it only] requires Time and good leadership to make them formidable."[13] Other German professionals with Howe noted that while American musket fire was particularly effective, the Continentals had difficulty maneuvering efficiently on the battlefield.[14] American leaders sought to correct these defects during the winter lull in operations.

Policy debates during the Valley Forge winter derived from opposite interpretations of the 1777 campaign. In Saratoga one group of Congressional delegates and military leaders saw evidence for a return to the concept of a small army supported in major battles by militia. Washington, most senior

[13] Johann Heinrichs, "Extracts from the Letter-Book of Captain Johann Heinrichs of the Hessian Jager Corps, 1778–1780," trans. Julian F. Sachse, *Pennsylvania Magazine of History and Biography* 22 (1898):137–40. Letters by professional German soldiers sent to other professional soldiers in Europe offer precise, objective military detail often missing from reports of British or American participants.

[14] Friedrich von Muenchhausen, *At General Howe's Side: The Diary of General Howe's Aide de Camp, Captain Friedrich von Muenchhausen*, trans. and ed. Ernst Kipping and Samuel S. Smith, (Monmouth Beach, N.J., 1974), pp. 31–32, 38–39; Carl Leopold Baurmeister, *Letters from Major Baurmeister to Colonel von Jungkenn Written during the Philadelphia Campaign 1777–1778*, trans. and ed. Bernard A. Uhlendorf and Edna Vosper (Philadelphia, 1937), pp. 5–27; Justin Winsor, ed., "Col. John Eager Howard's Account of the Battle of Germantown," *Maryland Historical Magazine* 4 (1909):314–20; Henry Hobart Bellas, ed., *Personal Recollections of Captain Enoch Anderson, An Officer of the Delaware Regiments in the Revolutionary War* (Wilmington, Del., 1896), pp. 43–46; "Diary of Joseph Clark, Attached to the Continental Army, from May, 1778 [1777], to November, 1779 [1778]," *Proceedings of the New Jersey Historical Society*, 1st ser. 7 (1854):98–101.

officers, and other delegates continued to support the 1777 plan. They called for further improvements, gradually achieved changes in organization and training, and codified tactical precepts.

Transformation of the Board of War into a permanent administrative body created the first conflict. Prompted by former Quartermaster General Thomas Mifflin, the delegates established the new board as Congress's sole official channel for dealing with the army and the states on military matters. Gates, the hero of Saratoga, became its president and Mifflin one of its key members. They then attempted to convert the board into an agency to control all military operations by planning an "irruption" into Canada in January 1778. Gates persuaded Congress to name the young marquis de Lafayette as the leader of this invasion, but expected the Frenchman to become a mere figurehead. Gates intended to have an Irish veteran of the French army, Maj. Gen. Thomas Conway, exercise real command. Conway had already informed Gates that he planned to use his official position as an inspector general to further the policies of the board. Lafayette's political skills and his refusal to participate in any activity that undermined Washington's authority brought the project to a halt on March 2.[15] Its demise and the publicity over a letter criticizing Washington ended this challenge to Washington's leadership. Conway and Mifflin resigned, and Gates left the board.

In a related development, Congress sent a "Committee of Conference" to Valley Forge to investigate ways to reduce

---

[15] Ford, ed., *Journals of Congress*, 7:241–42; 8:474n, 563; 9:809–11, 818–20, 874, 936, 941, 959–63, 971–72, 999–1001, 1026; 10:84–85, 87, 107, 216–17, 253–54; Edmund Cody Burnett, ed., *Letters of Members of the Continental Congress*, 8 vols. (Washington, D.C., 1921–36), 2:52, 574–76; 3:63–65, 124–30; Stanley J. Idzerda et al., eds., *Lafayette in the Age of the American Revolution: Selected Letters and Papers, 1776–1790*, 4 vols. to date (Ithaca, N.Y., 1977–), 1:xxiv–xxvi, 169–72, 204–7, 213–18, 245–385; Worthington C. Ford, ed., *Letters of Joseph Jones of Virginia* (Washington, D.C., 1889), pp. 5–8; Showman, ed., *Papers of Greene*, 2:259–61, 275–77; Thomas Conway to Horatio Gates, Nov. 11, 1777, and Jan. 4, 1778, Gates Papers, N.-Y. Hist. Soc.; James M. Varnum to Alexander McDougall, Feb. 7, 1778, McDougall Papers, N.-Y. Hist. Soc.

expenses. The pragmatic delegates who formed the committee met with Washington and his staff from January 28 until March 12. They filled the role that Mifflin and Gates had intended for the Board of War, but with a major difference: the members usually supported Washington's views. The committee guided Congressional action on a number of issues important to military leaders. Its intense lobbying, for example, contributed to the passage of a compromise that defused the explosive issue of half pay. Washington had hoped to use pensions worth half an officer's salary as a tool to upgrade the quality of the officer corps. Many delegates believed that pensions, common in European armies, implied a military aristocracy and violently opposed the concept. Congress rejected lifetime pensions but did agree to the committee's alternative of promising officers who served to the end of the war a sum equal to half of their pay for seven years.[16]

The committee also developed a compromise solution to the thorny problem of reconciling the large army authorized for 1777 with the reality of severe shortages of enlisted men. Congress lacked the legal authority to enforce a draft, the only practical way for Washington to obtain the manpower needed to fill his regiments. Many delegates wanted to trim expenses by lowering the ratio of officers to enlisted men. The committee's answer combined recommending permanent recruiting organizations and short-term drafting to the states, and new comprehensive legislation on regimental organizations. The latter, passed on May 22, 1778, lowered the percentage of officers but gave Washington certain new types of units.[17] The result of the committee's actions was expected

[16] Ford, ed., *Journals of Congress*, 10:39–41, 67, 285–86, 300–301; 11:502–3; Burnett, ed., *Letters*, 2:585–86; 3:31–34, 61–115, 123–24, 131, 160–63, 212–13, 219–21, 244–45, 255–56; Fitzpatrick, ed., *Writings of Washington*, 11:285–86, 290–92, 415.

[17] Fitzpatrick, ed., *Writings of Washington*, 11:475–76; 12:30–35, 60–62, 274–75; Burnett, ed., *Letters*, 3:263–66, 407, 431–32; Ford, ed., *Journals of Congress*, 11:538–43, 570, 633–34; 12:1154–60. It had also rejected a proposal by Charles Lee to adopt the "legion" of the comte de Saxe (Ford, ed., *Journals of Congress*, 11:514–15; "The Lee Papers," New-York Historical Society *Collections* for 1871–74 (New York, 1872–75), 2:382–89; Wor-

to be "a cleaver little snug Army, well clothed, well fed, and well deciplind."[18]

Under the legislation of May 27 an infantry regiment shrank to 29 officers and 553 enlisted men despite the addition of a light infantry company. The eight line companies now deployed only 448 muskets in the battalion, roughly the same total as a British regiment. Elimination of various regimental staff officers cut combat efficiency by reducing the reservoir of leaders available to replace casualties in combat. In contrast, a light dragoon regiment nearly doubled in size to 29 officers and 386 men. This change complemented Washington's attempt to upgrade the dragoon's combat potential. The four regiments of dragoons wintered at Trenton under Casimir Pulaski, a Polish volunteer, and received training in European-style cavalry shock action. Personality problems led Pulaski to resign as commander of horse in April. Washington never found a replacement, and strategic changes returned the light dragoons to their original reconnaissance role.[19]

Other European volunteers and ideas made a more dramatic impact on military engineering, a notorious weakness of the Continental army early in the war. Louis Duportail and three other French engineers arrived in mid-1777 on "loan" from the comte de Saint-Germain, the French minister of war. By the time of Valley Forge, Duportail's professional skills had earned him the trusted position of chief of engineers. He assembled a portable set of temporary bridges

---

thington C. Ford, ed., *Correspondence and Journals of Samuel Blachley Webb*, 3 vols. [New York, 1893–94], 1:84–87).

[18] Nathanael Greene to William Greene, Mar. 7, 1778, Showman, ed., *Papers of Greene*, 2:302; also see pp. 262–66; Ford, ed., *Journals of Congress*, 8:593–95, 670; 9:930; 10:39–40, 199–203; Fitzpatrick, ed., *Writings of Washington*, 8:440; 9:365–67, 406–7; 10:125–26, 153, 195, 197–98, 205, 221–25; 11:236–40.

[19] Ford, ed., *Journals of Congress*, 8:745; 12:897, 941; Burnett, ed., *Letters*, 3:408; Fitzpatrick, ed., *Writings of Washington*, 7:51, 190–91; 9:143–44, 305; 10:234–36; 11:446; 12:228, 276, 490; 13:14–15. Gates to Washington, May 23, 1778, Benjamin Tallmadge to Gates, June 1, 1778, Gates Papers.

that enhanced the main army's mobility, and he developed a complex fortress at West Point to serve as a strategic pivot. Duportail's suggestions led to the inclusion of three companies of combat engineers in the May 27 resolve. They served a dual purpose. In addition to a combat role, Duportail planned to give their officers training as apprentice engineers, a step that in time would produce a steady supply of competent American professional military engineers.[20]

Indirect French influence contributed to the formation of a second category of engineers. France's *Ingenieurs Géographes* emerged from the Seven Years' War as pioneers in the sphere of topographical engineering. Washington understood the value of accurate maps, and in July 1777 Congress approved his request to establish a topographical staff. Robert Erskine reported for duty in June 1778 and coordinated the efforts of up to six survey teams. That raw data emerged as a comprehensive survey of the main army's area of operations.[21] Erskine's maps lacked the polish of French maps, but they were highly accurate and gave Washington a planning tool superior to anything available to British leaders.

Other units created during 1777 and 1778 reflected European rather than colonial or British influences. Partisan corps under Henry Lee, Charles Armand-Tuffin (the marquis de La Rouerie), and Pulaski, each with a unique structure, followed French and German precedents. Armand-Tuffin's, for example, used the comte de Saxe's legionary

---

[20] Fitzpatrick, ed., *Writings of Washington*, 10:35, 433; 11:239, 241, 297–98, 311–12; John B. Reeves, ed., "Extracts from the Letter Books of Lieutenant Enos Reeves, of the Pennsylvania Line," *Pennsylvania Magazine of History and Biography* 20 (1896):458–59; W. F. Boogher, ed., "Captain James Duncan's Diary of the Siege of Yorktown," *Magazine of History* 2 (1905):408; Elizabeth S. Kite, *Brigadier-General Louis Lebegue Duportail: Commandant of Engineers in the Continental Army, 1777–1783* (Washington, D.C., 1933).

[21] Fitzpatrick, ed., *Writings of Washington*, 7:65; 8:372, 433, 495–96; 11:246; 12:21; 14:182–83; 23:68–69; Ford, ed., *Journals of Congress*, 8:580; 18:1118; 20:475–76, 738. The maps are in the Erskine–De Witt Collection, N.-Y. Hist. Soc. British headquarters maps are in the Henry Clinton Papers, William L. Clements Library, University of Michigan, Ann Arbor (copies in the N.-Y. Hist. Soc.).

concept; Pulaski's included a troop of lancers.[22] A special mounted police unit, the Marechaussee Corps, assisted the provost marshal in preserving order and preventing straggling; it was commanded by Capt. Bartholomew von Heer, a Prussian veteran.[23] Skilled workmen and technicians came under more efficient control when Congress created the Artillery Artificer and Quartermaster Artificer regiments. Another unit, the Corps of Invalids, contained men not fit for field duty but able to guard depots. Congress intended to have Col. Lewis Nicola, something of a military theorist, use the Invalids to train junior officers for ultimate reassignment to line units, but that was not done.[24]

The trends developed during the 1778 planning reached a peak in October 1780. Congress and Washington continued joint efforts to deal with economic and recruiting problems by arranging a further reorganization of the army. The "regular army of the United States" shrank on January 1, 1781, to fifty infantry and four artillery regiments, four legionary and two partisan corps, a regiment of artificers, the three companies of engineers, the Marechaussee Corps, and the Invalids. Changes in regimental structure restored some of the 1778 cuts and answered Washington's request for increased combat power. An infantry regiment was increased in size about 20 percent, to 36 officers and 681 enlisted men. It now deployed 544 rank and file under increased control in the eight line companies comprising the battalion. Cuts in the number of artillery companies were offset by increases in

[22] Ford, ed., *Journals of Congress*, 10:291, 294, 314–15, 364; 11:545, 642–45; Fitzpatrick, ed., *Writings of Washington*, 11:80–82, 205–6, 230; 12:152–53, 470; 13:41–43.

[23] Fitzpatrick, ed., *Writings of Washington*, 11:443; 12:26–27, 241; 13:61–63, 68–70; Ford, ed., *Journals of Congress*, 11:729. Von Heer to Steuben, Dec. 31, 1779, Steuben Papers, N.-Y. Hist. Soc.

[24] Ford, ed., *Journals of Congress*, 7:288–89; 8:485–86, 554–56; Lewis Nicola to Congress, Oct. 2, 1777, Record Group 360, National Archives. Nicola's reputation as a military expert stemmed from publishing a translation of the chevalier de Clairac's *L'Ingénieur de campagne: or, Field Engineer* (Philadelphia, 1776) and his own *A Treatise of Military Exercise, Calculated for the Use of Americans* (Philadelphia, 1776).

the enlisted men in each. The light dragoon regiment converted to a legionary corps by dismounting two of its six troops to gain a permanent infantry contingent for greater tactical stability. A partisan corps, which operated at a greater distance from a field army, adopted an arrangement of three mounted and three dismounted troops.[25]

The organizational changes initiated after 1777 sought to increase the military efficiency and sophistication of the Continental army. Shortages of men and other resources contributed to individual differences, but an overriding pattern of trans-Atlantic influence does emerge. By 1781 the Continental army resembled a small eighteenth-century European standing army, with adjustments such as a two-rank deployment and a much lower proportion of cavalry to meet specific conditions of North American geography and society. Individual foreign volunteers played an even larger role in the related development of unified training and the codification of tactical doctrine, a standard set of practices carefully supervised by Washington and his senior officers. Neither the early Continental army nor its provincial predecessors attained the degree of institutional permanence required to formulate written doctrine. Many individuals within the army attempted to read military books, particularly those written in England or available in translation, but it took an influx of European volunteers familiar with the latest French works on military theory to produce an American consensus on tactics.

European armies originally employed linear tactics (*l'ordre mince*) to take advantage of the musket. Most sacrificed some firepower by using a three-rank formation in order to gain greater stability and to employ the bayonet. Frederick the Great and his Prussian army epitomized this approach for most military men in the latter eighteenth century, although his *Instructions for His Generals* (available in translations after

[25] Ford, ed., *Journals of Congress*, 18:893–97, 959–62; Burnett, ed., *Letters*, 5:404, 407, 414–15, 417–18, 422–23, 428; Fitzpatrick, ed., *Writings of Washington*, 20:157–67, 263–64, 277–81, 311–12, 400; Steuben to Board of War, Feb. 5, 1780, Steuben to Washington, Oct. 23, 1780, Steuben Papers.

1760) hardly qualified as a comprehensive text. Several Frenchmen developed an alternative approach that called for dense infantry columns. These sacrificed still more firepower to maximize the bayonet's shock effect. Leaders of this school (*l'ordre profond*) included Jean-Charles de Folard, Joly de Maizeroy, and François-Jean de Mesnil-Durand. A new, comprehensive view, *l'ordre mixte*, emerged just before the Revolution. The comte de Guibert's 1772 *Essai général de tactique* espoused a flexible use of line and column according to the specific tactical situation and crosstraining soldiers for duty as both line and light infantry.[26]

The British army lagged behind the other leading powers in developing military theory. British officers learned their profession by actual service and generally ignored available European works. Most eighteenth-century British authors produced either simple drill manuals or handbooks on regimental duties. Humphrey Bland's 1727 *Treatise of Military Discipline* only outlined the practices of Marlborough's army. Under the duke of Cumberland and Lord Ligonier the British army came under Prussian influence. That trend culminated in 1764 with a new drill manual by Edward Harvey. "The '64" remained Britain's nominal official drill until 1795. Other popular manuals included Campbell Dalrymple's *Military Essay* (1761) and William Windham and George Townshend's *Norfolk Discipline*. Handbooks current at the time of the Revolution included James Wolfe's posthumous *Instructions to Young Officers*, several volumes by William Young, and Thomas Simes's *The Military Guide for Young Officers*.[27]

---

[26] Quimby, *Napoleonic Warfare*, pp. 233–48. Peter Paret, *Yorck and the Era of Prussian Reform, 1807–1815* (Princeton, 1966), pp. 13–15; *Frederick the Great: Instructions for His Generals*, trans. Thomas R. Phillips (Harrisburg, Pa., 1944), pp. 9–10.

[27] In addition to Glover, *Peninsular Preparation*, and Fuller, *British Light Infantry*, see Ira D. Gruber, "British Strategy: The Theory and Practice of Eighteenth-Century Warfare," in Don Higginbotham, ed., *Reconsiderations on the Revolutionary War: Selected Essays* (Westport, Conn., 1978), pp. 14–31; Rex Whitworth, *Field Marshal Lord Ligonier: A Story of the British Army, 1702–1770* (Oxford, 1958), pp. 32n, 34, 37n, 218; and Chandler, *The Art of Warfare*, pp. 106–7, 117.

Americans imported or reprinted many British, French, and German works before 1783 and read them avidly.[28] Technical artillery and engineering volumes included John Muller's treatises, translations of the chevalier de Clairac's *Field Engineer*, and J. C. Pleydell's *Essay on Field Fortifications*. Drill manuals, however, constituted the largest category of imports and reprints. A dozen American editions of Bland appeared between 1743 and 1759. Connecticut militia adopted it in 1743 and only discarded it in 1769 when officers complained that it was "prolix and encumbered with many useless motions."[29] Other popular works included the Prussian infantry drill, Cumberland's regulations, Simes's *Military Guide*, Dalrymple's *Military Essay*, the earl of Cavan's *New System of Military Discipline*, and Wolfe's *Instructions*. Washington himself owned copies of Bland, Cavan, Simes, Windham and Townshend's *Norfolk Discipline*, and Young's *Maneouvres*.

The popularity of the *Norfolk Discipline* in New England generated five editions of the book between 1768 and 1775 and its adoption by the Massachusetts and Connecticut militias. Although it simplified regular drills to some extent, its manual of arms still included 50 commands and 155 separate motions, 24 of which related to firing. Part of the book's value to Americans came from numerous references to various classical and contemporary European authors.[30] In addition,

---

[28] The following survey is based particularly on Charles Evans et al., eds., *American Bibliography*, 14 vols. (Chicago, 1903–59), Appleton P. C. Griffin, comp., *A Catalogue of the Washington Collection in the Boston Athenaeum* (Boston, 1897), and Henry Knox, *A Catalogue of Books Imported and to Be Sold by Henry Knox* (Boston, 1772). A more detailed treatment and full list of American imprints is found in Wright, "Organization and Doctrine," pp. 218–28, 310–12.

[29] James Hammond Trumbull and Charles J. Hoadley, eds., *The Public Papers of the Colony of Connecticut*, 15 vols. (Hartford, 1850–90), 8:568; 13:190; King Lawrence Parker, "Anglo-American Wilderness Campaigning, 1754–1764: Logistical and Tactical Developments," Ph.D. diss., Columbia University, 1970, p. 138n.

[30] Trumbull and Hoadley, eds., *Papers of Connecticut*, 13:190; 15:195; Windham, *A Plan of Discipline, Composed for the Use of the Militia of the County of Norfolk* (London, 1759), pp. x-xxiii.

Timothy Pickering, Thomas Hanson, Thomas Davis, and Lewis Nicola published their own drill manuals between 1775 and 1776, but these enjoyed lesser readership.

Harvey's "64" became the paramount manual for American officers between 1766 and 1777. Nineteen imprints appeared in cities from Boston to Williamsburg, especially in 1774, 1775, and 1776. Rhode Island and Massachusetts officially adopted it for militia use in 1774; Virginia, North Carolina, and Connecticut followed suit the next year for militia and Continentals. Harvey's popularity in the main army led Brigadier Generals Alexander McDougall and Samuel Parsons, with Washington's blessing, to make its use mandatory in their brigades on July 18, 1777.[31]

One significant British innovation during the French and Indian War solved the problem of operating with regular troops in the American wilderness. John Forbes and Henri Bouquet based their campaigns on ideas in the comte Turpin de Crissé's *Commentaires sur les Mémoires de Montecuccoli* and the comte de Saxe's *Mes reveries*. Americans, particularly Washington, who served as a brigade commander under Forbes in 1758, paid a great deal of attention to the Crisse-Saxe-Forbes-Bouquet line of thought. They valued refer-

---

[31] Force, ed., *American Archives*, 4th ser., 6 vols. (Washington, D.C., 1837–46), 1:843–49, 1145; 5th ser., 1:1346; Smith, ed., *Letters of Delegates*, 1:298–301; Showman, ed., *Papers of Greene*, 1:70–71; John Russell Bartlett, ed., *Records of the Colony of Rhode Island and Providence Plantations, in New England*, 9 vols. (Providence, 1856–65), 7:269–71; Trumbull and Hoadley, eds., *Papers of Connecticut*, 15:195; William Waller Henning, ed., *The Statutes at Large; Being a Collection of All the Laws of Virginia, from the First Session of the Legislature, in the Year 1619*, 3 vols. (Richmond, 1809–23), 9:9–35; William L. Saunders, ed., *The Colonial Records of North Carolina*, 10 vols. (Raleigh, 1886–90), 10:198; Worthington C. Ford, ed., *General Orders Issued by Major General Israel Putnam, When in Command of the Highlands, in the Summer and Fall of 1777* (Brooklyn, 1893), p. 31; Ford, ed., *Correspondence and Journals of Webb*, 1:247; Julian P. Boyd et al., eds., *The Papers of Thomas Jefferson*, 19 vols. to date (Princeton, 1950–), 1:160–62; Brent Tartar, ed., "The Orderly Book of the Second Virginia Regiment, September 27, 1775–April 15, 1776," *Virginia Magazine of History and Biography* 85 (1977):166; George Dudley Seymour, *Documentary Life of Nathan Hale . . .* (New Haven, 1941), p. 181.

ences to aimed musketry and the emphasis on practical training.[32]

Americans displayed intense interest in another group of relatively minor European works. Books on employing partisans in "petit guerre" imported or reprinted in America included Roger Stevenson's *Military Instructions for . . . Carrying on the Petit Guerre*, Jenny's *The Partisan*, and especially Grandmaison's *La petite guerre*, the text that Frederick the Great preferred. Americans such as Henry Jackson believed that partisan operations suited the nation's "natural genius." One significant native American text served as a tactical casebook: Thomas Church's 1716 account of his father Benjamin's campaigns against the Indians during the late seventeenth century.[33]

By 1777, commanders in the Continental army knew the general issues behind European theories and had read many of the important authors whose works existed in translation. Experience accumulated from colonial wars made Saxe and exponents of partisan operations more important to American generals than to their European counterparts. American traditions demanded emphasis on flexibility, simplicity, and marksmanship. These qualities are reflected in the list of basic works Washington cited in 1775: Harvey, Crisse, Stevenson, Jenny, and Young.[34] French and Hessian professional

---

[32] Quimby, *Napoleonic Warfare*, pp. 41–62; Fuller, *British Light Infantry*, pp. 97–98; Parker, "Wilderness Campaigning," pp. 252–342; John K. Mahon, "Anglo-American Methods of Indian Warfare, 1676–1794," *Mississippi Valley Historical Review* 45 (1958):268; Oliver L. Spaulding, Jr., "The Military Studies of George Washington," *American Historical Review* 29 (1924):675–80; Showman, ed., *Papers of Greene*, 1:89–90; Stille, *Wayne*, pp. 23, 75–76; Almon W. Lauber, ed., *Orderly Books of the Fourth New York Regiment . . .* (Albany, 1932), p. 816.

[33] Peter E. Russell, "Redcoats in the Wilderness: British Officers and Irregular Warfare in Europe and America, 1740 to 1760," *William and Mary Quarterly*, 3d ser. 35 (1978):629–52; Paret, *Yorck*, pp. 22–23; Force, ed., *American Archives*, 4th ser. 2:385–86; 5:717.

[34] Fitzpatrick, ed., *Writings of Washington*, 40:80–81; Worthington C. Ford, ed., *Defences of Philadelphia in 1777* (Brooklyn, 1897), pp. 179–88, 193–97, 229–31, 272–76; Smith, ed., *Letters of Delegates*, 4:115–16, 607–10; 5:35–

soldiers commented specifically on Continental officers' studies of the art of war.[35]

Washington hoped to establish a standard system of drill and evolutions prior to the start of the 1777 campaign. Events prevented him from achieving that goal. At Valley Forge several foreign volunteers turned their attention to that deficiency. The chevalier de Mauduit du Plessis, a graduate of the Grenoble artillery school, introduced the army's leaders to Guibert's writings.[36] Baron von Steuben played an even more important role.

Steuben arrived at Valley Forge on February 23, 1778. Although he was only a volunteer without rank, his reputation as a Prussian "lieutenant general" made him an expert on military affairs in American eyes. Washington directed him to prepare the drill regulations, and the main army adopted his system during the spring. Steuben later told Benjamin Franklin that "circumstances . . . obliged me to deviate from the Principles adopted in the European Armies. . . . Young as We are, We have already our Prejudices . . . [and] the pre-

---

36, 191–93, 262–63; Force, ed., *American Archives*, 4th ser. 2:385–86; "Diary of Captain Barnard Elliott," *Charleston Yearbook*, 1889 (Charleston, S.C., 1889), pp. 154–59. Greene summarized the American attitude in December 1777 when he told Washington, "Experience is the best of schools and the safest guide in human affairs, yet I am no advocate of blindly following all the maxims of European policy; but where reason corresponds with what custom has long sanctified, we may safely copy their Example" (Showman, ed., *Papers of Greene*, 2:232).

[35] Johann Ewald, *Diary of the American War: A Hessian Journal*, trans. and ed. Joseph P. Tustin (New Haven, 1979), pp. 108, 339–41; Fitzpatrick, ed., *Writings of Washington*, 8:29; C. Fiske Harris, ed., "Diary of a French Officer, 1781 (Presumed to be that of Baron Cromot du Bourg, Aide to Rochambeau)," *Magazine of American History* 7 (1881):295.

[36] Fitzpatrick, ed., *Writings of Washington*, 8:40–41, 108, 255, 268–69; 9:362–64; 11:163; *The Army Correspondence of Colonel John Laurens . . .* (New York, 1867), pp. 109–12, 134–41; George Fleming to Bauman, Feb. 6, 1778, Bauman Papers. In the fall of 1780 the marquis de Chastellux noted after visiting Maj. Gen. William Heath at West Point that Heath had "read our best authors on tactics, and especially the Tactics of Mr. Guibert, which he holds in particular estimation" (*Travels in North-America, in the Years 1780, 1781, and 1782*, 2 vols. [London, 1787], 1:79).

possession in favor of the British service, has obliged me to comply with many Things, which are against my Principles."³⁷

Steuben drew on many sources in compiling his system. A simple manual of arms emphasized improved execution, new techniques of marching, and use of the bayonet. He introduced movement in a column of fours to improve deployment. The standard pace became the Prussian norm of seventy-five two-foot steps per minute, not the British standard of sixty. Like Guibert and other theoreticians of the *ordre mixte* school, Steuben used both the column and line for tactical flexibility. Divisions and brigades practiced marching in closed columns for speed and control, and rapidly deployed into line for musket fire or bayonet work. Skirmishers covered the columns during movement and withdrew through gaps between regiments to reform. They maintained a distance of 100 yards (the effective range of musket fire) from a column to prevent enemy harassment.³⁸

In the fall of 1778, after the Battle of Monmouth, a board of general officers reviewed the drill. Washington agreed with their single suggestion for improvement and replaced the traditional command "Present!" with "Take Sight!" to emphasize the Continental army's continued reliance on marksmanship. The Board of War published the drill, after polishing by Steuben, as *Regulations for the Order and Discipline of the Troops of the United States, Part I*, and distributed copies to virtually every officer and state government.³⁹

---

³⁷ Steuben to Franklin, Sept. 28, 1779, Steuben Papers. Also *Army Correspondence of Laurens*, pp. 131–33, 145–49; and Showman, ed., *Papers of Greene*, 2:184–89.

³⁸ Idzerda, ed., *Lafayette*, 1:73–87, 91–103; Fitzpatrick, ed., *Writings of Washington*, 11:233, 335–36, 399–401; 12:4–7; "The Orderly Books of the Pennsylvania Line in the War of the Revolution," *Pennsylvania Archives*, 2d ser. 11 (1880):290–91, 304, 320–22, 410–11.

³⁹ Fitzpatrick, ed., *Writings of Washington*, 8:268; 12:360; 14:151–52, 227–31, 369, 444–46, 488–89; 15:46–49; 16:432–33, 447, 449, 468; Ford, ed., *Journals of Congress*, 13:384–85; Gates's notes on the Aug. 26, 1778, board meeting, Gates Papers. Steuben, *Regulations* (Philadelphia, 1779), had at least seven other editions by 1785; a second volume, "Baron von Steuben's

Steuben's second professional contribution to the Continental army gave substance to the office of inspector general. Congress recognized Steuben's credentials as a European expert on May 5, 1778, when it confirmed him in that staff assignment and gave him the rank of major general. Over the next few years Steuben created a hierarchy of subordinate officials which strengthened Washington's control over the army, a marked contrast to the role Conway had intended to play. This new staff gradually eliminated the need for most existing administrative officials. Steuben and his assistants at the division and brigade level served as training officers and as virtual chiefs of staff for their respective commanders.[40]

Steuben developed his powers and those of his subordinates without encountering significant opposition. Earlier growth in the size and role of Washington's personal staff of aides and secretaries had weakened the adjutant general, the one administrative official in a position to make a challenge for bureaucratic hegemony. Steuben's close relationships with Washington and the final two adjutants general cemented this arrangement. The rise of the inspector general stands in contrast to the situation in European armies, where either the adjutant general or the quartermaster general became paramount. It also illustrates that the Continentals borrowed

---

Regulations for the Cavalry or Corps Legionaire," was completed on Dec. 22, 1780, but never published; it is located in the Steuben Papers. For the implementation of Steuben's system in the South, see especially the "Order Book of John Faucheraud Grimké, August 1778 to May 1780," *South Carolina Historical and Genealogical Magazine* 14 (1913):50–51, 54–55, 165–68; 16 (1915):39–41.

[40] Ford, ed., *Journals of Congress*, 11:819–23; 13:111, 196–200, 403–4; 14:600–601; 16:47; 17:764–70; 18:855–61; Fitzpatrick, ed., *Writings of Washington*, 10:80–82, 245, 297, 332–33; 12:16, 66–68, 438–44; 14:224–27, 444–46, 486; 15:129–31, 288–90, 293, 356–58, 475–76; 16:11–13; 17:99–100, 495–96; Richard Peters to Steuben, June 2, 1778, William Davies to Steuben, June 18 and 21, and July 21 and 26, 1779, Benjamin Walker to Steuben, Feb. 2, and Mar. 10, 1780, Sub-Inspectors to Steuben, June 20, 1779, Alexander Scammell to Steuben, Sept. 22, 1779, Steuben Papers.

European ideas where appropriate but that they did not hesitate to experiment.[41]

The 1781 campaign demonstrated that the Continental army had matured into a small but effective military force. Washington and Nathanael Greene, with French military, naval, and financial support, wrested the strategic initiative from the British and brought the war to a virtual end at Yorktown. The main army, however, actually reached peak effectiveness in 1782 in the Hudson Highlands. Morale rose, long-established depots and housing kept the hardened veterans in good shape, and a comprehensive system of monthly brigade inspections prepared the troops for possible operations against New York City. The rigorous training program culminated on August 31, 1782, when Washington moved five brigades, complete with artillery and baggage, from Newburgh to Verplanck's Point. The units moved by small boat to test amphibious landing techniques. Boat assignments preserved unit integrity, and careful alignment insured cohesion and rapid deployment as the craft reached the beaches.[42]

Washington also implemented a reward system in 1782 to enhance morale. A chevron went to each soldier who "served more than three years with bravery, fidelity, and good Conduct." Two chevrons represented six years. The Badge of Military Merit, a purple heart edged with lace and worn over the left lapel, became a supreme award. Three individuals received it in 1783, all for a combination of exemplary service and conspicuous gallantry. Washington proudly proclaimed that these awards to sergeants proved that "the road

---

[41] S. G. P. Ward, *Wellington's Headquarters: A Study of the Administrative Problems in the Peninsula, 1809–1814* (Oxford, 1957), pp. 130–31; David G. Chandler, *The Campaigns of Napoleon* (New York, 1966), pp. 56, 144–61. "Instructions relatives au Département des Inspecteurs de l'armée," Steuben Papers.

[42] Sylvia J. Sherman, ed., *Dubros Times: Selected Depositions of Maine Revolutionary War Veterans* (Augusta, Maine, 1975), p. 9; Fitzpatrick, ed., *Writings of Washington*, 24:101, 303, 309–10, 322, 334, 358–59, 459–60; 25:93–96, 121.

to glory in a patriot army and a free country is thus open to all."⁴³

American officers in 1777 and early 1778 expressed confidence in the ability of the Continental army to learn how to fight effectively in open battle, the point made by Captain Heinrichs.⁴⁴ Although Monmouth was the last really large battle of the war, the Continentals trained at Valley Forge gave a good account of themselves in lesser engagements under a variety of circumstances. Capt. Johann Ewald, musing on the British defeat at Yorktown, summarized the change. "Concerning the American army," he wrote, "one should not think that it can be compared to a motley crowd of farmers. The so-called Continental, or standing, regiments are under good discipline." Others in the defeated army reached similar conclusions.⁴⁵

Victory in the War of American Independence depended on many factors. French aid played a key role. Militia and state troops maintained local control, but they could not carry out the long-term, long-distance burden of prosecuting the Revolutionary War any more than they could have performed similar tasks in the colonial era. Congress recognized this fact of life and created the regular Continental army early in the struggle.

Superior organization, arrived at in stages, offset many of the advantages inherent in Great Britain's control of the sea. The permanent brigade, introduced in 1777, enhanced the advantages of control and marksmanship built into the basic

---

⁴³ Fitzpatrick, ed., *Writings of Washington*, 24:487–88; 25:7, 142; 26:363–64, 481; James Hammond Trumbull, ed., *The Memorial History of Hartford County, Connecticut, 1633–1884*, 2 vols. (Boston, 1886), 2:514–15.

⁴⁴ Showman, ed., *Papers of Greene*, 2:10–13, 28–31; *Army Correspondence of Laurens*, pp. 109–12; Durand Echevarria and Orville T. Murphy, "The American Revolutionary Army: A French Estimate in 1777," *Military Affairs* 27 (1963):2–6, 155–61.

⁴⁵ Ewald, *Diary*, p. 340; also see pp. 229–30, 233, 241; Baurmeister, *Letters*, pp. 41–46; Heinrichs, "Letter-Book," pp. 168–70; C[harles] Stedman, *The History of the Origin, Progress and Termination of the American War*, 2 vols. (Dublin, 1794), 1:213; and [Banastre] Tarleton, *A History of the Campaigns*

regimental structure. It also helped to cement the cooperation between the infantry and artillery. Other types of units, each with a specialized role, combined with a staff system to form a well-rounded team. The development of a tactical doctrine in the form of Steuben's *Regulations* completed the transformation of the Continental army into a military institution typical in many ways of those in eighteenth-century Europe. Historians in the past have tended to look at the Revolution either as a continuation of colonial American military history or as an influence on the Napoleonic wars. It was, instead, a unique moment of transition that blended influences from both sides of the Atlantic.

---

of 1780 and 1781, in the Southern Provinces of North America (London, 1787), pp. 104–10, 214–22, 271–79.

STEVEN ROSSWURM

The Philadelphia Militia, 1775–1783:
Active Duty and Active Radicalism

IN MAY 1775, shortly after the formation of the Philadelphia militia, a "considerable number" of the militiamen met to consider the uniforms proposed by a committee of officers. Finding them "too expensive for the generality," these men demanded "equal consultation" for the "people." They suggested the adoption of a "Hunting Shirt," not only because it would be "within the compass of almost every person's ability" but also because it would "level all distinctions." "Hundreds" could not afford the proposed uniforms and "would never submit to ask any man for a coat," nor would they "appear in the ranks to be pointed at by those who had uniforms."[1]

While many historians have suggested the importance of the Philadelphia militia to the Pennsylvania Revolution, none have focused their entire attention on the militia, nor have any demonstrated the full significance of the militia radicalism that developed after the uniform incident.[2] In July 1775

The author would like to thank John Alexander, Don Higginbotham, Leslie Rowland, and, especially, Susan Figliulo and Alfred Young for their comments on earlier drafts of this essay.

[1] "To the Associators," May 18, 1775, 962.F.114, Library Company of Philadelphia. Radical militiamen apparently lost this battle (see Silas Deane to Elizabeth Deane, June 3, 1775, Eliphalet Dyer to Joseph Trumbull, June 8, 1775, Paul H. Smith et al., eds., *Letters of Delegates to Congress, 1774–1789*, 8 vols. to date [Washington, D.C., 1976–], 1:437, 459).

[2] See the following: J. Paul Selsam, *The Pennsylvania Constitution of 1776: A Study in Revolutionary Democracy* (Philadelphia, 1936), pp. 74–89, 126–29, 137; Theodore Thayer, *Pennsylvania Politics and the Growth of Democracy*

the associators—the name applied to those who joined the militia in its earliest months—began a nine-month struggle for equitable articles of association. This battle brought them and the resistance movement into conflict with the assembly and with moderates and helped delegitimize the assembly and radicalize the militia. Led by the Committee of Privates, a democratic steering committee composed of three representatives from each militia company, Philadelphia associators played an important role in the overthrow of the proprietary government and the establishment of the Revolution's most democratic constitution in the late spring and summer of 1776.

The militia's development of its own identity intensified when it went on active duty three times in 1776 and 1777. It came away from these tours with a firm sense of being exploited and, like Cromwell's New Model, had "its own history."[3]

The high point of popular insurgency in Philadelphia, and possibly during the Revolution as a whole, came in 1779. The militia played a principal role in the popular movement's attempt to punish tories, reduce prices, and defend the democractic constitution, and it took to the streets in 1779 bearing three-year-old grievances in mind; its refusal to accept the price-fixing committee's surrender led to the "Fort Wilson Riot" of October 4, 1779.

Soundly defeated at "Fort Wilson" and intimidated into calling off a demonstration in April 1780, the militia, as well

---

(Harrisburg, Pa., 1953), pp. 169–72 and ch. 13; David Hawke, *In the Midst of a Revolution* (Philadelphia, 1961); Charles S. Olton, *Artisans for Independence: Philadelphia Mechanics and the American Revolution* (Syracuse, N.Y., 1975), ch. 6; Eric Foner, *Tom Paine and Revolutionary America* (New York, 1976), pp. 63–66 and ch. 4; Richard Alan Ryerson, *The Revolution Is Now Begun: The Radical Committees of Philadelphia, 1765–1776* (Philadelphia, 1978), chs. 6, 8, and 9; Gary B. Nash, *The Urban Crucible: Social Change, Political Consciousness, and the Origins of the American Revolution* (Cambridge, Mass., 1979), ch. 13. Foner, *Paine,* and Robert L. Brunhouse, *The Counter-Revolution in Pennsylvania, 1776–1790* (Harrisburg, Pa., 1942), discuss the militia during the war.

[3] Mark A. Kishlansky, "The Army and the Levellers: The Roads to Putney," *Historical Journal* 22 (1979):824.

as the popular movement, sank into passivity. Poor militiamen, who comprised the bulk of the associators, began to avoid militia duty just as the "rich" had done all along. The militia, however, remained radical enough to be too unreliable to help suppress mutinies in 1781 and 1783.

This essay will explore the experience of what was probably the Revolution's most radical militia, a group of soldiers and citizens whose political views and activities closely approximated Cromwell's radical New Model and the *soldats-citoyens* of Year II.[4] It will consider the militia's formation, its role in the establishment of the radical constitution, its military activity, and, finally, its return to politics. This essay will demonstrate the usefulness—as Don Higginbotham suggested some time ago and as John Shy has argued forcefully—of situating military history within the broadest possible social and political context.[5]

From July 1775 to April 1776 the militia struggled for equitable articles of association. The associators found authorities unwilling to enfranchise the propertyless or enact a genuinely universal law that would minimize nonassociation. Although the militia was finally persuaded to sign flawed articles, the struggle for equitable articles radicalized it and convinced it of the need for internal revolution.

Since Pennsylvania did not have an established militia system, Philadelphians formed a volunteer association just after Lexington and Concord. Within days of the initial mass meeting, the city was transformed as these associators formed companies and elected officers. By the first week in June about

[4] Charles H. Firth, *Cromwell's Army: A History of the English Soldier during the Civil Wars, the Commonwealth, and the Protectorate*, 3d ed. (London, n.d.); H. N. Brailsford, *The Levellers and the English Revolution* (Stanford, Calif., 1961); Albert Soboul, *Les soldats de l'an II* (Paris, 1959); Jean-Paul Bertaud, *La Révolution armée: Les Soldats-citoyens et la Révolution française* (Paris, 1979).

[5] Higginbotham, "American Historians and the Military History of the American Revolution," *American Historical Review* 70 (1964):33–34; Shy, "The American Revolution: The Military Conflict Considered as a Revolutionary War," in Stephen G. Kurtz and James H. Hutson, eds., *Essays on the American Revolution* (Chapel Hill, N.C., 1973), pp. 121–56.

two thousand were organized into three battalions and various companies.[6]

While the staunchest militiamen in subsequent years would be the "lower sort"—free wage earners and "inferior" artisans and craftsmen—impressionistic evidence indicates that men of all ranks, occupations, and religions joined the association in the first few months. As a tory exile from Massachusetts noted in early May: "Gentlemen, Merchants, tradesmen, old, young, English, Irish, German and Dutch, Etc are [drilling?] and stand shoulder to shoulder."[7] Conservatives and moderates joined, and even many Quakers mustered.[8]

An analysis of the social composition of two early musters supports these observations. On the one hand, while men of wide-ranging wealth joined the association, poor men dominated numerically. On the other hand, a smaller percentage of the poor than the wealthy who could have mustered actually did so. A comparison of those who drilled in Middle Ward with those "able and willing to bear arms" yields the same result: those with "middling" taxable wealth "exercised" more enthusiastically than the poor.[9]

---

[6] Christopher Marshall Diary, B, June 8, 1775, Historical Society of Pennsylvania, Philadelphia. While the figure of 2,000 is an approximation, it is probably close to the truth (see, among others, Richard Caswell to William Caswell, May 11, 1775, Joseph Hewes to Samuel Johnston, May 11, 1775, Richard Henry Lee to Francis Lightfoot Lee, May 21, 1775, Dyer to Trumbull, June 8, 1775, Smith, ed., *Letters of Delegates*, 1:340, 342, 376, 459).

[7] Andrew Oliver, ed., *Journal of Samuel Curwen, Loyalist*, May 5, 1775, 2 vols. (Cambridge, Mass., 1974), 1:4. Also see *Memoir of Lieut. Colonel Tench Tilghman* (1876; reprint ed., New York, 1971), p. 14; Alexander Graydon, *Memoirs of a Life* (Harrisburg, Pa., 1811), pp. 107–8.

[8] Margaret Willard, ed., *Letters on the American Revolution* (1928; reprint ed., Port Washington, N.Y., 1968), p. 107; Marshall Diary, B, May 1, 1775. Also see Willard, ed., *Letters*, pp. 94, 101, 103; Oliver, ed., *Journal of Curwen*, May 5, 1775, 1:4–5; Graydon, *Memoirs*, p. 106; S. Deane to Samuel Webb, May 14, 1775, Smith, ed., *Letters of Delegates*, 1:348.

[9] "Those Associated with Captain John Little" [pencil notation, May 9, 1775], Daniel Clymer Manuscripts, 17; "Those in High Street who gener-

There were good reasons why the poor did not join in large numbers. First, there was the cost of arms and accoutrements, which a contemporary estimated at £10 to £12.[10] While patriots took up subscriptions for arms for poor associators and the Pennsylvania assembly voted some funds for that purpose, problems with manufacturing and limited resources slowed the supplying process.[11] Second, there was the problem of taking time from work for military training. Although one source indicated that drilling took place before and after work, associators complained that exercises occurred during normal laboring hours.[12]

On July 22, 1775, association officers met to discuss the assembly's minutemen resolves with the city and county resistance committees. The meeting ordered each captain to inquire who in his company would enroll as minutemen; each captain was to notify his colonel of the results. The responses of twelve companies and one battalion have been preserved,

---

ally attend," Richard Peters Papers, VIII, 47, both Hist. Soc. Pa.; "List of Persons in Middle Ward in the City of Philadelphia of the ages of eighteen upwards who are able and willing to bear arms, May 1, 1775," Clymer Manuscripts, 4; County Provincial Tax Duplicate, 1775, Philadelphia City Archives. For more detail and a discussion of the limitations of the data, see Rosswurm, "Philadelphia's Revolutionary Militia, 1775–1776" (Paper presented at the Seventy-third Annual Meeting of the Organization of American Historians, San Francisco, 1980), pp. 4–5.

[10] William Irvine to John Hancock, Mar. 23, 1776, Gratz Collection, Case 1, Box 12, Hist. Soc. Pa.

[11] Committee Chambers, May 24, 1775, Peters Papers, VIII, 46; Ryerson, *The Revolution Is Now Begun*, p. 119. In at least two cases arms were not distributed until the spring of 1776 (Journal of Sgt. William Young, May 4, 1776, Hist. Soc. Pa.; Peters Papers, VIII, 76). A number of men, "mostly servants," petitioned for arms in 1775; they were eager to fight but their "Circumstances" were such that they could not "afford to purchase Arms" (Petition of Simon Shaw et al., [May–June 1775], "Records of Pennsylvania's Revolutionary Governments, 1775–1790, in the Pennsylvania State Archives" [microfilm], reel 10, frame 203, Pennsylvania Historical and Museum Commission, Harrisburg [hereafter, "Records," 10/203]).

[12] S. Deane to E. Deane, May 12, 1775, Smith, ed., *Letters of Delegates*, 1:347; High Street Ward, Peters Papers, VIII, 54.

and they indicate a unanimous rejection of the resolves.¹³ While most captains simply noted that their men felt the pay was too low, one captain recorded the specific complaints of his company: drilling required "great pains and Time" for which they were not remunerated, the "Compensation" was "extremely inadequate and dissatisfactory," and the militiamen could not afford to leave their places of employment. The active duty pay was a "Trifle . . . not equal to the Time lost upon the Occasions," and would not support an associator's family while he was in the field. Furthermore, no provision had been made for an associator's family if he should die in battle. These men were willing to continue as militiamen, but not under the assembly's terms.¹⁴

All these considerations were economic. Poor militiamen, both artisans and wage earners, could not afford to take uncompensated time off work, and their precarious footing demanded some form of support for their families while they were gone. Increasingly battered after 1760 by long-run structural changes in both the world and local economies and by resistance strategies that meant they bore the brunt of the attack on British colonial policy, poor associators could only respond with a vehement *no* to the proposed plan.¹⁵

---

[13] Peters Papers, VIII, 50–64. The returns included one company of the first battalion, six of the second, one of the third, the two artillery companies, two companies of one Philadelphia County battalion, and the whole of another. The responses were unanimously negative except for Captain Wade's, which was silent on this point.

[14] Ibid., 54. Also see Wilcocks, 61 ("The Chief of them gave as a Reason their Occupations at Home by which they supported their families") and Shee, 62 ("Their Families would be in want and having no support but their daily Labour would render it impossible to comply with the Present Terms").

[15] For the "lower sort's" social situation after 1760, see Steven Rosswurm, "Arms, Culture, and Class: The Philadelphia Militia and 'Lower Orders' in the American Revolution, 1765 to 1783," Ph.D. diss., Northern Illinois University, 1979, pp. 23–27, 33–44, 70, 72, 149–50; Billy G. Smith, "The Material Lives of Laboring Philadelphians, 1750–1800," *William and Mary Quarterly*, 3d ser. 38 (1981):163–202; John K. Alexander, *Render Them Submissive: Responses to Poverty in Philadelphia, 1760–1800* (Amherst, Mass., 1980); Nash, *Urban Crucible*.

"Lower sort" militiamen not only knew their own interests, they were prepared to defend them. They had expressed egalitarian demands during the uniform controversy in May, and in July had spontaneously rejected articles that would have exploited them. Nevertheless, the formation of the Committee of Privates made their demands more pressing.

The first meeting of the "General Committee of Associators," the original and short-lived name for the Committee of Privates, was held on September 15, 1775.[16] The Committee met regularly until midsummer 1776, and militants briefly resurrected it in October 1779. Each company could send three representatives to the Committee meetings; by the end of September, thirty-three companies were sending delegates.[17]

It has been possible to identify fourteen members of the militia's "Advance-Guard," as the Committee of Privates once referred to itself.[18] Most were of the "middling sort," but some were of the "independent poor" while others were well-off, at least compared to the laboring poor. The eleven whose occupations could be found included a tailor, a cordwainer, two schoolmasters, a professor, a shopkeeper, a clerk, a bookseller, a merchant, a distiller, and a carpenter. Many members of the Committee were involved in Philadelphia's artisan and lower-class communities, and some had been members of the same organizations: five belonged to an English immigrant aid group, the Society of Englishmen, and others belonged to the "United Company . . . for Promoting American Manufactures." Samuel Simpson's ties to the artisan community were especially strong, though probably not exceptional. An original member of the Cordwainer's Fire

---

[16] The following is drawn from Rosswurm, "Arms, Culture, and Class," pp. 149–66.

[17] Marshall to S. H., Sept. 30, 1775, Marshall Letter Book, Hist. Soc. Pa. It has been impossible to determine whether every militia company sent representatives.

[18] "To the Privates of the Several Battalions of Military Associators in the Province of Pennsylvania," [June 14–21, 1776], Clymer Manuscripts, 13.

Company, he served as its only treasurer as well as performing committee assignments. Still others taught at schools that many apprentices, laborers, and artisans probably attended.

The Committee of Privates played an influential role in Pennsylvania's internal revolution. It took public positions on a wide range of issues relevant to its constituency and, with few exceptions, advocated the poorest associator's demands. The Committee's meetings themselves were a form of political education for the rank-and-file associators who participated in writing broadsides and petitions.[19]

The associators, however, had not needed the Committee of Privates' advice to reject the original articles, and even before most companies had been polled, it had been clear that few, if any, would subscribe to the articles.[20] The officers and comittees decided to petition the recently established Committee of Safety to frame new articles of association and submit them to the men.

A subcommittee sent a memorial to the assembly-appointed Committee of Safety, which strongly supported the associators: the "Majority" were "of the poorer sorts of People whose public spirit" exceeded "their abilities in the point of Fortune."[21] The officers had their own reasons for new and more complete articles. They commanded men with a strong sense of egalitarianism and wanted "some Regulation to oblige the Associators to yield due obedience to them in all cases where the Service requires." Fines were suitable for "divers In-

---

[19] Such discussion undoubtedly occurred elsewhere as well. The taverns were important social institutions in which much spirited conversation probably took place. See John Adams to Abigail Adams, Apr. 13, 1776, in which he discussed his barber's visits to a "Beer House kept by one weaver" where he had many "curious Disputes and Adventures," Lyman H. Butterfield et al., eds., *The Adams Family Correspondence*, 3 vols. (Cambridge, Mass., 1963), 1:392.

[20] John Coxe to Joseph Reed, July 26, 1775, Joseph Reed Papers (microfilm), reel 1, New-York Historical Society, New York City.

[21] "To the honourable Committee of Safety, for the Province of Pennsylvania, the Memorial of a Number of the Committees of the City & Liberties & County of Philadelphia & the Body of Officers of the Several Battalions in the said City & County," Peters Papers, VIII, 66.

stances of Misbehaviour," but the officers wanted a "stricter more sever discipline" for active duty.

On August 19 the Committee of Safety adopted new articles of association and recommended them to the militia, but in late September all the companies repudiated these as well.[22] In a "free state" all ought to be bound by the same laws, the Committee of Privates argued, but the Committee of Safety had not made the association compulsory.[23] The associators would not subscribe to a militia law that did not "equally extend to every inhabitant."[24] Since the "present stoppage of trade" would "necessarily throw many poor people out of bread," the Committee of Privates suggested that poor associators be enlisted with pay for six months.[25]

[22] *Minutes of the Provincial Council of Pennsylvania*, 10 vols. (Philadelphia, 1851–52), 10:297, 307, 308–12. See "Papers Relating to the War of the Revolution, 1775–1777," *Pennsylvania Archives*, 2d ser. 1 (1879):578, for what appears to be a subcommittee's discussion notes. The Committee of Safety's articles differed from Congress's of June 30, 1775, in two important matters of discipline: they were more lenient in the amount and type of punishment and provided for noncommissioned representation on both regimental and general courts martial. A two-thirds vote, not a majority, was necessary for conviction.

[23] *Pennsylvania Evening Post*, Sept. 28, 1775.

[24] Two companies had complained in July that few had mustered (Peters Papers, VIII, Furman, 63, Morgan, 59). The officers' petition noted that "poor associators" were particularly angry at the many who were "setting at their Ease & bearing no part in the Expence or Labour of the Association" (ibid., 66).

[25] The Committee of Privates' position on the question of a standing army was ambiguous. On the one hand, traditional whig theory influenced it—"every citizen a soldier and every soldier a citizen" ("Caractacus," *Pennsylvania Packet*, Aug. 21, 1775). (For the most recent summary of the literature, see Lawrence Delbert Cress, "Radical Whiggery on the Role of the Military: Ideological Roots of the American Revolutionary Militia," *Journal of the History of Ideas* 40 [1979]:43–60). It therefore sounded the alarm about mercenaries and standing armies (*Pennsylvania Evening Post*, Sept. 28, 1775; "To the Non-Commissioned Officers and Privates of the Several Associators, belonging to the City and Liberties of Philadelphia," [probably 1776], Ab 1775–2, Hist. Soc. Pa.). On the other hand, the situation of poor associators pressed upon the Committee, and it therefore pushed for public employment in the association.

ARMS AND INDEPENDENCE

An officers' group and the Committee of Safety, which had written the rejected articles, sent the assembly strongly worded petitions of support for the Committee of Privates. These and other petitions provoked the Quaker Meeting into an attempt to block a general militia law; such a law, the Meeting argued, would violate liberty of conscience.[26] The Quakers also advocated reconciliation with Britain. The Committee of Privates, an officers' group, and the popularly elected Committee of Inspection immediately attacked the Quakers.[27] Each argued that liberty and equality demanded a universal association; the last two groups contended that wealth had influenced the Meeting's position.

After sharp debate, the assembly met a number of associator demands in its articles of November 1775.[28] It provided for the support of poor associators' families, enacted the first universal militia law in the colony's history, and voted substantial funds for defense. From the militia's viewpoint, however, the assembly had not gone far enough. Though it fined nonassociators, the fines were far lower than the associators' expenses in time and equipment. It did not raise militia pay above the Continental rate, or fine nonassociators in proportion to their wealth. Furthermore, it instructed Pennsylvania's delegates in the Continental Congress to refuse to accept any plan to separate from Britain.

Since militiamen had twice rejected articles of association, the Committee of Privates' position on the newest ones would be of capital importance for the defense of the colony, as well as for the decision of the associators. In January 1776 the

---

Some associators were aware that good whigs frowned upon the use of mercenaries. Two companies indicated in July that they would "remain in their present situation" rather than be exposed to the "Appellation of Mercenaries without the actual receipt of Pay" (Peters Papers, VIII, 54, 63).

[26] *Pennsylvania Archives*, 8th ser. 8 (1935):7259–62, 7311–13; "The Address of the People Called Quakers," Oct. 27, 1775, Ab 1775-37, Hist. Soc. Pa.

[27] *Pennsylvania Archives*, 8th ser. 8:7339–43, 7337–39, 7334–37.

[28] Ibid., pp. 7369–84. For the important preliminary resolves, see pp. 7351–52.

Committee urged privates and noncommissioned officers to sign the articles; in so doing, it asked poor associators to put patriotism above their immediate interests.[29]

The Committee of Privates agreed that the articles were defective, but expected "redress" since officers had pledged to support the effort. Not to sign could mean that an expected invasion would not be repelled, or that the colony's defense might rest in the hands of mercenaries. The Committee argued that "discipline" and "subordination" were not incongruous with an "equality of rank and fortune." The militia required regulations to differentiate its "regular and united exertions" from the "tumultuous and disorderly movements of an armed mob." Only the "cowardly and treacherous" had anything to fear from "sanctions and punishments."[30] Perhaps the Committee of Privates' most potent argument was that the associators ought to "banish . . . all considerations of interest, ambition or convience" and "preserve a fixed attention to the public good." Those who would not sign, the Committee hinted, were tories: "its greatest enemy could not strike a more fatal blow."

Rank-and-file associators evidently were convinced by these arguments for within weeks signing had "become very general in the city and districts" and "like to become universal."[31]

---

[29] There are three essential documents: "To the Non-Commissioned Officers and Privates of the Several Companies of Associators, Belonging to the City and Liberties of Philadelphia," Ab 1775-2, Hist. Soc. Pa.; "Gentlemen and Fellow-Soldiers," 1776, 962.F.95, Libr. Co. Phila.; and "To the Privates of the Military Association Belonging to the Province of Pennsylvania," *Pennsylvania Gazette*, Feb. 7, 1776. For a discussion of the chronological ordering of the documents, including the argument that the first appeared in 1776, see Rosswurm, "Arms, Culture, and Class," p. 132, n. 75.

[30] For a discussion of the discipline problem within the militia, see Rosswurm, "Arms, Culture, and Class," pp. 135-40. There is a useful discussion in a different context in Charles Royster, *A Revolutionary People at War: The Continental Army and American Character, 1775-1783* (Chapel Hill, N.C., 1979), pp. 213-27.

[31] *Pennsylvania Gazette*, Feb. 14, 1776. See "We the Officers and Soldiers . . .," n.d., "Records," 11/686, for what appears to be a draft of the subscription agreement that the associators were signing.

The Committee of Privates provided a further incentive for subscribing when it petitioned the Committee of Safety to give signers preference in public works.[32]

As promised, in early March the Committee of Privates issued detailed criticisms of the articles.[33] Expenses already incurred would not be reimbursed, and the articles gave the "Strongest Temptations" to "avoid the Danger and Fatigue" to the "Lazy, Timid, and Disaffected," who were ridiculing the militia by "representing" the assembly as "rating their lives at 50s a Piece" (the fine for nonassociation). A stiffer nonassociation fine was needed to "entice very many of suitable age and strength (not truly scrupulous) to join in the association."

Most important among the Committee of Privates' other points was its suggestion that the assembly enfranchise poor militiamen and unnaturalized German associators. In denying the connection between property-holding and voting rights, disenfranchised militiamen broke decisively with contemporary political thought and practice.[34]

Pressure on the assembly mounted, both from Philadelphia officers and the increasingly politicized backcountry.[35]

---

[32] This was significant because the association was "principally" composed of "Tradesmen and others who earn their living by their Industry." The cessation of trade in 1775 and the freezing of the Delaware in the winter of 1775–76 created much unemployment. This, in turn, produced a scrambling for war-related public works jobs (Rosswurm, "Arms, Culture, and Class," pp. 24–25 and 149–50; petitions in "Records," 10/43, 156, 182–83, 304, 319, 354). Although one observer argued that public works meant that the "City scarce feels the interruption of Trade," the extant evidence contradicts this (William Hooper to James Iredell, Jan. 6, 1776, Smith, ed., *Letters of Delegates*, 3:45).

[33] *Pennsylvania Archives*, 8th ser. 8:7403–7.

[34] For the contemporary view see J. Adams to James Sullivan, May 26, 1776, Charles Francis Adams, ed., *The Works of John Adams*, 10 vols. (Boston, 1850–56), 9:376.

[35] *Pennsylvania Archives*, 8th ser. 8:7383, 7397–7401, 7409–10, 7424–26, 7429–30, 7433–35, 7438–40, 7448–49. During the early disputes over the minutemen resolves, backcountry associators exhibited less displeasure than their city compatriots, if York County is representative. In August a number subscribed as minutemen, but problems developed later. See "Minutes

On April 4, "A Friend to Government by Assembly" warned that if the assembly did not make significant changes in the militia articles, no one could prevent the associators "from seeking redress where they know they can find it."[36] The assembly's revised articles of April 6, 1776, met some associator demands but ignored others and tried to compromise on the rest.[37] Although the assembly raised nonassociation fines, militiamen still considered the penalty too low. As for the suffrage question, the assembly merely recommended that Germans and other "Foreigners" be granted citizenship and the vote in the future, and did not even suggest the vote for poor "natural-born subjects."

Events during the next few months demonstrated that control of the militia was essential to an orderly revolution. The elite and moderates in other states more or less met this challenge: those in Pennsylvania did not. Pennsylvania's ruling class refused to support independence or to make qualitative concessions to the militia. Unlike other provincial elites, it refused to "yield to the torrent" and so lost control of the revolutionary process.[38] "Under the sense of being oppressed by the very men whose liberties and estates" they would be called on to defend, the militia supported internal revolution in May and June 1776, and in July played an im-

---

of the York County Militia Officers Committee," July 28, 1775, "We, the Subscribers," Aug. 7, 1775, Richard McCalister et al. to Benjamin Franklin and John Dickinson, Aug. 31, 1775, James Smith et al. to the Committee of Safety, Sept. 14, 1775, "Records," 10/16, 32, 54, 66.

[36] *Pennsylvania Evening Post*, Apr. 4, 1776.

[37] *Pennsylvania Archives*, 8th ser. 8:7473–505.

[38] Robert R. Livingston to William Duer, June 12, 1777, quoted in Alfred F. Young, *The Democratic Republicans of New York: The Origins, 1763–1797* (Chapel Hill, N.C., 1967), p. 15. Two Philadelphians, both of whom eventually became loyalists, joined the militia hoping to control it, but their efforts proved fruitless ("Diary of James Allen, Esquire, of Philadelphia," Oct. 14, 1775, *Pennsylvania Magazine of History and Biography* 9 [1885]:186; Wallace Brown, *The King's Friends: The Composition and Motives of the American Loyalist Claimants* [Providence, 1965], p. 133).

portant role in the establishment of the era's most democratic constitution.[39]

The major reason for this ruling class failure to ride out the storm was fear of social upheaval. This threat, present in Philadelphia from at least late 1774, worsened through early 1776 and became ominous as the spring progressed. The acrimonious political debate over frames of government before the May 1 Philadelphia by-election intensified ruling class paralysis and fear.[40] Radical polemicists advocated unicameralism and stridently reiterated the Committee of Privates' demand for suffrage expansion.[41]

Some Committee members were involved in selecting the pro-independence ticket for the May 1 election. When the results proved disappointing, local radicals, including James Cannon of the Committee of Privates, began a series of meetings with Congressional radicals.[42] These meetings led to Congress's May 10 resolution and May 15 preamble establishing the framework within which local radicals could lead a revolution.

Radicals, again including some of the Committee of Privates, organized a "town meeting," or demonstration, for May 20. This meeting, attended by four thousand despite rain, created the machinery that abolished proprietary government. It directed county Committees of Inspection to elect representatives to a provincial conference whose charge was to arrange a constitutional convention.[43]

The Committee of Privates helped foil attempts by con-

[39] "Memorial of the Committee of Privates of the City and Liberties of Philadelphia," May 11, 1776, Peter Force, ed., *American Archives*, 4th ser., 6 vols. (Washington, D.C., 1837–46), 4:421–22.

[40] "The plot thickens; peace is scarcely thought of—Independency predominant, thinking people uneasy irresolute, & inactive. The mobility triumphant" ("Diary of Allen," Mar. 6, 1776, p. 186).

[41] See Rosswurm, "Arms, Culture, and Class," pp. 208–14.

[42] David Hawke, *In the Midst of a Revolution*, pp. 130–32, 156–57.

[43] Marshall Diary, C, May 20, 1776; *Pennsylvania Gazette*, May 22, 1776. While the immediate events from May 1 to May 15 contributed to the ease with which radicals succeeded (Hawke, *In the Midst of a Revolution*, pp. 116–27), long-term "middling" and "lower sort" hostility toward the as-

servatives and moderates to retain proprietary government by asking battalion officers to poll their men about Congress's May 15 preamble and the town meeting's May 20 resolves. The four battalions that were polled overwhelmingly supported the resolves. The two polled about independence unanimously supported that as well.[44]

The Committee of Privates again flexed its political muscle when it, along with officers, refused to allow the assembly to appoint the colony's brigadier generals. Both groups decided that each provincial battalion should send two officers and two privates to Lancaster to elect those officers.[45] Before the meeting, the Committee issued a circular that urged their provincial compatriots to send delegations to Lancaster and summarized a year's worth of grievances;[46] all the Philadelphia battalions sent representatives. Privates and officers chose, for the first and last time, their top field officers.[47]

Meeting from June 18 to June 25, the Provincial Conference altered the colony's instructions to its Congressional delegates, allowing them to support independence. The Conference also established procedures for electing delegates to the constitutional convention, disenfranchised most conservatives and some moderates, and enfranchised all associators who paid taxes.[48]

The Committee of Privates exploited the opportunity pre-

---

sembly and the "rich & the powerful," as well as the necessities of the continental independence movement, were far more significant.

[44] Marshall Diary, C, June 10, 1776; *Pennsylvania Evening Post*, June 11, 1776; *Pennsylvania Packet*, June 17, 1776; Ryerson, *The Revolution Is Now Begun*, pp. 219–28. The lieutenant colonel of the third battalion refused to put the question at "great umbrage to the men." For the questions as put to a backcountry battalion, see "Questions Proposed on the 10th of June 1776 to Colonel Hunter's Battalion in Northumberland," "Records," 10/609.

[45] "At a Meeting of a Board of Officers . . . and the Committee of Privates . . . the 14th of June, 1776," Clymer Manuscripts, 12.

[46] "To the Privates of the Several Battalions," ibid., 13.

[47] The minutes of the meeting can be found ibid., 29.

[48] "Resolves of the Committee for the Province . . .," *Pennsylvania Archives*, 2d ser. 3 (1875):557–82.

sented by the large number of associators now able to vote. Seeking to ensure that "no rank" above that of "Freeman" developed in America, the Committee made overt class appeals in a circular sent to all associators about the upcoming constitutional convention elections. Among those incapable of pursuing the Committee's goals the circular included "great and overgrown rich men," "Gentlemen of the learned Professions," anyone "at any time solicitous to be [a] representative," and those who were "very backward in declaring you a free people." Associators should select "Men of like Passions and Interests"; honesty, common sense, and "plain understanding" were sufficient qualifications, "when unbiased by sinister motives." If the militia chose "improper" delegates, "an Aristocracy, or Government of the Great" would result.[49]

The convention did not write a frame of government for the "Great," but rather drew up the Revolution's most democratic constitution, a small-property-holder's document.[50] It adopted almost every proposal made by the author of *Four Letters* (possibly James Cannon) and the Committee of Privates.[51]

The political role of the Philadelphia associators in Pennsylvania in 1775 and 1776 was nothing less than extraordinary. Without the "lower sort's" mobilization and politicization in the militia, there probably would have been no internal revolution, no democratic constitution. The militia experience had been instructive. No longer did the "lower sort" think it not their right, or beyond their potential, to control

---

[49] "To the Several Battalions of Military Associators in the Province of Pennsylvania," June 26, 1776, Ab 1776–19, Hist. Soc. Pa. The Committee of Privates was involved in the nomination of the city delegates but did not have the final approval. For a discussion of the contradiction between the social composition of the Committee of Privates and its recommendations for election to the constitutional convention, see Rosswurm, "Arms, Culture, and Class," pp. 228–31.

[50] Selsam, *Pennsylvania Constitution of 1776*; Rosswurm, "Arms, Culture, and Class," pp. 227–40.

[51] *Four Letters on Interesting Subjects* (Philadelphia, 1776); "To the Several Battalions."

The Philadelphia Militia

their lives: the Committee of Privates had helped them to break through that ideological barrier. This growing political power and consciousness, among other factors, led "middling" and "lower sort" men to join the Philadelphia militia.[52]

We shall now examine the active duty experience of the Philadelphia militia on its three tours of active duty: in July 1776, in the winter of 1776–77, and in the summer of 1777. Its performance often confirmed the worst expected of the Revolutionary militia—tardiness in turning out, ill-discipline, maltreatment and wasteful use of equipment, and an unwillingness to remain in the field longer than agreed upon, if that long.[53] At the same time, it fought extremely well in the winter campaign and bore up well under harsh conditions, earning the praise of George Washington. Furthermore, it brought its radicalism into the field and sooner or later refused to accept unequal militia burdens. The militia was now not as ready to subordinate its interests as it had been when it agreed to sign the flawed articles of association.

Philadelphia associators responded well to their first call-up of the war in July 1776.[54] By the third week in July, almost nineteen hundred rank and file had arrived at camps in

---

[52] For more on motivations for joining the militia, see Rosswurm, "Arms, Culture, and Class," pp. 167–73. For recent thinking on line troops and motivation, see Royster, "A Note on Statistics and Continental Soldiers' Motivation," *A Revolutionary People*, pp. 373–78, and Robert Middlekauff, "Why Men Fought in the American Revolution," *Huntington Library Quarterly* 43 (1980):135–48.

[53] For a summary of these attitudes toward the militia, see Higginbotham, "The American Militia: A Traditional Institution with Revolutionary Responsibilities," in Higginbotham, ed., *Reconsiderations on the Revolutionary War: Selected Essays* (Westport, Conn., 1978), pp. 84–86. This perception was embodied in the comment that one group of associators had "behaved with as much good Order and fidelity as can be expected from Malitia" (Peter DeHaven et al. to the Committee of Safety, n.d., "Records," 12/100).

[54] George Read to Gertrude Read, July 14, 1776, Abraham Clark to Elias Dayton, July 14, 1776, William Whipple to John Langdon, July 16, 22, 1776, Smith, ed., *Letters of Delegates*, 4:455, 451, 477, 520. According to Clark, Congress had to "stop part of the Militia of Philada or the City would have been left wholly defenseless."

northeastern New Jersey.[55] An initial report indicated that the men were in "high spirits," but this did not last long.[56] Within a week the militia was uneasy and desertions began. Commanders did everything they could to alleviate the unrest, but nothing—not speeches by Gen. Daniel Roberdeau of the Pennsylvania militia and by General Washington nor a popular minister's sermon—seems to have worked. By August 14 at least 20 percent of the rank and file had left.[57] Gen. Hugh Mercer, commander of the Flying Camp (specially designated militia from Delaware, Maryland, and Pennsylvania), finally relieved the troops on August 19; by the end of August all but the artillery were at home.[58]

No city associators exhibited much discipline, but Col. Thomas McKean's 4th Battalion seems to have been the most unruly of the lot. McKean thought these men "some of the most rude, turbulent, lazy, dirty fellows" he had "ever beheld."[59] As early as July 19 they were expressing dissatisfaction, and almost 40 percent had left by August 14.[60] Those

---

[55] To be precise, 1,879 (Gen. Hugh Mercer to George Washington, July 25, 1776, Peter Force, ed., *American Archives*, 5th ser., 3 vols. [Washington, D.C., 1848–53], 1:574). This return corrected that of the previous day, which had a "very capital error." There is also a July 22 return for the first three battalions (ibid., 556–57, 575).

[56] "Extract from a Letter of an Officer in the Second Philadelphia Battalion," July 22, 1776, ibid., 499.

[57] Ibid., 963–64. Roughly another 7 percent were either sick or on furlough.

[58] See Rosswurm, "Arms, Culture, and Class," pp. 247–57. The following were also useful: "Military Papers," Box 2, D–16–2/no. 2, John Dickinson Papers (R. R. Logan Collection); Benjamin Loxley Journal; Sharpe Delaney Orderly Book; John Dickinson Papers (Libr. Co. Phila. Collection), all Hist. Soc. Pa.; Gen. Hugh Mercer's correspondence, Force, ed., *American Archives*, 5th ser., vol. 1; "Orderly Books of Mercer, Sullivan, and Stirling," *American Historical Review* 3 (1897–98):303–7.

[59] McKean to J. Reed, Aug. 29, 1780, Reed Papers, reel 2.

[60] Gen. Daniel Roberdeau to the Committee of Safety, July 19, 1776, Gratz Collection, Case 4, Box 14; Mathew Clarkson to Dickinson, Aug. 17, 1776, Dickinson Papers, no. 353 (Libr. Co. Phila. Coll.), Hist. Soc. Pa.

who had not deserted mutinied on August 14, and violence was narrowly averted.[61]

The Philadelphia militia acted poorly as patriots and as soldiers. The important question, however, is why they did so. Some of the reasons were no doubt among the familiar explanations for militia incompetence. But scholars have ignored another—and probably more important—reason for their behavior: their sense that they bore the brunt of active duty while the rich and "disaffected" reaped the benefits.

A rations problem made the militiamen uneasy and continual boredom irritated them, but it was events in Philadelphia that angered them.[62] The militia knew about developments in the city because many took authorized or unauthorized leaves there[63] and found that "some of rank and fortune" had not only remained at home but refused to do their duty in the city guard. One angry associator asked officers to enroll all those who had not gone to camp, but they refused to do so "without respect of persons." In retaliation, he declared that he would turn out for duty only if all the delinquents' names appeared with his. If not, his obligation was to serve in the cause of equality, not the militia.[64]

---

[61] William Bradford, Jr., to Mother, Wallace Papers, I, 47, Hist. Soc. Pa.; Loxley Journal, Aug. 15, 1776; Howard H. Peckham, ed., *Memoirs of the Life of John Adlum in the Revolutionary War* (Chicago, 1968), p. 15. The social composition of this battalion is not precisely known; by late November most of the men had enlisted in the Continental Line (McKean to Committee of Safety, Nov. 30, 1776, Gratz Collection, Case 1, Box 50).

[62] For these problems, see Rosswurm, "Arms, Culture, and Class," pp. 247–49. The associators were engaged in only one small skirmish with the British (McKean to Sally McKean, July 26, 1776, McKean Papers, VI, 2, Hist. Soc. Pa.; Mercer to the President of Congress, July 26, 1776, "Extract of a letter from the Camp at Perth-Amboy," July 26, 1776, Force, ed., *American Archives*, 5th ser. 1:599, 600).

[63] See the furlough recommendations in the Dickinson Papers, no. 76 (Libr. Co. Phila. Coll.), Hist. Soc. Pa. Also see Dickinson et al. to [?], Nov. 8, 1776, Provincial Delegates, II, 66, Hist. Soc. Pa.

[64] "To the Commanding Officer of the detachment of Associators left for the defense of the city," *Pennsylvania Evening Post*, Aug. 10, 1776. This writer was responding to the threat that those in the home guard who did not do their duty would be dealt with "seriously" (ibid., Aug. 8, 1776).

ARMS AND INDEPENDENCE

The rising cost of the "necessities" of life was another fundamental grievance. Some associators had paid high prices for canteens, and a number of innkeepers either refused to sell them provisions for their march to camp or charged the "most extravagant prices."[65] Prices rose in July and August and hurt the associators' families.[66] What concerned them, in Roberdeau's words, was that others were "meanly seeking to enrich themselves."[67]

Responding to the militia's unrest, Roberdeau addressed the associators on August 10. After urging the men to ignore "those (should there be such among us) who would stir up discontent and uneasiness," he agreed that their complaints were just.[68] These grievances, however, did not justify the militia's deserting before the Flying Camp arrived. The associators ought to serve with at least as much dedication, Roberdeau argued, as the conscripted British soldiers.

Roberdeau sought from the associators what the Committee of Privates had obtained in February: the submergence of class interests in favor of patriotism. This time, however, the militia resisted. It refused to remain long in the field, refused to march to Washington's aid, even refused to relieve state troops who marched to New York. Although many contemporaries argued that the militia's recalcitrance was selfish

---

Problems in the home guard continued. See Richard Peters to the Committee of Safety, Aug. 17, 30, 1776, "Records," 10/910, 976; Peters and John Bayard to the Committee of Safety, Sept. 2, 1776, *Pennsylvania Archives*, 1st ser. 5 (1853):17.

[65] "Complaint against Jacob Brandt," [late July–early Aug. 1776], "Whereas . . .," [mid-July 1776], "Records," 11/691, 759.

[66] According to Anne Bezanson, *Prices and Inflation during the American Revolution* (Philadelphia, 1951), p. 12, prices did not begin to rise steeply until September, but impressionistic evidence suggests there was movement before then. See Marshall Diary, D, July 31, Aug. 5, 1776; Force, ed., *American Archives*, 5th ser. 2:27, 29; Thomas Nelson to John Page, Aug. 13, 1776, Smith, ed., *Letters of Delegates*, 4:676; Philadelphia Committee of Inspection Resolve, Aug. 23, 1776, Force, ed., *American Archives*, 5th ser. 1:1119; John Mitchell to the Council of Safety, Sept. 5, 1776, "Records," 10/990.

[67] *Pennsylvania Gazette*, Aug. 21, 1776.

[68] Ibid.

and cowardly, state officers received an entirely different interpretation when they met with militia officers in November 1776 to consider how best to get the associators into the field for their second call-up of the war.[69]

The condition of the militia, the officers asserted, was a "public Calamity." Not only was it not "supported by law," but the militiamen were angry because they had fought while others remained at home in "the peaceable Enjoyment of their Professions." The associators had expected to see nonassociators punished, but instead found their own "patriotic Exertions . . . sneered at" and the "distresses of their families . . . made a jest of."[70] Given these complaints—and there is every reason to believe they were legitimate[71]—the Committee of Safety was not hopeful that the militia would turn out: "What can we Expect from the Class of Men, who live from day to day on the produce of their industry?" "Can it be expected," the Committee continued, "under these disappointments and insults, that they will consent to bear the whole Burthen and face alone the dangers of defending the State?" Patriotic platitudes would not induce them "to forget the unequal Burthens" and turn out. Only justice and respect would do that.

State authorities took three avenues of action to ensure a good turnout. First, they cooperated with Congress's order to use Thomas Mifflin, a splendid orator, to rouse the mili-

---

[69] John Witherspoon to David Witherspoon, Aug. 26, 1776, Hooper to Jonathan Trumbull, Jr., Aug. 28, 1776, Smith, ed., *Letters of Delegates*, 5:69, 80; Hooper to Johnston, Sept. 26, 1776, William Saunders, ed., *Records of North Carolina*, 10 vols. (Raleigh, 1886–90), 10:817.

[70] Committee of Safety Representation to the House, Nov. 26, 1776, "Records," 11/276. Also see Board of War to Washington, Oct. 24, 1776, Smith, ed., *Letters of Delegates*, 5:376.

[71] See, for example, William Will's complaint that while he was in the field, he "lost the Opportunity (which others who remained here improved to their advantage) of purchasing Block Tin." Will, a pewterer, needed tin "to carry on his business for the Support of himself and family"; if he could not get any, he would have to close his shop (Petition, Sept. 4, 1776, "Records," 10/986). Also see Privates of Captain Cowperthwaite's Company to Colonel Dickinson, [Aug. 2–6(?), 1776], Dickinson Papers, no. 77 (Libr. Co. Phila. Coll.), Hist. Soc. Pa.

tia.[72] Mifflin spoke to the militia on November 27, addressed a town meeting the next day, and "harrangued" a single battalion on November 29.[73] He not only stirred their emotions, but assured them their grievances would be alleviated.[74] Second, the Committee of Safety gave the militia power to enforce the decree of December 7 that all associators must turn out. Third, the Committee of Safety, as well as the assembly, offered bounties to get the militia into the field as soon as possible.[75]

For the associators, the care of their families was at least as important as the equality of burden; the Committee of Safety provided money for this while they were in the field.[76] One captain increased his turnout when he went to each associator and promised that authorities would look after their families.[77]

[72] On Mifflin, see Kenneth R. Rossman, *Thomas Mifflin and the Politics of the American Revolution* (Chapel Hill, N.C., 1952); Rosswurm, "Arms, Culture, and Class," p. 260.

[73] Mifflin to Washington, Nov. 27, 1776, Reed Papers, reel 1; *Pennsylvania Evening Post*, Nov. 28, 1776; Charles Willson Peale Diary, no. 2, Nov. 29, 1776, American Philosophical Society, Philadelphia.

[74] "The Memorial and Petition of the First Company of Philadelphia Militia Artillery," May 12, 1779, *Pennsylvania Archives*, 1st ser. 7 (1853):392.

[75] "Committee of Safety Representation to the House," Nov. 26, 1776; "At a Meeting of Real Whigs," Society Hall, Dec. 1, 1776, "In Assembly," Nov. 29, 30, 1776, "In Council," Dec. 1, 1776, "Records," 11/350, 303, 330, 346; "In Assembly," Dec. 5, 1776, 5805.F.13, Libr. Co. Phila.; "In Council," [early Dec. 1776], "Records," 11/784; "A Diary of Trifling Occurrences [Sarah Logan Fisher]," *Pennsylvania Magazine of History and Biography* 82 (1958):414; "In Council of Safety," Dec. 7, 1776, Ab 1776–2, Hist. Soc. Pa.; Council of Safety to [Colonel (?)], [Dec. 8–10(?), 1776], "Records," 12/111; "In Assembly," Dec. 12, 1776, Ab 1776–12; "Philadelphia, December 18, 1776," Society Miscellaneous, Box 15c, folder 1, both Hist. Soc. Pa.

[76] "In Council," Nov. 30, 1776 (three items), "Records," 11/333–34; Resolution of Committee of Safety, *Minutes of Council*, Dec. 5, 1776, 11:32. For the record of disbursement of funds to the families of two companies, see "Minute Book of the Board of War," Apr. 2, 11, 1777, "Records," reel 35.

[77] Peale Diary, 2, Dec. 2, 1776; Peale Autobiography (typescript), 42, Am. Phil. Soc.

The Philadelphia Militia

Official attention to grievances as well as patriotism apparently spurred militiamen to turn out enthusiastically.[78] Between fifteen hundred and two thousand Philadelphians had joined Washington's army by December 18.[79] If the associators had not responded so well, Washington's force would have been much smaller since few militiamen from the Pennsylvania backcountry or New Jersey came out immediately.[80]

The Philadelphia associators guarded the ferries along the Delaware until December 26 when, under the command of Gen. John Cadwalader, they failed in their attempt to cross the river.[81] Washington called Cadwalader's brigade into ac-

[78] There is no direct proof of cause and effect, but see the following: Hooper to Hewes, Dec. 1, 3, 1776, R. H. Lee to Patrick Henry, Dec. 3, 1776, Robert Morris to William Bingham, Dec. 4, 1776, Smith, ed., *Letters of Delegates*, 5:561, 564, 565, 574; Elias Boys to the Council of Safety, Dec. 17, 1776, Council of Safety Orders to constables, Dec. 23, 1776, "Records," 11/517, 578.

[79] Washington to Gov. Jonathan Trumbull, Dec. 12, 1776, to John A. Washington, Dec. 18, 1776, John C. Fitzpatrick, ed., *The Writings of George Washington . . .*, 39 vols. (Washington, D.C., 1931–44), 6:352, 397.

[80] See, for example, Nathanael Greene to Catharine Greene, Dec. 4, 1776, Richard K. Showman et al., eds., *The Papers of General Nathanael Greene*, 2 vols. to date (Chapel Hill, N.C., 1976–), 1:365; Washington to Lund Washington, Dec. 10, 1776, Fitzpatrick, ed., *Writings of Washington*, 6:345–46. The Council of Safety called out the backcountry militia at the same time as the city militia, but there was little enthusiasm in most counties and outright resistance in others. See, for Berks, John Patton to James Read, Dec. 4, 1776, James Read Papers, Hist. Soc. Pa., Capt. Elias Waggoner to John Linle, Dec. [?], 1776; for Chester, William Dewes, Jr., to Council of Safety, Dec. 12, 1776; for Cumberland, Committee of Cumberland County to Council of Safety, Dec. 2, 1776; for Westmoreland, John Carnahan to John Moore, Dec. 24, 1776; for York, York County Committee to Council of Safety, Dec. 27, 1776, "Records," 11/679, 461, 377, 592, 623.

[81] Washington to Colonel Cadwalader, Dec. 12, 1776, in William S. Stryker, *The Battles of Trenton and Princeton* (Boston, 1898), p. 311; "Quarter of the several parts of Colonel Cadwalader's Brigade," Dec. 14, 1776, Cadwalader Collection, General Cadwalader, Box 15, folder misc., 1776, Hist. Soc. Pa.

Among the best sources for this campaign are *Diary of Captain Thomas Rodney, 1776–1777*, Papers of the Historical Society of Delaware, vol. 8 (1888); "Journal of Sergeant William Young," *Pennsylvania Magazine of History and Biography* 8 (1884):255–78; John F. Reed, ed., "Journal of Captain

tion on January 1, 1777, and on January 3 he moved them in to reinforce the Assunpunk Bridge in Trenton in the face of a heavy Hessian grenadier attack. An anonymous major general attested to the militia's "brave" behavior, and Capt. Joseph Moulder's artillery company fought particularly well at the bridge.[82]

Philadelphia associators were at the very center of the Battle of Princeton on January 3, 1777. Although some panicked and fled on the night march from Trenton, most did well. After the British routed General Mercer's men, Cadwalader's city militia came up to meet them. "Rashly," according to one witness, Cadwalader ordered his men to charge. When the enemy opened fire, the "front broke" and "threw the whole into confusion," and all the militia began to run except for Moulder's artillery which kept the British from advancing.[83] Cadwalader and Washington rallied their men who then counterattacked. After another minor panic they finally defeated the British 17th Regiment, and the American forces soon captured the whole town.[84]

The Philadelphia militia had fought well, and the artillery had fought even better. Although the associators had panicked, they "reformed," according to an observer, "in the face of grapeshot and pushed on with a spirit that would do honor

---

Samuel Massey, 1776–1778," *Bulletin of the Historical Society of Montgomery County* 20 (1976):215–19 (I am thankful to Mr. Reed for sending me a copy of this issue); Peale Diary, no. 3; Peale Autobiography.

[82] *Pennsylvania Evening Post*, Jan. 14, 1777. First-hand accounts of the fighting at the bridge include "Journal of Massey," p. 217; Peale Diary, no. 3, Jan. 2, 1777; Peale Autobiography, 43; "Journal of Young," p. 263; Charles C. Haven, *Thirty Days in New Jersey* (Trenton, 1867), p. 45; Johann Ewald, *Diary of the American War: A Hessian Journal*, trans. and ed. Joseph P. Tuslin, Jan. 2, 1777 (New Haven, 1979), p. 49; Col. John Haslett to Caesar Rodney, Jan. 2, 1777, "Sergeant Joseph White's Narrative," in Stryker, *Trenton and Princeton*, pp. 376–77, 479.

[83] *Diary of Rodney*, pp. 35–36; Samuel Stelle Smith, *The Battle of Princeton* (Monmouth Beach, N.J., 1967), p. 24.

[84] For first-hand accounts see, among others, [Cadwalader] to [Council of Safety], Jan. 6, 1777; "Memorial of Thomas Hanson," June 4, 1777, "Records," 11/888, 12/388.

to veterans."[85] Furthermore, the militiamen had not slept for nearly two days before the Battle of Princeton, and many had been without shoes and stockings since before Christmas.[86] Washington praised them highly when he noted that they had "undergone more fatigue and hardship" than he had "expected Militia (especially citizens) would have done at this Inclement Season."[87] But he knew the Philadelphia militia would not remain much longer in the field.

As early as January 6, 1777, the city associators wanted to leave camp. Although officers convinced them to remain beyond their six-week tour of duty, most were gone by January 20.[88] Their grievances were the same as they had been in August 1776: militia duty was unequally distributed and too much leniency was shown to "Cowards, disaffected Men, and open Enemies to the Liberties of America." These militiamen, according to officers who agreed that their complaints were just, wanted the Committee of Safety to force all associators to do their duty or "be banish'd [from] the Country and their Estates forfeited."[89]

Some associators had felt aggrieved as early as Christmas, but nevertheless stayed in camp. Capt. Alexander Boyd's

[85] *Pennsylvania Evening Post*, Jan. 14, 1777. Also see Major Hubley to Brother, Jan. 4, 1777, "Records," 11/848.

[86] "Extract of letter from S. C. Morris to Council of Safety," Dec. 24, 1776, "Records," 11/598; "Journal of Massey," p. 218; Maj. Samuel Meredith to [?], Jan. 9, 1777, in Stryker, *Trenton and Princeton*, p. 469; "The Humble Petition of Sundry Officers and Privates," Mar. 10, 1777; Council of Safety to Washington, Dec. 18, 1776, "Records," 12/134, 11/527; Rosswurm, "Arms, Culture, and Class," p. 269, n.114.

[87] Washington to the President of Congress, Jan. 5, 1777, Fitzpatrick, ed., *Writings of Washington*, 6:470.

[88] Peale Diary, no. 3, Jan. 12, 13, 15, 16, 1777; "Journal of Young," Jan. 16, 17, 18, 19, 1777, pp. 268, 269; Thomas Proctor to Owen Biddle, Jan. 17, 1777, "Records," 11/1017; Washington to the President of Congress, Jan. 19, 1777, to the Pennsylvania Council of Safety, Jan. 19, 1777, Fitzpatrick, ed., *Writings of Washington*, 7:29, 34; Col. Timothy Matlack to Cadwalader, Jan. 21, 1777, John Cadwalader Papers, I, Hist. Soc. Pa.

[89] Address to the Council of Safety, Jan. 15, 1777, Cadwalader Papers, I, 18.

company was angry because the Committee of Safety had not forced James Allen, a member of the most powerful family in Pennsylvania and whom they had been questioning about suspected toryism, to join it in camp. Boyd's associators wanted authorities to enforce the laws impartially, "there being no difference between the Rich & poor associators."[90] If the "rich & the Great" were allowed to remain at home and the "poorer kind" forced into the field, few would serve at the next militia turnout. In the companies at camp, "hardly one Man in ten . . . [was] . . . a Man of Property."[91]

Associators returned to Philadelphia from their duty to find conditions similar to those of the previous August: prices had risen and trade had been taken over by those who had not turned out. Although, as a radical artillery company recalled, it "had Arms in . . . its . . . hands and knew the use of them," it decided to wait "patiently" for the "Interference of the Legislative Authority."[92] Legislative action came with the militia law of March 1777.

The assembly began work on the state's first militia law in late January or early February and finished the primary law on March 13, 1777.[93] Legislators tried to alleviate the militia's grievances by establishing an orderly procedure known as

[90] Capt. Alexander Boyd et al. to the Council of Safety, Dec. 26, 1776, "Records," 11/609. Allen had originally joined the militia because of both a desire to influence it and community pressure (see note 38 above) but had refused to sign the articles.

[91] On December 17 Elias Boys sent to the Council a list of those in his company who had stayed at home "(mostly) through trifling Excuses" ("Records," 11/517). While most men on the list were rather poor, two were significantly wealthier than the others, and Boys's associators probably felt the same as Boyd's.

[92] "The Memorial . . . of the First Company . . .," *Pennsylvania Archives*, 1st ser. 7:393. There again is evidence that those who turned out came back to find their trade appropriated (Petition of Jeremiah Baker, Feb. 20, 1777, Petition of Stynes and Cist, Mar. 10, 1777, "Records," 12/8, 130).

[93] James T. Mitchell and Henry Flanders, comps., *The Statutes at Large of Pennsylvania from 1682 to 1801*, 16 vols. (Harrisburg, 1896–1915), 9:75–95. For additions and clarifications, see ibid., 131–36, 167–69, and 185–89.

The Philadelphia Militia

"classing" for active duty calls. Militia authorities placed each man in a class, numbered from one to eight. They then called out the classes in numerical order; no class was eligible for a second tour of duty until all eight had been called. While there was criticism of classing, it was a reasonable attempt to equalize the burdens and ensure that nonassociation fines could be collected.[94] The assembly also established punitive measures to deal with nonassociation and maintained the discrepancy between the more lenient disciplinary articles of the state and the harsher ones of Congress. It continued the election of officers, set up a pension system, and organized a relief system for the families of poor associators.[95]

The "System in the main . . . [was] . . . a good one," according to Joseph Reed, a Continental Line veteran.[96] Law abstracted from social reality, however, often has little meaning, and the Philadelphia associators, having lost their political naiveté some time before, acted accordingly in the third major turnout of the war in June 1777. Washington ordered the mobilization, and Pennsylvania authorities again called upon Mifflin to rouse the militia. Mifflin used his immense oratorical skills on June 13 in an attempt to convince fifteen hundred associators to respond immediately regardless of class.[97] The

[94] For criticism, see "Hampden," *Pennsylvania Evening Post*, Mar. 13, 1777; Jonathan Mifflin to R. H. Lee, Nov. 12, 1777, Richard Henry Lee, *Memoirs . . .*, 2 vols. (Philadelphia, 1825), 2:174. Washington was pleased when he heard the assembly was planning to equalize the burdens (to the Pennsylvania Council of Safety, Jan. 29, 1777, Fitzpatrick, ed., *Writings of Washington*, 8:79). For a detailed explanation of the system, see Hannah Benner Roach, "The Pennsylvania Militia in 1777," *Pennsylvania Genealogical Society* 23 (1964):162–64.

[95] There is more detail on these points in Rosswurm, "Arms, Culture, and Class," pp. 274–81.

[96] Reed to Thomas Wharton, Feb. 1, 1778, *Pennsylvania Archives*, 1st ser. 7:219–20.

[97] *Pennsylvania Gazette*, June 18, 1777. For reports on the speech, see Abraham Robinson to Anthony Wayne, June 13, 1777, Anthony Wayne Papers, III, 98, Hist. Soc. Pa.; Thomas Paine to R. H. Lee, July 1, 1777, Lee Correspondence, I, 333, Am. Phil. Soc.; "Diary of Allen," July 2, 1777, p. 284.

ARMS AND INDEPENDENCE

militia refused, and its reluctance compelled state authorities to enforce the militia law's classing provisions, which the assembly had enacted because of militia dissatisfaction.[98] The militia would fight, but only within an egalitarian context. Pennsylvania authorities called out two city classes at once and, by mid-September, had four more out, as well as the artillery.[99] Philadelphia militiamen did turn out more enthusiastically than those in the backcountry, where county officials had trouble enforcing the militia law.[100] Nevertheless, substitutes in Philadelphia as well as in the backcountry demanded high fees. The radical artillery company later criticized the substitution clause for its looseness, and in December 1777 the assembly restricted who could be substitutes.[101]

The militia emerged from its three call-ups having learned one important lesson: it had borne the brunt of active duty while others remained at home, raising prices and profiting in its absence. In short, others had exploited the efforts of the "Midling and poor." Its behavior in 1779 also indicates that the militia had developed a sense of self-identity and importance: *it* was virtuous, and *it* had turned out against the enemy. It had not always fought well, but it had performed at least adequately in most cases, even courageously at Trenton and Princeton. This active duty experience greatly influenced the militia in 1778 and 1779.

[98] "Diary of Allen," July 2, 1777, p. 284. Other developments from January to June probably affected their decision; see Rosswurm, "Arms, Culture, and Class," pp. 282–91.

[99] Wharton to Delegation in Congress, July 3, 1777, "Records," 12/504; Muster Returns for Bradford and Delaney Battalions, July 10, 1777, Records, 47/927; Roach, "The Pennsylvania Militia," pp. 176, 189, 190; Supreme Executive Council to Lt. William Henry, Aug. 23, 1777, Wharton to Jehu Eyre, Sept. 6, 1777, "Records," 12/856, 981.

[100] This generalization is based upon a reading of the June, July, and August correspondence in "Records," reel 12.

[101] Lt. Kirkbride to Wharton, Aug. 24, 1777, "Records," 12/860; "The Memorial . . . of the First Company . . .," *Pennsylvania Archives*, 1st ser. 7:393; Mitchell and Flanders, comps., *Statutes at Large*, 9:167–69. Evidence relating to substitution is scattered throughout "Records," reel 12, but see, for example, Robert Smith to Wharton, July 12, 1777, 12/546. Smith sent 320 men to camp, and 200 of them were substitutes.

The Philadelphia Militia

Philadelphia radicalism reached its high point in 1779 when the popular movement sought to lower prices, defend the radical constitution, and implement a strong antitory program. The militia, with its active duty experience clearly in mind, took the lead in pursuing the popular movement's goals. It took to the streets in May to administer popular justice and continually pressured price-fixing committees to take militant action. Resistance to radicalism increased, however, and the attempt to control prices failed. By September the situation was at a stalemate.

As the locus of the war moved south and war-related production declined, labor scarcity apparently turned to labor glut.[102] The laboring poor found it difficult, if not impossible, to maintain their standard of living as currency depreciated and many constituencies competed for scarce goods. Worse, merchants exploited the situation to reap handsome profits, and some intensified it by withholding goods. Although Philadelphia and Pennsylvania authorities, many of whom were radical, tried to alleviate the problems, the popular movement's patience came to an end in early May.

On May 12 the First Company of City Artillery, then at Mud Island in the Delaware River, presented a petition to the Supreme Executive Council. The artillerymen had served in all three active duty campaigns, and they were as angry as their grievances were old. They had defended citizens who had shirked their duty and had returned from the battlefield to find prices raised. Although the assembly had heavily fined nonassociators, there was enough money to be made in a day of "monopolizing" to "defray all their Expences or Fines or Penalties in a whole year." The "Midling and poor" bore the dual burden of militia duty and speculation and now demanded that the assembly either fine nonassociators in proportion to their wealth or put the "Fines and Penalties" aside and allow the patriotic militia to "Compell every able Bodied man to join them in some Station."[103]

---

[102] For a survey of the impressionistic evidence, see Rosswurm, "Arms, Culture, and Class," pp. 343–47.

[103] *Pennsylvania Archives*, 1st ser. 7:393–95; also see Rosswurm, "Arms, Culture, and Class," pp. 360–69.

The next day the Constitutional Society, formed in March to defend the frame of government and composed largely of the "middling sort," began to plan a town meeting for May 25. Even before the town meeting, however, the militia acted on its own in the streets.

No doubt spurred on by a tremendous price increase the previous week, but also clearly influenced by long-standing grievances, copies of a broadside signed "Come on Coolly" were distributed throughout Philadelphia on May 23, the night before a militia exercise day.[104] The broadside urged the people to lower prices and raised the threat that popular military participation always entailed: guns could be used against internal as well as external enemies. "We have turned out against the enemy," the broadside thundered, "we will not be eaten up by monopolizers and forestallers."

The militia's activity in the streets from May 24 to May 30 indicates that many associators shared the writer's anger. On the morning of May 24, before the militia exercise, militiamen pummelled some who were tearing down the broadside and took others prisoner. On May 25 associators seized some of those suspected of toryism or speculation as well as a man who laughed at them. Sporadic seizures continued for the next week as radical militiamen meted out popular justice.[105] While a number of observers called the militia a "mob," others noticed a regularity in its proceedings quite unlike the traditional crowd action.[106] The "lower sort" apparently had internalized its military training: it now evidenced discipline and orderly methods of action.

It was in this context that Philadelphians, including the mi-

---

[104] Come on Coolly, "For Our Country's Good," transcription in William Blodgett to Greene, May 24, 1779, Greene Correspondence, V, no. 64, Am. Phil. Soc. For the price increases, see Chaloner and White to Gouveneur Morris and Committee of Congress, May 22, 1779, to Jeremiah Wadsworth, May 24, 1779, Chaloner and White Letter Books (Mar. 15–Sept. 18, 1779), Hist. Soc. Pa.

[105] Rosswurm, "Arms, Culture, and Class," pp. 370–71, 375–77.

[106] Charles Pettit to Greene, May 24, 1779, Greene Correspondence, VI, no. 61; Gérard to Vergennes, May 24, 1779, John J. Meng, ed., *Despatches and Instructions of Conrad Alexandre Gérard* (Baltimore, 1939), p. 677.

litia, attended their first major town meeting since 1776. There they heard speeches, including one by General Roberdeau, whom militia officers and privates had elected as the state's first brigadier general in 1776, which harshly attacked speculators and tories. The meeting then passed resolutions establishing a price-fixing committee and prohibiting tories from remaining in Philadelphia.[107]

The militia's activity, the town meeting, and the formation of the price-fixing committee seemed to indicate that the popular movement was well situated to score impressive victories. These achievements, however, proved minor. Merchants evaded the regulations, refused to sell their goods, and slowed importations. The price-fixing committee tried a variety of tactics, but none worked. From June 28 to July 26, the May 25 committee fought a holding action: "While our Committee of Regulators reigns supreme their Conduct had obliged the Merchants to secret his property and many to remove."[108]

In late June the radical artillery, frustrated with the situation, presented a fiery petition to the price-fixing committee.[109] Much good had come from the May 25 resolves, the petitioners acknowledged, but "indefatigable attention and vigilence" were needed to cope with "designing and interested persons" who tried to evade the committee's edicts. "We have arms in our hands and know the use of them—and are ready and willing to support your Honorable Board," the artillerymen pledged. They would support the price-fixing committee in "relieving the oppressed and punishing the agressors," no matter the "rank or the Station." They would stand up for the "virtuous, innocent, and suffering part of the community." After reading the address, the company gave three cheers and fired three salutes.

Radical leaders called another town meeting at the end of July to assess the deteriorating situation. Rousing speeches,

---

[107] *Pennsylvania Packet*, May 27, 1779.

[108] Chaloner and White to Wadsworth, July 12, 1779, Chaloner and White Letter Books.

[109] *Pennsylvania Packet*, July 1, 1779.

the presentation of a "plan for Improving the Currency," and the approval of a price-fixing "Association" highlighted the first day's activities.[110] On the second day of the meeting, July 27, members of the crowd, probably militiamen, angrily refused to allow conservatives to speak. They pounded "large Staves or Bludgeons" and shouted until the conservatives withdrew.[111]

Although radicals won an overwhelming victory in the election for a new price-fixing committee on August 2, the situation worsened. Those who had goods refused to sell, and importers restricted their efforts or directed shipments to other ports. Few goods changed hands in August and September; doubts multiplied as to the efficacy of price-fixing. On September 10 "merchants and traders" issued a sharply worded ideological attack on price-fixing and publicly refused to obey the committee's resolves.[112] On September 18 the price-fixing committee petitioned the assembly to deal with the crisis and six days later suspended all activity until it acted.[113] The committee feared that its actions might "increase the avaricious disposition for removing goods." There was little choice except, perhaps, to push on with regulations, then seize goods and sell them at a just price. To do that, however, would have meant further militia action.

To most "middling" radicals, the militia had already acted quite enough. The militia had been the most militant sector of the popular movement and had pushed it to the left. Silas Deane had interpreted the developments in late July as class struggle between "the respectable Citizens, of Fortune &

[110] Unless otherwise noted, information on this meeting is from *Proceedings of the General Town Meeting ... on Monday the Twenty-Sixth ...* (Philadelphia, 1779).

[111] No source identifies those who disrupted the meeting, but the following account warrants the interpretation that they were militiamen: Silas Deane to Simeon Deane, July 28, 1779, *Pennsylvania Magazine of History and Biography* 17 (1893):350. The radical account argued that the men brought "sticks" because it had been "rumoured" that those opposed to the regulations were bringing sailors (*Proceedings*, p. 25). This strikes me as self-serving.

[112] *Pennsylvania Packet*, Sept. 10, 1779.

[113] Ibid., Sept. 18, 25, 1779.

Character, opposed to the Constitution of the State" and "People in lower Circumstances, & Reputation."[114] The militia had played an important role in this struggle. Would they now accept the price-fixing committee's surrender?

The radical militia refused to capitulate and on October 4, 1779, tried to expel tories and support the price-fixing committee. The resulting incident, known as the "Fort Wilson Riot," pitted the militia against conservatives, moderates, and radical state authorities. The confrontation, the culmination of four years of conflict, was a defeat for the militia as well as the popular movement.

The militia's discontent was as deep as its grievances were old. The "Midling and poor" continued to bear an unequal share of the active duty burden. While the militia law of April 1777 had rectified these grievances on paper, the law, according to the militia, had not become fact. Authorities collected some nonassociation fines in Philadelphia, but the militia felt there were still too many nonassociators and that the fines were too low.[115] The problem of unequal burdens related to the militia's second grievance: rising prices. Every time they returned from duty, the militia found that prices had been raised and their trade appropriated. By 1779 more than enough could be made by "monopolizing" to pay the nonassociation fine. The militia's final grievance lay in the indul-

---

[114] Silas Deane to Simeon Deane, July 27, 1779, *Pennsylvania Magazine of History and Biography* 17 (1893):348.

[115] *Pennsylvania Archives*, 1st ser. 7:393. For evidence of collection in Philadelphia, see Samuel Rowland Fisher to Jabez Maude Fisher, Feb. 19, 1779, Logan-Fisher-Fox Collection, Box 3, folder 4, Hist. Soc. Pa.; Henry D. Biddle, ed., *Extracts from the Journal of Elizabeth Drinker from 1759 to 1807*, June 14, 1779 (Philadelphia, 1889), p. 117. For evidence that fines were not being collected outside Philadelphia County, see "Records," reel 12; James Thompson to Reed, June 16, 1779, Stauffer Collection, X, 676, Hist. Soc. Pa.; William Coats to Wharton, Feb. 2, 1778, Gratz Collection, Case 1, Box 17.

For continued militia unrest, see Reed to Washington, May 8, 1779, in William B. Reed, *The Life and Correspondence of Joseph Reed*, 2 vols. (Philadelphia, 1847), 2:104; Thomas Bradford to Reed, July 17, 1779, Matlack to T. Bradford, July 19, 1779, Bradford Manuscripts, British Army Prisoners, II, 48, 42, Hist. Soc. Pa.

gence which they felt was shown tories and neutralists, especially those who had cooperated with the British occupation of Philadelphia. "Tory" had become the epithet for those who did not do their part in the Revolutionary struggle as well as those who aided the British.

Late in August, "Come on Warmly" urged the people "to rouse up as a Lyen out of his den" against a "few overbearing Merchants, a swarm of Monopolizers and Speculaters, and an infernal gang of Tories."[116] There was no immediate response to this broadside's suggestions to defend the price-fixing committee; that action came when the prospects for the winter began to look bleak.[117]

Radical militiamen met on September 27 on the city commons, prepared to begin the task of exiling the families of tories who had fled Philadelphia.[118] Charles Willson Peale, a popular militia captain, refused to lead them and convinced them not to march. The Committee of Privates, revived on September 27, issued a summons to meet again on the commons on October 4.[119] This time Peale and three other radicals were not able to stop the militia from marching. The associators went ahead, pursuing by their own methods the goals they largely shared with the radical "middling sort."

The militiamen were in a serious, even arrogant, mood as they began their march. They seized four men they identi-

---

[116] Come on Warmly, "Gentlemen and Fellow-Citizens," [Aug. 29, 1779], Hist. Soc. Pa.; Biddle, ed., *Drinker Journal*, Aug. 30, 1779, p. 120. "Gentlemen and Fellow-Citizens" is dated 1776, Ab 1776–46, Hist. Soc. Pa.; the Drinker entry provides the correction.

[117] From September 22 to October 2 food prices rose about 50 percent (Coxe to Greene, Oct. 2, 1779, Greene Correspondence, III, no. 27). The price of firewood, furthermore, was rising since "vast quantities" were being consumed for the production of molasses and lump sugar. This practice was "generally oppressive to all but the first rank of People" (Overseers of the Poor Minutes [1774–May 1782], Sept. 16, 1779, Phila. Arch.).

[118] The following is drawn from Rosswurm, "Arms, Culture, and Class," pp. 428–65. Also see the excellent article by John K. Alexander, "The Fort Wilson Incident of 1779: A Case Study of the Revolutionary Crowd," *William and Mary Quarterly*, 3d ser. 31 (1974):589–612.

[119] *Pennsylvania Packet*, Oct. 2, 1779; "Journal of Samuel Rowland Fisher," Sept. 27, 1779, *Pennsylvania Magazine of History and Biography* 41 (1917):169.

fied as tories, taking them "about ye Streets with the Drum after them, beating ye Rogue's March."[120] The march continued through the city streets and approached the home of James Wilson, an attorney who had defended tories and who opposed the constitution. Wilson, convinced he was the marchers' target, had gathered armed friends and political allies in his house.

When a state official tried to detour the militia away from Wilson's house, a militia captain denied his men meant to "meddle" with Wilson. The associator's goals, according to the captain, were "to support the constitution, the laws, and the Committee of Trade. The labouring part of the city had become desperate from the high prices of the necessaries of life."[121] Two poor militiamen, both of whom had served on the popular committees, successfully ordered the march to continue. One of them emphasized the order with a fixed bayonet.

Firing did not begin until the militiamen were almost past Wilson's house. There are conflicting accounts about who initiated the shooting, which continued for about ten minutes.[122] Joseph Reed, state president and Constitutionalist, arrived on horseback, accompanied by Timothy Matlack, a well-known radical, and others. They began fighting the associators; the City Light Horse and some Continental Dragoons joined the battle just before the artillery readied its cannon. The horsemen, aided by those inside "Fort Wilson," quickly subdued the militia and soon had twenty-seven in jail.

Popular support for the militia who marched made the authorities' task more difficult. People threw "large stones and bricks" at the Light Horse as they rounded up the militia, and others tried to free those jailed.[123] Unrest continued

[120] Biddle, ed., *Drinker Journal*, Oct. 4, 1779, p. 121.

[121] "Allen McLane's Narrative," in Reed, *Life and Correspondence*, 2:151.

[122] The five eyewitness accounts are discussed in Rosswurm, "Arms, Culture, and Class," pp. 447–48.

[123] Horace E. Hayden, ed., "The Reminiscences of David Hayfield Conyngham, 1750–1834," *Proceedings and Collections of the Wyoming Historical and Geological Society* 8 (1904):212, 215; "Journal of Fisher," p. 171; Biddle, ed., *Drinker Journal*, Oct. 4, 1779, p. 122.

through the night and the next day, finally forcing Matlack to release the prisoners, "who drew up in a line, [and] gave three very loud huzzas."[124] The militia suffered the most casualties during the battle: five killed and fourteen wounded. In "Fort Wilson" only one "gentleman" was killed and three wounded.[125]

By October 8 calm had returned to the city.[126] Although anger about the battle continued for weeks, and in some cases for years, the affair was over.[127] On November 13 the assembly passed an "act of oblivion"; in March 1780 the Supreme Executive Council granted a universal pardon.

October 4 was a major defeat for the militia as well as for the popular movement. Conservatives and moderates were both pleased and surprised that "middling" radicals deserted their erstwhile allies and defended those in Wilson's house. The militia had overstepped the "middling" radicals' boundaries of acceptable behavior.[128] Most militia officers agreed that their men had gone too far in their "forceable attempts to redress themselves," and few joined the militia on its march. Many presented a petition on October 8 to the Supreme Executive Council that attested to the legitimacy of the militia's

---

[124] "Journal of Fisher," p. 172.

[125] Samuel Shaw to Winthrop Sargent, Oct. 10, 1779, Society Collection, Hist. Soc. Pa.; Samuel Patterson to Rodney, Oct. 6, 1779, George H. Ryden, ed., *Letters to and from Caesar Rodney, 1756–1784* (Philadelphia, 1933), p. 324.

[126] Chaloner and White to Wadsworth, Oct. 8, 1779, Chaloner and White Letter Books (Sept. 21, 1779–May 18, 1780).

[127] "General Militia Orders," Oct. 27, 1779, Ab 1779–4, Hist. Soc. Pa.; "Sydney," *Freeman's Journal*, Mar. 20, 1782; anecdote told William B. Reed, Feb. 20, 1838, Reed Papers, reel 3.

[128] Arthur St. Clair to Joseph Reed, Oct. 10, 1779, William H. Smith, ed., *The St. Clair Papers* . . ., 2 vols. (Cincinnati, 1882), 1:488; Bernard Dougherty to Joseph Reed, Jan. 22, 1781, Reed Papers, reel 3; Benjamin Rush to J. Adams, Oct. 12, 1779, Lyman H. Butterfield, ed., *Letters of Benjamin Rush*, 2 vols. (Princeton, 1951), 1:240; "Philip Hagner's Narrative" (Arnold statement), in Reed, *Life and Correspondence*, 2:427; "Journal of Fisher," p. 172; Rosswurm, "Arms, Culture, and Class," pp. 457–58.

grievances, but condemned the men's solutions to the problems.[129]

At "Fort Wilson" the militia faced the city's total apparatus of law enforcement. Decisive to its defeat was the Light Horse, formed in 1775. This unit, which included many from gentry social clubs, wore ornate and expensive uniforms; many of its members actively opposed the democratic constitution.[130] It acted not simply as an agent of law and order, but as a decidedly partisan force. The militia officers' request that the corps be either disbanded or placed under militia discipline underscored the mutual hostility.

All evidence indicates that it was poor militiamen who marched on October 4.[131] For many years before 1775 they had endured dependent social relations; although the war years brought them increased political power and importance, total justice and equality continued to elude them. If the militiamen did not intend to attack Wilson's house, most were ready to fight as they would not have been in 1775. Four years of military and political activity had prepared the militia to act on its own on October 4.

Although moderate whigs were appalled at the "licentiousness" of "Fort Wilson" and feared the "many headed monster" would spread its "baneful influence," the split in the popular movement prevented that eventuality.[132] Notwithstanding some short-term goals, the "lower sort" suffered

[129] "The Memorial and Representation of a Deputation from the Several Battalions of Militia of the City and Liberties of Philadelphia," Oct. 8, 1779, Stauffer Collection, IX, 663.

[130] Rosswurm, "Arms, Culture, and Class," pp. 461–62.

[131] *Pennsylvania Packet*, Oct. 9, 1779; *Minutes of Council*, Oct. 9, 1779, 12:125.

[132] For example, see J. Adams to Rush, Nov. 14, 1779, Adams, ed., *Works of Adams*, 9:507; Rev. John Clarke to Timothy Pickering, Oct. 21, 1779, in Octavius Pickering and Charles W. Upham, *The Life of Timothy Pickering*, 2 vols. (Boston, 1867–73), 1:242; Francis Holland to James Wilson, Oct. 19, 1779, James Wilson Papers, IV, no. 5, Hist. Soc. Pa.; Rush to R. H. Lee, Oct. 24, 1779, Butterfield, ed., *Letters of Rush*, 1:244.

through the rest of the war and could only defend its interests at the risk of taking on all state authorities.[133] "Fort Wilson" had shown that such a battle could not be won, and the "Slow & Sure" incident in the spring of 1780 reinforced the lesson. Demoralization intensified, and associators responded poorly to the war's final call-up in August 1780. Neither the militia nor the popular movement offered effective resistance to Robert Morris's political-economic program in 1781.

The winter of 1779-80 must have been hard on Philadelphia's laboring poor. Although trade revived, prices rose to extraordinarily high levels. The winter was cold, some said the coldest they remembered, and firewood went quickly. Depreciation continued, and paper money became almost useless. As the Overseers of the Poor noted, "many worthy families . . . have . . . seen better days."[134]

On April 4 a broadside signed "Slow & Sure" urged the militia to meet on matters of concern on April 17, the day on which new officers were to be elected.[135] The grievances, according to "Slow & Sure," were the same as before: rising prices and unequal militia burdens. There had been few qualitative changes in the new militia law of March 1780.[136] While it retained the democratic features of the 1777 law and placed the Light Horse under militia discipline, the assembly

---

[133] On October 9 the Supreme Executive Council ordered the state to buy 100 barrels of flour to be given first to those families whose members had performed militia duty (*Minutes of Council*, Oct. 9, 1779, 12:125). The assembly passed the same resolution but ruled that the flour must first go to the families of those who would turn out for the upcoming militia campaign (*Journals of the House of Representatives of the Commonwealth of Pennsylvania, November 28, 1776–October 2, 1781* [Philadelphia, 1782], p. 387). It also enacted strong laws against the "disaffected," passed a law against engrossing, and ruled that militia fines be levied in proportion to the nonassociator's wealth (*Pennsylvania Packet*, Oct. 12, 1779).

[134] These generalizations are based on Rosswurm, "Arms, Culture, and Class," pp. 466–67. The quotation is from Overseers of the Poor to Dickinson, Dec. 30, 1779, Overseers of the Poor Minutes.

[135] "Journal of Fisher," p. 283.

[136] Mitchell and Flanders, comps., *Statutes at Large*, 10:144–73.

again allowed militiamen to hire substitutes from outside their households. Furthermore, it lowered the nonassociation fines that it had raised in the aftermath of "Fort Wilson."

Reed angrily examined printers for the identity of "Slow & Sure," offering a substantial reward for the names of the printer and the author.[137] He accused the writer of inciting "Tumults and Divisions" and promoting the "like tragical Scenes which but a few months ago involved the City in the greatest distress and Confusion." Those who met on April 17 would do so "at their own Peril," he declared, adding that current militia officers were to supervise their companies until new officers were elected. The radical Constitutional Society's "handbill" attacking "Slow & Sure" offered final evidence of the split in the popular movement.[138]

April 17 came and went without an uprising or even a demonstration. "People seem much dissatisfied," George Nelson wrote, "but know not how to help themselves."[139] The aristocratic Light Horse as well as "many of the Citizens" were "stirring and very active on the morning of the 17th."[140] Not content with this show of force, the authorities also withheld ammunition from the exercising militia.

It appears that "Fort Wilson" and the "Slow & Sure" incident, as well as high prices and currency depreciation, affected the militia's morale and commitment to the Revolution. Philadelphia's final major turnout of the war, in August 1780, produced fewer men than previously. Although war-weariness played a role in the poor turnout, the poor, according to Reed, had decided the war was not worth fighting. "It is too obvious that the bulk of the People are weary of war. The rich pay their fines and avoid Duty. The poor having little or no stake in the Game seek their Indulgences also."[141] Advance pay-

---

[137] George Nelson Diary, Apr. 15, 1780, Hist. Soc. Pa.; "By His Excellency Joseph Reed . . . A Proclamation," Apr. 16, 1780, Ab 1780–1, both Hist. Soc. Pa.

[138] Nelson Diary, Apr. 17, 1780.

[139] Ibid.

[140] "Journal of Fisher," p. 284.

[141] Joseph Reed to Esther Reed, Aug. 18, 1780, Reed Papers, reel 2.

ment brought out only 530 Philadelphians.¹⁴² Even so, more came out from the city than from Philadelphia County and Bucks County. Although some uneasiness developed in camp, it was minimal compared to previous years.¹⁴³

Militia unrest continued in 1781. During the first week of May, sailors demonstrated against depreciation amid hints that the militia might do the same. A proclamation issued by Reed, however, apparently reinforced the reluctance of officers to lead their men and the unwillingness of the militia to act on its own.¹⁴⁴ During the spring, Robert Morris met little opposition to the implementation of his political economy. Its central focus was the retirement of paper money upon which depended, according to "Brutus," the "subsistence of a number of brave and valuable soldiers and citizens . . . 'tho poor."¹⁴⁵ Specie gradually replaced the depreciating paper money, and in June 1781 the assembly abolished the legal tender basis of paper money.

As the war sputtered to an end, the "lower sort" relapsed into traditional "mobbing" activities, which although expressing hostility to wealth and toryism, led nowhere and achieved nothing. The militia, however, retained a certain radicalism. An artillery company refused to fight against the 1781 Pennsylvania mutineers unless they tried to "form a junction with the Enemy," and officers offered their services as arbitrators between Congress and the Pennsylvania troops.¹⁴⁶ In 1783 militia officers again reported that their men were too unreliable to turn out against Pennsylvania Line troops who demonstrated at the State House in June.¹⁴⁷

---

¹⁴² Joseph Reed to [William Moore], Aug. 21, 1780, ibid.

¹⁴³ Among the sources for this campaign are John Lacey Orderly Book, Memoir and Correspondence, II, N.-Y. Hist. Soc.; Reed Papers, reel 2.

¹⁴⁴ Nelson Diary, Apr. 26, 30, May 6, 7, 10, 1781; "Proclamation," May 11, 1781, 953.F.46, Libr. Co. Phila.

¹⁴⁵ *Pennsylvania Packet*, Mar. 14, 1780.

¹⁴⁶ Nelson Diary, Jan. 6, 17, 1781.

¹⁴⁷ "Rough Minutes of the Council Meeting with Militia Officers," (June 24[?], 1783), Dickinson Papers, no. 52 (Libr. Co. Phila. Coll.), Hist. Soc. Pa.

The Philadelphia Militia

The experience of the Philadelphia militia during the American Revolution supports contentions that military history cannot be isolated from the history of society, that the military aspect of the Revolution was central to its other aspects, and that the war had "revolutionary effects," at least in Pennsylvania. At every point from 1775 to 1781, the Philadelphia militia affected the development of the state revolution and often that of the Revolution as a whole.

In 1775 and 1776 the experience of serving in the militia politicized and mobilized the Philadelphia "lower sort" who previously had little or no control over their lives. Beginning with the conflict over the articles of association, the militiamen's consciousness of their political position in society and the possible solutions to their grievances increased as they struggled for equitable and just articles. The Committee of Privates led the militia's struggle against both the assembly and moderate resistance leaders and further politicized rank-and-file associators who attended its meetings and read its petitions and broadsides.

In 1776 radicals in Congress and Philadelphia cooperated in the overthrow of Pennsylvania's proprietary government. Some leaders from the Committee of Privates participated in planning this revolution, but more important, many, perhaps most, associators had come to consider the established government their primary enemy by May 1776. The assembly had not only refused to pass equitable articles of association and to expand the suffrage, but had also opposed independence. The overthrow of proprietary government did not mean merely that Pennsylvania no longer obstructed the drive for independence. Given the militia's politicization and the radical political theories that had come to dominate the most powerful sector of the resistance movement, internal revolution meant that Pennsylvania's new constitution was the most democratic of the era. The people had chosen "governors from among themselves" as well as a democratic constitution.[148]

Just as the militia experience had politicized the "lower sort,"

---

[148] "Extracts from the Diary of James Clitherall, 1776," *Pennsylvania Magazine of History and Biography* 22 (1898):469.

so political views affected the militia's performance in the field in 1776 and 1777. It often acted as poorly as critics charged, but the militia's fighting and forebearance in the winter campaign of 1776-77 earned General Washington's praise. Behind much of its ill-disciplined and erratic behavior lay egalitarian politics, the conviction that there was "no difference between the Rich & poor associators."[149] Inequality of the fighting burden forced associators to choose between patriotism and equality, and they consistently demanded they be able to fight within a just political and social context. In the frequent absence of justice, the militia chose equality over patriotism, as they had not done in February 1776. The militia emerged from its active duty tours having discovered one important fact: the "Midling and poor" had done the fighting while those who had stayed at home exploited both them and their families.

The militiamen's active duty experience deeply influenced their political activities in Philadelphia in 1779. They fought with their more "middling" allies in the popular movement for price-fixing, a firmer policy toward tories, and the democratic constitution. At the same time, the militia was willing to take more direct action to obtain these goals than were its allies, and it went into the streets in May 1779 to seize speculators and tories.

Out of the militia's politicization during the previous four years, and its three active tours of duty in 1776 and 1777, came its refusal to accept the surrender of the price-fixing committee in September 1779.[150] The militiamen had come too far to give up simply because their "middling" allies had done so. On October 4 the militia marched to "support the constitution, the laws, and the Committee of Trade." The radical "middling sort" turned on their allies and joined the

---

[149] Boyd et al. to the Council of Safety, Dec. 24, 1776, "Records," 11/609.

[150] For an analysis of the political-economic debate that raged in Philadelphia during the summer of 1779, see Rosswurm, "'As a Lyen out his den': Philadelphia's Popular Movement, 1776-1780," in Margaret C. and James R. Jacob, eds., *The Origins of Anglo-American Radicalism* (forthcoming).

The Philadelphia Militia

City Light Horse and Continental Dragoons to suppress the militia.

The militia's refusal to surrender meekly had two important results. First, the popular movement split decisively into its constituent parts. Neither group could effectively challenge Morris's political economy of self-interest in 1780 and 1781. Although Morris's political economy undoubtedly would have triumphed eventually, the militia indirectly hastened its victory. Price-fixing, according to many observers, produced popular committees and, even more ominously, direct action. Free trade, on the other hand, meant order and calm.[151] Second, the militiamen's defeat profoundly affected their commitment to the Revolution. Few associators turned out for the last major active duty call of the war in August 1780 because they "had no stake in the Game." Once again, politics affected military performance.

How typical was the Philadelphia militia? What does its experience tell us about other militia and the Revolution's military history? While it appears the Philadelphia militia's radicalism was unmatched, its history raises important questions. First, did military participation raise the issue of suffrage rights in other states? There are indications it did, but these must be examined systematically.[152] Second, was elite control of the militia necessary for a moderate revolution? Again, there is evidence for this view, but more research is necessary.[153] Third, did other militias face the choice between patriotism and egalitarianism? If so, how did they choose

---

[151] George Wall, Jr., to John Lacey, Feb. 17, 1780, Miscellaneous Manuscripts, L., N.-Y. Hist. Soc.; Peletiah Webster, *Political Essays on the Nature and Operation of Money, Public Finances, and Other Subjects* (Philadelphia, 1791), p. 10. Webster's piece first appeared publicly in August 1779 under the pseudonym "A Citizen of Philadelphia."

[152] Ronald Hoffman, *A Spirit of Dissension: Economics, Politics, and the Revolution in Maryland* (Baltimore, 1973), p. 171 (see pp. 186 and 189–90 for demands for company elections of officers); Chilton Williamson, *American Suffrage: From Property to Democracy, 1760–1860* (Princeton, 1960), pp. 80–81.

[153] Staughton Lynd, "The Revolution and the Common Man: Farm Tenants and Artisans in New York Politics, 1777–1788," Ph.D. diss., Co-

and on what basis? These questions cannot yet be answered. But the history of the Philadelphia militia from 1775 to 1781 makes it clear that they are legitimate and ripe for further study.

---

lumbia University, 1962, pp. 85–90; Hoffman, *A Spirit of Dissension*, chs. 8 and 9; William F. White, "The Independent Companies of Virginia, 1774–1775," *Virginia Magazine of History and Biography* 86 (1978):149–62.

JAMES KIRBY MARTIN

A "Most Undisciplined, Profligate Crew":
Protest and Defiance in the Continental Ranks, 1776–1783

A SEQUENCE OF EVENTS inconceivable to Americans raised on patriotic myths about the Revolution occurred in New Jersey during the spring of 1779. For months the officers of the Jersey brigade had been complaining loudly about everything from lack of decent food and clothing to pay arrearages and late payments in rapidly depreciating currency. They had petitioned their assembly earlier, but nothing had happened. They petitioned again in mid-April 1779, acting on the belief that the legislature should "be informed that our pay is now only *minimal*, not *real*, that four months' pay of a private will not procure his wretched wife and children a single bushel of wheat." Using "the most plain and unambiguous terms," they stressed that "unless a speedy and ample remedy be provided, the total dissolution of your troops is inevitable."[1] The Jersey assembly responded to this plea in its usual fashion—it forwarded the petition to the Continental Congress without comment. After all, the officers, although from

---

[1] Memorial dated Apr. 17, 1779, *Selections from the Correspondence of the Executive of New Jersey, from 1776 to 1786* (Newark, N.J., 1849), pp. 144–45. I am deeply indebted to Mark Edward Lender of Rutgers University for his assistance with this paper. Many of the conclusions contained herein also appear in James Kirby Martin and Mark Edward Lender, *A Respectable Army: The Military Origins of the Republic, 1763–1789* (Arlington Heights, Ill., 1982). Spelling in all quotations in this text has been updated to conform to modern usage.

ARMS AND INDEPENDENCE

New Jersey, were a part of the Continental military establishment.

The assembly's behavior only further angered the officers, and some of them decided to demonstrate their resolve. On May 6 the brigade received orders to join John Sullivan's expedition against the Six Nations. That same day, officers in the First Regiment sent forth yet another petition. They again admonished the assembly about pay and supply issues. While they stated that they would prepare the regiment for the upcoming campaign, they themselves would resign as a group unless the legislators addressed their demands. Complaints had now turned into something more than gentlemanly protest. Protest was on the verge of becoming nothing less than open defiance of civil authority, and the Jersey officers were deadly serious. They had resorted to their threatened resignations to insure that the assembly would give serious attention to their demands—for a change.[2]

When George Washington learned about the situation, he was appalled. "Nothing, which has happened in the course of the war, . . . has given me so much pain," the commander in chief stated anxiously. It upset him that the officers seemingly had lost sight of the "principles" that governed the cause. What would happen, he asked rhetorically, "if their example should be followed and become general?" The result would be the "ruin" and "disgrace" of the rebel cause, all because these officers had *reasoned wrong about the means of obtaining a good end.*"[3]

So developed a little known but highly revealing confrontation. Washington told Congress that he would have acted very aggressively toward the recalcitrant officers, except that "the causes of discontent are too great and too general and the ties that bind the officers to the service too feeble" to force the issue. What he did promise was that he would not countenance any aid that came "in [such] a manner ex-

---

[2] Memorial dated May 6, 1779, *Selections Correspondence Executive N.J.*, pp. 156–57.

[3] To Brig. Gen. William Maxwell, May 7, 1779, John C. Fitzpatrick, ed., *The Writings of George Washington* . . ., 39 vols. (Washington, D.C., 1931–44), 15:13–16.

torted."[4] On the other hand, the officers had been asking the assembly for relief since January 1778, but to no avail. They, too, were not about to be moved.[5]

The New Jersey legislature was the political institution with the ability to break the deadlock. Some of the legislators preferred disbanding the brigade. The majority argued that other officers and common soldiers might follow the First Regiment's lead and warned that the war effort could hardly succeed without a Continental military establishment. The moment was now ripe for compromise. The assemblymen agreed to provide the officers with whatever immediate relief could be mustered in return for the latter calling back their petitions. That way civil authorities would not be succumbing to intimidation by representatives of the military establishment, and the principle of subordination of military to civil authority would remain inviolate. The assembly thus provided an immediate payment of £200 to each officer and $40 to each soldier. Accepting the compromise settlement as better than nothing, the brigade moved out of its Jersey encampment on May 11 and marched toward Sullivan's bivouac at Easton, Pennsylvania.[6] Seemingly, all now had returned to normal.

The confrontation between the New Jersey officers and the state assembly serves to illuminate some key points about protest and defiance in the Continental ranks during the years 1776–83. Most important here, it underscores the mounting anger felt by Washington's regulars as a result of their perceived (and no doubt very real) lack of material and psychological support from the society that had spawned the

[4] To the President of Congress, May 11, 1779, ibid., pp. 43–44.

[5] Captains and Subalterns of the First Regiment of New Jersey to George Washington, May 8, 1779, *Selections Correspondence Executive N.J.*, pp. 164–66.

[6] A more detailed description of this incident may be found in Mark Edward Lender, "The Enlisted Line: The Continental Soldiers of New Jersey," Ph.D. diss., Rutgers University, 1975, pp. 219–28. See also Leonard Lundin, *Cockpit of the Revolution: The War for Independence in New Jersey* (Princeton, 1940), pp. 435–38.

Continental army. It is common knowledge that Washington's regulars suffered from serious supply and pay shortages throughout the war. Increasingly, historians are coming to realize that officers and common soldiers alike received very little moral support from the general populace. As yet, however, scholars have not taken a systematic look at one product of this paradigm of neglect, specifically, protest and defiance. The purpose of this essay is to present preliminary findings that will facilitate that task.[7]

Given that there was a noticeable relationship between lack of material and psychological support from the civilian sector and mounting protest and defiance in the ranks, it is also important to make clear that patterns of protest were very complex. A second purpose of this essay is to outline those basic patterns and to indicate why protest and defiance did not result in serious internal upheaval between army and society in the midst of the War for American Independence. To begin this assessment, we must bring Washington's Continentals to the center of the historical arena.

During the past twenty years, historians have learned that there were at least two Continental armies. The army of 1775–76 might be characterized as a republican constabulary, consisting of citizens who had respectable amounts of property and who were defending hearth and home. They came out for what they believed would be a rather short contest in which their assumed virtue and moral commitment would easily carry the day over seasoned British regulars not necessarily wedded to anything of greater concern than filling their own pocketbooks as mercenaries.

The first army had a militialike appearance. Even though phrases of commitment were high sounding, there was not much discipline or rigorous training. These early soldiers had responded to appeals from leaders who warned about "our wives and children, with everything that is dear to us, [being] subjected to the merciless rage of uncontrolled despotism." They were convinced that they were "engaged ... in the cause

---

[7] For further comments, beyond those presented here, consult Martin and Lender, *A Respectable Army*, esp. chs. 3–5.

of virtue, of liberty, of *God.*" Unfortunately, the crushing blows endured in the massive British offensive of 1776 against New York undercut such high-sounding phrases about self-sacrifice. The message at the end of 1775 had been "Persevere, ye guardians of liberty."[8] They did not.

The second Continental establishment took form out of the remains of the first. Even before Washington executed his magnificent turnabout at Trenton and Princeton, he had called for a "respectable army," one built on long-term enlistments, thorough training, and high standards of discipline.[9] The army's command, as well as many delegates in Congress, now wanted soldiers who could stand up against the enemy with more than notions of exalted virtue and moral superiority to upgird them. They called for able-bodied men who could and would endure for the long-term fight in a contest that all leaders now knew could not be sustained by feelings of moral superiority and righteousness alone.

To assist in overcoming manpower shortages, Congress and the states enhanced financial promises made to potential enlistees. Besides guarantees about decent food and clothing, recruiters handed out bounty moneys and promises of free land at war's end (normally only for long-term service). Despite these financial incentives, there was no great rush to the Continental banner. For the remainder of the war, the army's command, Congress, and the states struggled to maintain minimal numbers of Continental soldiers in the ranks.

In fact, all began to search diligently for new recruits. Instead of relying on propertied freeholders and tradesmen of

---

[8] "To the American Soldiery," Nov. 14, 1775, and "To the Worthy Officers and Soldiers in the American Army," Nov. 24, 1775, Peter Force, ed., *American Archives*, 4th ser., 6 vols. (Washington, D.C., 1837–46), 3:1557–59, 1667–68. Besides reflecting the rhetoric of the Revolution, these statements are evidence that there were already serious difficulties in convincing individuals to sign up, even for short-term enlistments. Thus these appeals were written to stimulate reenlistments and new enlistments for the 1776 campaign.

[9] For Washington's classic statement, see his letter to the President of Congress, Sept. 24, 1776, Fitzpatrick, ed., *Writings of Washington*, 6:106–16.

the ideal citizen-soldier type, they broadened the definition of what constituted an "able-bodied and effective" recruit. For example, New Jersey in early 1777 started granting exemptions to all those who hired substitutes for long-term Continental service—and to masters who would enroll indentured servants and slaves. The following year Maryland permitted the virtual impressment of vagrants for nine months of regular service. Massachusetts set another kind of precedent in 1777 by declaring blacks (both slave and free) eligible for the state draft. Shortly thereafter, Rhode Islanders set about the business of raising two black battalions. Ultimately, Maryland and Virginia permitted slaves to substitute for whites. The lower South, however, refused to do so, even in the face of a successful British invasion later in the war.

The vast majority of Continentals who fought with Washington after 1776 were representative of the very poorest and most repressed persons in Revolutionary society. A number of recent studies have verified that a large proportion of the Continentals in the second establishment represented ne'er-do-wells, drifters, unemployed laborers, captured British soldiers and Hessians, indentured servants, and slaves.[10] Some of these new regulars were in such desperate economic straits

[10] Mark Edward Lender, "The Social Structure of the New Jersey Brigade: The Continental Line as an American Standing Army," in Peter Karsten, ed., *The Military in America: From the Colonial Era to the Present* (New York, 1980), pp. 27–44; John R. Sellers, "The Common Soldier in the American Revolution," in Stanley J. Underdal, ed., *Military History of the American Revolution: Proceedings of the Sixth Military History Symposium, United States Air Force Academy* (Washington, D.C., 1976), pp. 151–61; Sellers, "The Origins and Careers of the New England Soldier: Noncommissioned Officers and Privates in the Massachusetts Continental Line" (Paper presented at the Eighty-seventh Annual Meeting of the American Historical Association, New Orleans, 1972); and Edward C. Papenfuse and Gregory A. Stiverson, "General Smallwood's Recruits: The Peacetime Career of the Revolutionary War Private," *William and Mary Quarterly*, 3d ser. 30 (1973):117–32. Comparing the social characteristics of the new American soldier with his British and Hessian counterparts may be done qualitatively by relating the articles herein to Sylvia R. Frey, "The Common British Soldier in the Late Eighteenth Century: A Profile," *Societas* 5 (1975):117–31, and idem, *The British Soldier in America: A Social History of Military Life in the Revolutionary Period* (Austin, Tex., 1981), pp. 3–20.

that states had to pass laws prohibiting creditors from pulling them from the ranks and having them thrown in jail for petty debts. (Obviously, this was not a problem with the unfree.)

The most important point to be derived from this dramatic shift in the social composition of the Continental army is that few of these new common soldiers had enjoyed anything close to economic prosperity or full political (or legal) liberty before the war. As a group, they had something to gain from service. If they could survive the rigors of camp life, the killing diseases that so often ravaged the armies of their times, and the carnage of skirmishes and full-scale battles, they could look forward to a better life for themselves at the end of the war. Not only were they to have decent food and clothing and regular pay until the British had been irrevocably beaten, they had also been promised free land (and personal freedom in the cases of indentured servants, black slaves, and criminals). Recruiters thus conveyed a message of personal upward mobility through service. In exchange for personal sacrifice in the short run, there was the prospect of something far better in the long run, paralleling and epitomizing the collective rebel quest for a freer political life in the New World.

To debate whether these new Continentals were motivated to enlist because of crass materialism or benevolent patriotism is to sidetrack the issue.[11] A combination of factors was no doubt at work in the mind of each recruit or conscript. Far more important, especially if we are to comprehend the ramifications of protest and defiance among soldiers and of-

[11] Charles Royster, *A Revolutionary People at War: The Continental Army and American Character, 1775–1783* (Chapel Hill, N.C., 1979), pp. 373–78, argues in favor of the importance of ideological motivation while castigating the work of Lender, Sellers, and Papenfuse and Stiverson as being too oriented toward materialistic factors. Royster has only blurred the issue by pressing too hard for his side while needlessly simplifying the findings of others. Far more balanced on motivation for service are Robert Middlekauff, "Why Men Fought in the American Revolution," *Huntington Library Quarterly* 43 (1980):135–48, and John Shy, "Hearts and Minds in the American Revolution: The Case of 'Long Bill' Scott and Peterborough, New Hampshire," *A People Numerous and Armed: Reflections on the Military Struggle for American Independence* (New York, 1976), pp. 165–79.

ficers, we must understand that respectably established citizens after 1775 and 1776 preferred to let others perform the dirty work of regular, long-term service on their behalf, essentially on a contractual basis. Their legislators gave bounties and *promised* many other incentives. Increasingly, as the war lengthened, the civilian population and its leaders did a less effective job in keeping their part of the agreement. One significant outcome of this obvious civilian ingratitude, if not utter disregard for contractual promises, was protest and defiance coming from Washington's beleaguered soldiers and officers.

That relations between Washington's post-1776 army and Revolutionary society deteriorated dramatically hardly comes as a surprise to those historians who have investigated surviving records. Widespread anger among the rank and file became most demonstrable in 1779 and 1780, at the very nadir of the war effort. Pvt. Joseph Plumb Martin captured the feelings of his comrades when he reflected back on support for the army in 1780. He wrote: "We therefore still kept upon our parade in groups, venting our spleen at our country and government, then at our officers, and then at ourselves for our imbecility in staying there and starving in detail for an ungrateful people who did not care what became of us, so they could enjoy themselves while we were keeping a cruel enemy from them."[12] Gen. John Paterson, who spoke out in March 1780, summarized feelings among many officers when he said, "It really gives me great pain to think of our public affairs; where is the public spirit of the year 1775? Where are those flaming *patriots* who were ready to sacrifice their lives, their fortunes, their all, for the public?"[13] Such thoughts were

---

[12] George F. Scheer, ed., *Private Yankee Doodle: Being a Narrative of the Adventures, Dangers and Sufferings of a Revolutionary Soldier* (Boston, 1962), p. 186.

[13] To William Heath, Mar. 31, 1780, *Heath Papers*, Massachusetts Historical Society Collections, 5th ser., vol. 4, 7th ser., vols. 4–5 (1878–1905), 5:44–45. For similar comments, see Alexander McDougall to Nathanael Greene, Mar. 24, 1779, Greene Correspondence, American Philosophical

not dissimilar from those of "A Jersey Soldier" who poured his sentiments into an editorial during May 1779 in support of those regimental officers who were trying to exact some form of financial justice from their state legislature. The army, he pointed out, had put up with "a load ... grown almost intolerable." "It must be truly mortifying to the virtuous soldier to observe many, at this day, displaying their cash, and sauntering in idleness and luxury," he went on, including "the gentry ... [who] are among the foremost to despise our poverty and laugh at our distress." He certainly approved the actions of his comrades because he resented "the cruel and ungrateful disposition of the people in general, in withholding from the army even the praise and glory justly due to their merit and services," just as he resented society's failure to live up to its contract with the soldiers.[14] These statements, which are only a representative sampling, indicate that the army had come to believe that Revolutionary civilians had taken advantage of them—and had broken their part of the contract for military services.

There were real dangers hidden behind these words. With each passing month beginning in 1777, Washington's regulars, especially that small cadre that was signing on for the long-term fight, became more professional in military demeanor. Among other things, including their enhanced potential effectiveness in combat, this meant that soldiers felt the enveloping (and reassuring) bonds of "unit cohesion." The immediate thoughts of individual soldiers, whether recruited, dragooned, or pressed into service, became attached to their respective primary units in the army, such as the particular companies or regiments in which they served. The

---

Society, Philadelphia; Benedict Arnold to Greene, Sept. 12, 1780, Peter Force Transcripts, Library of Congress; and Ebenezer Huntington to Andrew Huntington, July 7, 1780, "Letters of Ebenezer Huntington, 1774–1781," *American Historical Review* 5 (1900):725–26. Consult also Richard H. Kohn, "American Generals of the Revolution: Subordination and Restraint," in Don Higginbotham, ed., *Reconsiderations on the Revolutionary War: Selected Essays* (Westport, Conn., 1978), pp. 104–23.

[14] *New Jersey Journal*, May 6, 1779, *Documents Relating to the Revolutionary History of the State of New Jersey*, 2d ser. 3 (1906):307–9.

phenomenon was nothing more than a developing comradeship in arms. Any threat or insult thus became an assault on the group, especially if that threat or insult were directed at all members of the group.[15] The bonding effect of unit cohesion suggests that collective protest and defiance would become more of a danger to a generally unsupportive society with each passing month, unless civilians who had made grand promises started to meet their contractual obligations more effectively.

Indeed, the most readily observable pattern in Continental army protest and defiance was that it took on more and more of a collective (and menacing) character through time. At the outset, especially beginning in 1776, most protest had an individual character. Frequently it was the raw recruit, quite often anxious for martial glory but quickly disillusioned with the realities of military service once in camp, who struck back against undesirable circumstances. Protest could come through such diverse expressions as swearing, excessive drinking, assaulting officers, deserting, or bounty jumping. One source of such behavior was the dehumanizing, even brutal nature of camp life. Another had to do with broken promises about pay, food, and clothing. A third was a dawning sense that too many civilians held the soldiery in disregard, if not utter contempt.

It must be remembered that middle- and upper-class civilians considered Washington's new regulars to be representative of the "vulgar herd" in a society that still clung to deferential values. The assumption was that the most fit in terms of wealth and community social standing were to lead while the least fit were to follow, even when that meant becoming little more than human cannon fodder. Perhaps James Warren of Massachusetts summarized the social perceptions of "respectable" citizens as well as any of the "better sort" when he described Washington's troops in 1776 as "the most

---

[15] Samuel A. Stouffer et al., *The American Soldier: Adjustment during Army Life*, Studies in Social Psychology in World War II, vol. 1 (Princeton, 1949), pp. 106–30, employs the concept of unit cohesion in discussing troop behavior during World War II. For application to the Revolutionary War period, see Lender, "The Enlisted Line," pp. 203–8, and Middlekauff, "Why Men Fought," pp. 143–48.

undisciplined, profligate Crew that were ever collected" to fight a war.[16]

While civilians often ridiculed the new regulars as riffraff, troublemakers, or mere hirelings (while conveniently ignoring the precept that military service was an assumed obligation of all citizens in a liberty-loving commonwealth), individual soldiers did not hold back in protesting their circumstances. In many cases, they had already acknowledged the personal reality of downtrodden status before entering the ranks. Acceptance of these circumstances and the conditions of camp life did not mean, however, that these new soldiers would be passive. Thus it may be an error to dismiss heavy swearing around civilians or repeated drunkenness in camp as nothing more than manifestations of "time-honored military vices," to borrow the words of one recent student of the war period.[17]

At least in some instances, individual soldiers could have been making statements about their sense of personal entrapment. Furthermore, protest through such methods as drunkenness (this was a drinking society but not one that condoned inebriety) was a defensive weapon. One of Washington's generals, for instance, bitterly complained in 1777 that too many soldiers consistently made it "a practice of getting drunk ... once a Day and thereby render themselves unfit for duty."[18] To render themselves unfit for duty was to give what they had received—broken promises. Defiance that came in the form of "barrel fever" for some soldiers thus

---

[16] To Elbridge Gerry, Apr. 16, 1776, in C. Harvey Gardiner, ed., *A Study in Dissent: The Warren-Gerry Correspondence, 1776–1792* (Carbondale, Ill., 1962), p. 17.

[17] Royster, *A Revolutionary People*, p. 71, otherwise provides a good discussion of the camp behavior of many common soldiers. Frey, *British Soldier in America*, pp. 63–66, also attributes heavy drinking to boredom and treats it as a traditional military vice. She also points out, however, that drinking provided a channel of escape as well as release for more aggressive behavior. Thus she hints that drinking may have been a form of or a basis for protest, but she does not follow up on the point.

[18] Peter Muhlenberg, Sept. 5, 1777, "Orderly Book, ... March 26–December 20, 1777," *Pennsylvania Magazine of History and Biography* 34 (1910):455.

translated into statements about how society looked upon and treated them.

Only over time did individual acts of protest take on a more collective character. That transition may be better comprehended by considering the phenomenon of desertion. While it is true that a great many soldiers did not think of desertion as a specific form of protest, they fled the ranks with greater frequency when food and clothing were in very short supply or nonexistent, as at Valley Forge. However, primary unit cohesion worked to militate against unusually high desertion levels. Sustained involvement with a company or regiment reduced the likelihood of desertion. Hence as soldiers came to know, trust, and depend upon one another, and as they gained confidence in comrades and felt personally vital to the long-term welfare of their primary group, they were much less likely to lodge a statement of individual protest through such individualized forms as desertion.

So it appears to have been with Washington's new regulars. Thad W. Tate discovered that, in the regiments of New York, Maryland, and North Carolina, about 50 percent of all desertions occurred within six months of enlistments.[19] Mark Edward Lender, in studying New Jersey's Continentals, also found that the rate of desertion dropped off dramatically for those soldiers who lasted through just a few months of service.[20] The first few days and weeks in the ranks were those in which these poor and desperate new regulars asked themselves whether vague promises of a better lot in life for everyone, including themselves, in a postwar republican polity was worth the sacrifice now being demanded. Many enlistees and conscripts concluded that it was not, and they fled. Since they had little proof that they could trust the civilian population and its leaders, they chose to express their defiance through

[19] "Desertion from the American Revolutionary Army," M.A. thesis, University of North Carolina, 1948, pp. 7–12.

[20] Lender found the desertion rate among New Jersey Continentals to be 42 percent in 1777, 21 percent in 1778, 10 percent in 1779, and 10 percent in 1780 (see "The Enlisted Line," pp. 204–16). For a general discussion, consult James Howard Edmonson, "Desertion in the American Army during the Revolutionary War," Ph.D. diss., Louisiana State University, 1971.

desertion. Unit cohesion, in turn, helped sustain those who read the equation differently, and it eased the pain of enduring a long war in return for the remote prospect of greater personal freedom, opportunity, and prosperity.

Then there were those individuals who neither deserted nor became hard-core regulars. By and large, this group defied civil and military authority through the practice of bounty jumping. The procedure, which Washington once referred to as "a kind of business" among some soldiers, was straightforward.[21] It involved enlisting, getting a bounty, and deserting, then repeating the same process with another recruiting agent in another location. Some of the most resourceful bounty jumpers got away with this maneuver seven, eight, or even nine times, if not more. Most jumpers appear to have been very poor young men without family roots. The most careful of them went through the war unscathed.[22] Bounties thus provided a form of economic aggrandizement (and survival) in a society that generally treated its struggling classes with studied neglect. To accept a bounty payment, perhaps even to serve for a short period, and then to run off, was a strongly worded statement of personal defiance.

Bounty jumping was invariably the act of protesting individuals; looting and plundering (like desertion) combined individual with collective protest. Certainly there were numerous occasions when hungry soldiers looted by themselves. Just as often, groups of starving men "borrowed" goods from civilians. Even before the second establishment took form, looting had become a serious problem. Indeed, it probably abetted unit cohesion. One sergeant, for example, described how he and his comrades, searching desperately for food, "liberated" some geese belonging to a local farmer in 1776 and devoured them "Hearty in the Cause of Liberty of taking what Came to their Hand." Next "a sheep and two fat turkeys" approached this band of hungry soldiers, but "not being able to give the countersign," they were taken prisoner, "tried

---

[21] To John A. Washington, Feb. 24, 1777, Fitzpatrick, ed., *Writings of Washington*, 7:197–99.

[22] This assessment is based on the findings of Lender, "The Enlisted Line," pp. 208–16.

by fire and executed" for sustenance "by the whole Division of the freebooters."[23]

When army looting of civilian property continued its unabated course in 1777, General Washington threatened severe penalties. He emphasized that the army's "business" was "to give protection, and support, to the poor, distressed Inhabitants; not to multiply and increase their calamities."[24] These pleas had little impact. Incident after incident kept the commander in chief and his staff buried in a landslide of civilian complaints. Threats of courts martial, actual trials, and severe punishments did not deter angry, starving, protesting soldiers. In 1780 and 1781 Washington was still issuing pleas and threats, but to little avail. Not even occasional hangings contained an increasingly defiant and cohesive soldiery that wondered who the truly poor and distressed inhabitants were—themselves or civilians ostensibly prospering because of the army's travail. To strike back at hoarding, unsupportive citizens, as they had come to perceive the populace whom they were defending, seemed only logical, especially when emboldened by the comaraderie of closely knit fellow soldiers.

Above all else, two patterns stand out with respect to common soldier protest. First, as the war effort lengthened, defiance became more of a collective phenomenon. Second, such protest had a controlled quality. While there was unremitting resentment toward civilians who were invariably perceived as insensitive and unsupportive, protest rarely metamorphosed into wanton violence and mindless destruction. Soldiers may have looted and pillaged, they may have grabbed up bounties, and they may have deserted. But they rarely maimed, raped, or murdered civilians. Pvt. Joseph Plumb Martin attempted to explain why. Even though "the monster Hunger, ... attended us," he wrote, and the new regulars "had borne as long as human nature could endure, and to bear longer we considered folly," he insisted that his comrades had be-

---

[23] Louise Rau, ed., "Sergeant John Smith's Diary of 1776," *Mississippi Valley Historical Review* 20 (1933–34):252–56.

[24] General Orders, Jan. 21, 1777, Fitzpatrick, ed., *Writings of Washington*, 7:46–47.

Protest and Defiance in the Ranks

come, in the end, "truly patriotic." They were persons who "loved their country, and they had already suffered everything short of death in its cause."[25] The question by 1779 and 1780 was whether these hardened, cohesive veterans would be willing to endure even more privation.

In reflecting positively on the loyalty of his comrades, Martin was commenting on a near mutiny of the Connecticut Line in 1780. Indeed, the specter of collective defiance in the form of line mutinies had come close to reality with the near insubordination of the New Jersey officers in 1779. They had not demonstrated in the field, but they had made it clear that conditions in the army were all but intolerable—and that civil society, when desperate to maintain a regular force in arms, could be persuaded to concede on basic demands. Washington had used the phrase "extorted"; he had also pointed out that, "notwithstanding the expedient adopted for a saving appearances," this confrontation "cannot fail to operate as a bad precedent."[26] The commander in chief was certainly right about the setting of precedents.

Among long-term veterans, anger was beginning to overwhelm discipline. There had been small-scale mutinies before, such as the rising of newly recruited Continentals at Halifax, North Carolina, in February 1776. In 1779 Rhode Island and Connecticut regiments threatened mutinies, but nothing came of these incidents. Then in 1780 another near uprising of the Connecticut Line occurred. Invariably, the issues had the same familiar ring: lack of adequate civilian support as demonstrated by rotten food, inadequate clothing, and worthless pay (when pay was available). On occasion, too, the heavy hand of company- and field-grade officers played its part. The near mutiny of the Connecticut Line in 1780 had been avoided by a fortuitous shipment of cattle and by promises from trusted officers of better treatment. In the end, the Connecticut Line calmed itself down, according to Martin, because the soldiery was "unwilling to desert the cause

---

[25] Scheer, ed., *Private Yankee Doodle*, p. 182.

[26] To the President of Congress, May 11, 1779, Fitzpatrick, ed., *Writings of Washington*, 15:43–44.

of our country, when in distress." Nevertheless, he explained that "we knew her cause involved our own, but what signified our perishing in the act of saving her, when that very act would inevitably destroy us, and she must finally perish with us."[27]

By the end of 1780, there were some veterans who would have disputed Martin's reasoning. They had all but given up, let come what might for the glorious cause. On January 1, 1781, the Pennsylvania Line proved that point. Suffering through yet another harsh winter near Morristown, New Jersey, the Pennsylvanians mutinied. Some one thousand determined comrades in arms (about 15 percent of the manpower available to Washington) ostensibly wanted nothing more to do with fighting the war. On a prearranged signal, the Pennsylvanians paraded under arms, seized their artillery, and marched south toward Princeton, their ultimate target being Philadelphia. These veterans had had their fill of broken promises, of the unfulfilled contract. They maintained that they had signed on for three years, not for the duration. If they were to stay in the ranks, then they wanted the same benefits (additional bounty payments, more free land, and some pay in specie) that newer enlistees had obtained.

Formal military discipline collapsed as the officers trying to contain the mutineers were brushed aside. The soldiers killed one and wounded two other officers, yet their popular commander, Anthony Wayne, trailed along, attempting to appeal to their sense of patriotism. Speaking through a committee of sergeants, the soldiers assured Wayne and the other officers that they were still loyal to the cause, and they proved it by handing over two spies that Sir Henry Clinton had sent out from New York to monitor the situation. Moreover, the mutineers, despite their anger and bitterness, behaved themselves along their route and did not unnecessarily intimidate civilians who got in their way.

Later checking demonstrated that many of the mutineers were duration enlistees, yet that was a moot point. When the soldiers reached Trenton, representatives of Congress and the Pennsylvania government negotiated with them and

[27] Scheer, ed., *Private Yankee Doodle*, p. 186.

agreed to discharge any veteran claiming three years in rank. Also, they offered back pay and new clothing along with immunity from prosecution for having defied their officers in leaving their posts. Once formally discharged, the bulk of the mutineers reenlisted for a new bounty. By late January 1781 the Pennsylvania Line was once more a functioning part of the Continental army.

These mutineers won because Washington was in desperate need of manpower and because they had resorted to collective defiance, not because their society wanted to address what had been grievances based on the contract for service. Unlike their officers, who had just won a major victory in driving for half-pay pensions, they were not in a position to lobby before Congress. Hence they employed one of the most threatening weapons in their arsenal, collective protest against civil authority, but only after less extreme measures had failed to satisfy their claims for financial justice. They were certainly not planning to overthrow any government or to foment an internal social revolution against better-placed members of their society. They had staked their hopes on a better life in the postwar period and had already risked their lives many times for the proposed republican polity. All told, the extreme nature of this mutiny demonstrated, paradoxically, both that Washington's long-term Continentals were the most loyal and dedicated republican citizens in the new nation, and that they were dangerously close to repudiating a dream that far too often had been a personal nightmare because of the realities of societal support and of service in the Continental army.[28]

More worrisome in January 1781 than the matter of appropriate appreciation of the soldiers' actions was whether this mutiny, and its stillborn predecessors, would trigger further turbulence in the ranks. Also camped near Morristown during the winter of 1780–81 were veteran soldiers of the New Jersey Line. Their officers were aware that the Jersey regulars sympathized with the Pennsylvanians and had been

[28] The best general history of the Pennsylvania mutiny is Carl Van Doren, *Mutiny in January: The Story of a Crisis in the Continental Army* . . . (New York, 1943). For the mutiny in the context of soldier protest, see Martin and Lender, *A Respectable Army*, esp. ch. 5.

in constant communication with them. Then, on January 20, 1781, the New Jersey Line, having witnessed the success of its comrades, also mutinied. The soldiers had each recently received $5 in specie as a token toward long overdue pay, but they were bothered by the better bounties and terms of enlistment offered newer recruits. Their leaders urged them on by shouting: "Let us go to Congress who have money and rum enough but won't give it to us!"[29]

Within a few days, the Jersey Line had won acceptable concessions and was back under control. Washington, however, had decided that enough was enough. "Unless this dangerous spirit can be suppressed by force," he wrote to Congress, "there is an end to all subordination in the Army, and indeed to the Army itself."[30] To back up his strong words, the commander ordered Gen. Robert Howe and about five hundred New England troops near West Point to march to the Jersey camp at Pompton to make sure that the mutineers were back in line and summarily to execute the most notorious leaders. Howe did as instructed. He reached Pompton on January 27, three days after grievances had been redressed. Deploying his men around the campsite just before dawn, Howe caught the Jersey soldiers off guard. He ordered them to fall in without arms, then singled out three ringleaders and ordered their summary execution, to be shot to death by nine of their comrades. A Jersey officer intervened in one case, but the other two were put to death by firing squad.[31]

It was a brutal ending for men who had dreamed of a better future despite all of society's violations of the contract. Perhaps because of the calculated coldheartedness of Washington's orders, or perhaps because the war picture began to

---

[29] J. N. Cumming to John L. Howell, Mar. 5, 1781, New Jersey Society of Pennsylvania, *Year Book*, 1930 (Philadelphia, 1931), p. 78.

[30] To the President of Congress, Jan. 23, 1781, Fitzpatrick, ed., *Writings of Washington*, 21:135–36.

[31] For good descriptions of the details of the New Jersey line mutiny, see Lender, "The Enlisted Line," pp. 238–45, and Van Doren, *Mutiny in January*, pp. 204–27.

Protest and Defiance in the Ranks

brighten in 1781, there were no major uprisings among Washington's regulars after the mutiny of the New Jersey Line. Then again, the soldiery may have been too worn down physically and mentally to continue their protest and defiance in the name of financial justice, humane treatment, and psychological support. They may have passed beyond the point of despair to that of quiet acceptance of whatever came their way, whether just or unjust.

An important question that must be raised in conclusion has to do with political perceptions and fears: given real concerns in Revolutionary society that a regular army could obtain too much power, could corrupt the political system, and could threaten the civilian sector with some form of tyranny, such as a military dictatorship, why did officers and soldiers never unite effectively and put maximum pressure on the frail Revolutionary political structure by protesting in unison? They could have easily played on fears of a coup. But about the closest such union was the Jersey officers' defiance of 1779. Thus, while common soldiers got drunk, deserted, looted, or mutinied, officers pursued their own (and largely separate) avenues of protest. This is curious, especially since the officers too worried about the personal financial cost of service; they too came to resent civilian indifference, ineptitude, and greed; and they too were dismayed over society's inability to treat them with respect. They feared that their virtuous behavior and self-sacrifice would go unappreciated if not completely unrecognized and unrewarded. Having so much in common with their brethren in the rank and file, then, it is worth considering why the officers almost never aligned with them. For if they had, the alliance might have been powerful enough to have fomented something truly menacing to the vitals of Revolutionary society.

The officer corps developed its own forms of protest, and the pattern paralleled that of the common soldiers. The movement was from a dominant expression of individual defiance (resignations in 1776 and 1777) to collective protest (the drive for half-pay pensions which began in earnest during the fall of 1777 and climaxed with the Newburgh Conspiracy of 1782–83).³² Like common soldiers, the officers had collectivized their protest. In that sense, unit cohesion among comrades had come into play, but such cohesion never broke through the vertical hierarchy of military rank.

Part of the reason lay in the social gulf separating the two groups. As befit the deferential nature of their times as well as their concern for maintaining sharp distinctions in rank as a key to a disciplined fighting force, officers, many of whom were drawn from the "better sort" in society, expected nothing less than steady, if not blind obedience to their will from the rank and file. In their commitment to pursuing the goals of the Revolution, the officers were anything but social levelers. Indeed, many of them feared that the Revolution might get out of hand and lead to actual internal social upheaval, particularly if the "vulgar herd" gained too much influence and authority, whether in or out of the army. They hesitated to turn their troops against society because these same soldiers could always turn against them as well and, through brute force, undermine all assumed claims to economic and social preeminence in Revolutionary America.

Washington's veteran officers, even though they complained and protested with vehemence, also willingly accepted their responsibilities as the army's leadership cadre. The officers administered harsh discipline to deserters, looters, bounty jumpers, and mutineers whenever it seemed necessary—and sometimes when it was not. They generally supported Washington's desire to set the legal limit for lashes at 500 strokes, and many of them often sanctioned whippings of more than 100 lashes, despite the Articles of War of 1776. For example, officers took with relish to Washington's general orders at Morristown in 1780 to inflict 100 to 500

---

[32] The strongest analysis of the Newburgh crisis remains Richard H. Kohn, "The Inside History of the Newburgh Conspiracy: America and the Coup d'Etat," *William and Mary Quarterly*, 3d ser. 27 (1970):187–220. For increasing turmoil in the officer corps as background to Newburgh, consult Kohn's "American Generals," pp. 104–23. For other patterns of protest among officers, consult James Kirby Martin, "Benedict Arnold's Treason as Political Protest," *Parameters* 11 (1981):63–74.

lashes on duly tried plunderers and to administer up to 50 lashes on the spot, even before formal hearings, when soldiers were caught breaking military laws.

Many officers thus used their authority with impunity and rarely expressed sympathy for the plight of common soldiers in the ranks. They were much more concerned with societal stability and the protection of property, as well as with military decorum and hierarchy, all of which precluded the officer corps from working in harmony with the soldiery when protesting common grievances against the civilian sector.[33]

Washington's officers, in reality, were caught between the rank and file, for which they had little sympathy, and the larger society, which had little sympathy for them. They pursued their half-pay pension demands, resorting to such defiant acts as threatening to resign en masse during the late summer of 1780. Later they became even more extreme as some toyed with the idea of a full mutiny, if not the possibility of a coup, during the Newburgh crisis.[34] In the end, they failed in their short-term quest for pensions or commutation, as the soldiery fell short in its drive for minimal levels of respectable support. Perhaps those quests would have been more successful had officers and regulars been able to unite

---

[33] Martin and Lender, *A Respectable Army*, esp. chs. 4 and 6.

[34] Interesting parallels emerge between collective military protest, defiance, and threats of violence, and crowd activity in the Revolutionary period. Military protest was controlled; it had specific targets and goals; it did threaten property but rarely human lives. Thus it seems to be in the tradition of popular protest in defense of the community—in this case the survival of the army. For general observations about the nature of eighteenth-century crowd activity, see E. P. Thompson, "The Moral Economy of the Crowd in the Eighteenth Century," *Past & Present* 50 (1971):76–136; George Rudé, *The Crowd in History, 1730–1848* (New York, 1964); and Pauline Maier, *From Resistance to Revolution: Colonial Radicals and the Development of American Opposition to Britain, 1765–1776* (New York, 1972). Protest and defiance in the Continental ranks lacked the quasi-Marxist dimension suggested by Jesse Lemisch in his "Jack Tar in the Streets: Merchant Seamen in the Politics of Revolutionary America," *William and Mary Quarterly*, 3d ser. 25 (1968):371–407. Soldiers were not challenging the nature of the system; rather they were attempting to establish a more legitimate base within their society through collective protest.

in a common bond transcending social class and military rank. If they had, the story of the Revolution might have been quite different. Recalling the common well of bitterness, the ending might well have had more of a Napoleonic cast to it.

That it did not is more than a mere testament to class, hierarchy, and rank. It is also a statement about the evolving feelings among both hard-core officers and regulars, regardless of the multifold reasons that brought them to the service in the first place, that they were fighting for something worthwhile, something of consequence for their particular lives. If they protested, they still maintained residual faith in their personal dreams. They also came to comprehend that, for all of the pain and suffering that was their lot, they could make a lasting contribution. Henry Knox stated the proposition aptly in 1783 when he noted that there was "a favorite toast in the army," that of "'A hoop to the barrel,' or 'Cement to the Union.'"[35] That is the way that these protesting, defying, long-term Continentals should be remembered, not as a "most undisciplined, profligate Crew," but as individuals who, for all of their defiance, made the necessary personal sacrifice to insure that the Revolution and its ideals would succeed when so many about them in their society did not.

[35] To Gouverneur Morris, Feb. 21, 1783, quoted in Richard H. Kohn, "The Creation of the American Military Establishment, 1783–1802," in Karsten, ed., *Military in America*, p. 75.

RICHARD BUEL, JR.

Samson Shorn:
The Impact of the Revolutionary War on Estimates of the Republic's Strength

THE FIRST ACTS OF RESISTANCE to British authority did not spring from any deliberate calculations of America's chances in a military confrontation: few dreamed it would come to that. But by the early 1770s the colonists had begun to think about the unthinkable, and their thoughts were governed by a number of assumptions about their military capability.[1] One of these assumptions rested on a theory concerning republics at war. The republican tendency of colonial social systems

---

[1] For obvious reasons public discussion of this subject did not begin until it was raised by tory pamphleteers. It was first broached by the author of *A Friendly Address to All Reasonable Americans, on the Subject of Our Political Confusions: In Which the Necessary Consequences of Violently Opposing the King's Troops . . . Are Fairly Stated* (New York, 1774), pp. 26–27. The pamphlet, probably written by Thomas B. Chandler, inspired several newspaper discussions of the issue, especially "Americanus" in the *Connecticut Gazette*, Dec. 30, 1774, and unsigned in the *Virginia Gazette* (Purdie), Feb. 3, 1775. Alexander Hamilton alluded to the issue Chandler had raised in his *A Full Vindication of the Measures of Congress* (New York, 1774), p. 12, and Charles Lee answered Chandler in a pamphlet entitled *Strictures on a Pamphlet Entitled a "Friendly Address"* . . . (New York, 1775), which was widely reprinted. Samuel Seabury touched on Hamilton's allusion to the subject in his *A View of the Controversy between Great-Britain and Her Colonies* (New York, 1774), pp. 30–32, to which Hamilton replied in *The Farmer Refuted* (New York, 1775), pp. 70–72. The colonists had obviously been thinking about the subject before it came up for public discussion.

was widely acknowledged even before the imperial controversy began, and when independence became a possibility both patriots and loyalists believed that, if it were achieved, it would confirm that tendency. Therefore when the Revolutionaries had taken stock of their strategic assets—distance from Europe, a large and diffuse population, skills acquired during the Seven Years' War, and an economy able to support an armed force—they placed their inventory in the context of an ancient ideological theory. Its origins reached at least as far back as the account that Herodotus gave of the Persian Wars, though the colonists probably knew it best from Harrington's gloss on Machiavelli.[2]

According to this theory, a republic at war had one important advantage over monarchical or aristocratic states: it could call upon the services of free citizens who had a stake in their society, hence more incentive to fight than soldiers procured only with the money or under the compulsion of less happy governments. One result of its application to the American colonies was to spawn some utterly unrealistic estimates of the number of men who would take the field when hostilities began. For instance, Charles Lee, who had seen military service in North America during the Seven Years' War, declared that the British would find themselves having "to conquer two hundred thousand active, vigorous yeomen."[3] Still more inflated than these notions of the quantity of citizen soldiers who would leap to arms were the expectations of their quality. Thus the young Alexander Hamilton countered the apprehensions of those who pointed to the superior skill and discipline of Britain's professional army by asserting "a certain enthusiasm in liberty, that makes human nature rise above

---

[2] See J. G. A. Pocock, "Machiavelli, Harrington, and English Political Ideologies in the Eighteenth Century," *William and Mary Quarterly*, 3d ser. 22 (1965):549–83; also Harrington's discussion of the Roman Republic's military system in Pocock, ed., *The Political Works of James Harrington* (Cambridge, 1977), pp. 312, 686–87.

[3] Lee, *Strictures*, p. 6; see also "Solon" and "Caius," *Massachusetts Spy*, Oct. 20, 1774; unsigned, ibid., Oct. 27; "Cosmopolitan," ibid., Nov. 17 and Dec. 8. Hamilton advanced the most inflated figure of 500,000 men, an estimate he argued was conservative (*Farmer Refuted*, p. 72).

itself in acts of bravery and heroism," which, added to the "superior numbers" and "natural intrepidity" of Americans, might well "overballance those [tactical] advantages" enjoyed by the British.[4] And the historical success of Holland and Switzerland in defending themselves against ostensibly mightier states received frequent mention in support of this point.[5] One writer of dubious revolutionary credentials, who signed himself "Caractacus," nevertheless added his voice to the chorus of those who admired the huge reserves of popular strength and power enjoyed by countries that could call every citizen a soldier, every soldier a citizen.[6]

America's optimism about her own popular resources found some confirmation in the initial experiences of the Revolutionary War. A spontaneous mobilization of armed citizenry greeted the outbreak of hostilities in most areas, and, though it soon became clear that spontaneity alone would not suffice to maintain a force in the field over long periods of time, many of the Revolutionary governments succeeded in maintaining the first, powerful momentum for several years. Moreover, even after their early enthusiasm gave way to war weariness, patriotic citizens continued to rally their energies whenever fresh emergencies arose.[7] Charles Royster has reminded us that the revolutionary commitment of the troops

[4] Hamilton, *Farmer Refuted*, pp. 70, 72; also idem, *A Full Vindication*, p. 12. Washington stressed the mercenary character of the British army in his General Orders, Jan. 3, 1776, John C. Fitzpatrick, ed., *The Writings of George Washington . . .*, 39 vols. (Washington, D.C., 1931–44), 4:207.

[5] See *Massachusetts Spy*, Nov. 3, 1774, and Feb. 9, 1775. Tory pamphleteers like Charles Inglis tried to disabuse the colonists of the idea that the Swiss and Dutch examples were ones the colonists should be following; see *Plain Truth . . .* (Philadelphia, 1776), pp. 18–20.

[6] Peter Force, ed., *American Archives*, 4th ser., 6 vols. (Washington, D.C., 1837–46), 3:220.

[7] See, for instance, Connecticut's response to the coastal raids of 1779 and the efforts of the towns to raise troops for combined operations against New York in 1780, described in Richard Buel, Jr., *Dear Liberty: Connecticut's Mobilization for the Revolutionary War* (Middletown, Conn., 1980), pp. 190–94, 232.

themselves was an essential ingredient in the cohesion and survival of the beleaguered Continental army.[8] Nor should we forget the heroism that continued to manifest itself amongst the people at large, whether through action, for which they had more limited opportunity, or through simple endurance.

It is true that where the people found themselves in direct confrontation with the British they tended to compromise their commitment to the Revolution in order to survive.[9] But few faced such intense pressure for any length of time, and what seems more worthy of remark is that so many of those drawn into danger by the vast sweep of British operations, particularly in the South, still chose continued resistance over collaboration or capitulation.[10] Though the leadership often worried about the people's ability to hold out,[11] and though

[8] *A Revolutionary People at War: The Continental Army and the American Character, 1775–1783* (Chapel Hill, N.C., 1979), pp. 143–46.

[9] John Shy has convincingly argued this point in "Hearts and Minds in the American Revolution: The Case of 'Long Bill' Scott and Peterborough, New Hampshire," *A People Numerous and Armed: Reflections on the Military Struggle for American Independence* (New York, 1976), pp. 177–78.

[10] David Ramsay, *The History of the Revolution of South-Carolina from a British Province to an Independent State*, 2 vols. (Trenton, 1785), 2:112, 115–25. Kenneth Coleman, *The American Revolution in Georgia, 1763–1789* (Athens, Ga., 1958), pp. 122, 133–35. North Carolina had as great an incidence of active loyalism as any state, but the patriot militia repeatedly concentrated to repress the loyalists; see Hugh F. Rankin, *The North Carolina Continentals* (Chapel Hill, N.C., 1971), pp. 36–42, 193, 239, 250–51, 393. See also the case of Col. Josiah Parker of Isle of Wight County, Virginia, who rallied patriot resistance to the British in the exposed southeastern counties of the state, as reported in William P. Palmer et al., eds., *Calendar of Virginia State Papers and Other Manuscripts*, 11 vols. (Richmond, 1875–93), 3:91–93; also extract of Parker to the Speaker of the House of Delegates, June 8, 1781, Julian P. Boyd et al., eds., *The Papers of Thomas Jefferson*, 19 vols. to date (Princeton, 1950–), 4:83–84.

[11] See, for instance, Hamilton to Robert Morris, Apr. 30, 1781, E. James Ferguson, ed., *The Papers of Robert Morris*, 5 vols. to date (Pittsburgh, 1973–), 1:55. See also Charles Carroll of Carrollton to William Carmichael, May 31, 1779, Edmund Cody Burnett, ed., *Letters of Members of the Continental Congress*, 8 vols. (Washington, D.C., 1921–36), 4:240; and Meriwether Smith to Thomas Jefferson, June 29, 1779, Boyd, ed., *Papers of Jefferson*, 3:16.

some of the governments within the Confederation succumbed to enemy pressure while others showed signs of cracking under the strain,[12] I know of no evidence that a majority of the American people ever seriously considered abandoning the objective of establishing an independent republic by force of arms.

My concern here, however, is not with those ways in which the war experience confirmed Revolutionary preconceptions, but with the ways in which it forced their revision or abandonment. And of all those that had to go, perhaps the most cherished was the idea that an army of loyal citizens could by enthusiasm alone outclass a disciplined professional force. The point has usually been made in terms of the tactical advantage that well-trained soldiers led by experienced officers enjoyed on the battlefield over ill-trained, inexperienced, badly led men. Recognition of this fact did influence Congress in its consideration of the best way to fight the war, a recognition in which Washington's lament that he could not take the offensive with an army composed wholly of militia figured prominently.[13] But economic factors played an equally important part in promoting the eventual decision to form a permanent army. So long as manpower remained the essential determinant of agricultural productivity,[14] and so long as farmers remained the segment of society from which the militia drew most of its men, military objectives would stand in direct opposition to the needs of the economy. The government could not call out the militia en masse without jeopardizing the ability of the farmers even to support themselves, let alone produce a surplus for consumption by others.[15]

---

[12] For instance, Connecticut, as described in Buel, *Dear Liberty*, pp. 272–90.

[13] Worthington C. Ford, ed., *Journals of the Continental Congress, 1774–1789*, 34 vols. (Washington, D.C., 1904–37), 5:762. See also Washington to the President of Congress, Feb. 9 and Sept. 24, 1776, Fitzpatrick, ed., *Writings of Washington*, 4:316, 6:150.

[14] James A. Henretta, *The Evolution of American Society, 1700–1815: An Interdisciplinary Analysis* (Lexington, Mass., 1973), pp. 15–18.

[15] See, for instance, Jeremiah Wadsworth to Joseph Trumbull, Sept. 4, 1776, Jeremiah Wadsworth Papers, box 123, Connecticut Historical Soci-

ARMS AND INDEPENDENCE

At the beginning of the war the colonists had taken over a system that had been developed during the late colonial wars for raising men to serve extended terms of duty. In those days, whenever the demand arose for men to serve in expeditionary forces, they were raised from the militia by voluntary enlistment more often than by ordering men to march. Drafting was routinely threatened and occasionally employed, but when that happened the authorities usually took care to select the wealthier candidates who could afford to hire their own replacements if they did not choose to serve.[16] This led to the eventual selection of those who could best be spared, and provided both them and their families with bounties and wages in exchange for a commitment that never lasted longer than one campaign. The Revolutionaries quickly found, however, that a system which had worked for expeditionary warfare did not work so well for them.

The most obvious difficulty they encountered was that of maintaining a constant number of troops in the field. During the Seven Years' War the men who had enlisted for only one campaign performed the function of auxiliaries to a permanent, professional force supplied by Great Britain. During the Revolutionary War, Americans were forced back entirely upon their own resources. Even when the recruiting officers succeeded in raising their quotas from the militia, and for the terms specified, as they did at first,[17] they never fully solved the problem of how to have the successor force in place before the period of service set for the first rotation of troops had expired. There was always a hiatus. At the end of the first campaign, for instance, the hardships of winter discour-

---

ety, Hartford; Joseph Jones to Jefferson, June 30, 1780, Boyd, ed., *Papers of Jefferson*, 3:473; Charles J. Hoadley et al., eds., *Public Records of the State of Connecticut*, 11 vols. to date (Hartford, 1894–), 1:207–8.

[16] Douglas E. Leach, *Arms for Empire: A Military History of the British Colonies in North America, 1607–1763* (New York, 1973), pp. 21–22, 263–64; Harold Selesky, "Connecticut Goes to War . . .," Wesleyan University Honors Essay, 1972, pp. 45–46; see also John Adams to Jefferson, May 26, 1777, Boyd, ed., *Papers of Jefferson*, 2:21.

[17] See Buel, *Dear Liberty*, pp. 36–43.

aged reenlistment. It was the lack of timely replacements that led Montgomery to mount his ill-fated assault on Quebec in the last hours of 1775, before the terms of such men as he had with him would expire. The same lack also left Washington's army at Boston seriously undermanned that winter, at least until he received emergency aid from the militia.[18] And in the following autumn it seemed to threaten the continued existence of any army at all.[19] A system designed to solve an economic problem had led to the creation of an acute military problem.

As it turned out, the reliance on annual rotations of men through the ranks raised fresh economic problems too. Unless a large number of the soldiers reenlisted at the expiration of their terms, the army would embark on each new campaign as a hodgepodge of raw recruits who needed training before they could begin to justify their cost to society.[20] In addition, each large secession from the ranks was accompanied by an equally large loss of equipment. When replacements were not immediately at hand to take possession of equipment from outgoing men, much of it tended to disappear; or, when it did not, the newcomers found that men who were approaching the end of their own dependence upon their weapons, ammunition, camp utensils, and so on, could become careless in their use of them to the detriment of those who followed.[21] Yet another difficulty concerned the fitness of the new recruits. Men unused to camp life and unsea-

---

[18] Washington to the President of Congress, Feb. 9, 1776, Fitzpatrick, ed., *Writings of Washington*, 4:315–16. See also Washington to Joseph Reed, Nov. 28, 1775, and Jan. 4, 1776, ibid., pp. 124–25, 211.

[19] Washington to John A. Washington, Nov. 6, 1776, to Lund Washington, Dec. 10, and to the President of Congress, Dec. 24, ibid., 6:245, 346, 432.

[20] This was the central point of Washington's letter to the President of Congress, Sept. 24, 1776, ibid., pp. 110–11. See also 4:316.

[21] Washington to the President of Congress, Feb. 9, 1776, ibid., 4:317. See also Washington to Philip Schuyler, Oct. 22, and to the President of Congress, Dec. 5, ibid., 6:223–24, 332; Palmer, ed., *Virginia State Papers*, 2:517–18.

ARMS AND INDEPENDENCE

soned to the microbiological environment they encountered there sickened faster and recovered more slowly than veteran soldiers would have done.[22] This made it difficult, even while the first flush of enthusiasm lasted, to keep enough effective men in the field without resorting to short-term calls on the militia. In 1776, in some jurisdictions, the whole body of the militia had to turn out in answer to such calls.[23] And on each of these occasions society paid an enormous price in marching money, not to mention foregone productivity, while receiving very little in return. The constant shuffling of men from farm to army, and from army to farm, quickly came to be recognized as a ruinous expedient, far more costly and far less efficient than a clear division of labor between soldiers and cultivators would have been.[24]

By the autumn of 1776 the desirability of an army raised for the duration had made itself clear in economic as well as military terms. The question was how to raise it, since by then it had become equally clear that "the duration" might mean a long time. Furthermore, the money that Congress had earmarked to serve as bounty payments and wages had begun to lose its value, and therefore its power to attract recruits, as a consequence of rising doubts about the nation's ability to sustain its cause.[25] Congress tried to resolve the difficulty by

---

[22] Washington to the President of Congress, Feb. 9, 1776, Fitzpatrick, ed., *Writings of Washington*, 4:317. See also Washington's account of the health of the army around New York during the following summer in his letter to Jonathan Trumbull, Aug. 7, ibid., 5:390. The statistical information about the percentage of rank and file who were sick in the army presented in Charles H. Lesser, ed., *The Sinews of Independence: Monthly Strength Reports of the Continental Army* (Chicago, 1976), pp. xxx–xxxi, despite some anomalies, in general confirms the point.

[23] See Buel, *Dear Liberty*, pp. 77–80.

[24] Washington to the President of Congress, Sept. 24, 1776, to Lund Washington, Sept. 30, to Patrick Henry, Oct. 5, to Samuel Washington, Oct. 5, Fitzpatrick, ed., *Writings of Washington*, 6:112, 137, 166, 169. See also Jefferson to the Speaker of the House of Delegates, Mar. 1, 1781, Boyd, ed., *Papers of Jefferson*, 5:34; Ramsay, *Revolution of South-Carolina*, 2:104; Buel, *Dear Liberty*, p. 100.

[25] Ramsay, *Revolution of South-Carolina*, 2:81; Buel, *Dear Liberty*, p. 84. See also, Fitzpatrick, ed., *Writings of Washington*, 6:399n.

adding a land bounty to the monetary one and by allowing those who enlisted for three years to qualify for both,[26] but when it appeared that this gesture would fail to satisfy the need, Congress passed the problem to the individual states. Most of them tackled it by offering additional bounties, but with mixed results. And when all else failed, the states passed the problem on yet again, this time to the localities, whether by assigning quotas to each township or county, by resorting to the device known as classing, or by employing both methods at once. Classing called for the division of local populations into as many classes as there were places to fill, with each class obligated to produce its own recruit. If any failed to do so, the law required that the place be filled, as before, by drafting a man from within the class; but the evidence suggests that this was rarely necessary since the classes in general preferred to raise the incentives they offered until someone came forward.[27]

Fortunately the states had formed the nucleus of a permanent army by the summer of 1777, before the currency had so far depreciated as to deprive it of all value as an incentive for long-term enlistment. Less fortunately, the ranks still fell far short of the number that both Washington and Congress thought they ought to reach. Increasingly the states found themselves driven to make up the difference by drafting, a method they abhorred, to judge from their obvious reluctance to impose a long term of service on men selected in this way and from the lengths to which some went in attempting to persuade draftees to enlist if only for the short term.[28]

From 1778 on, the army became ever more dependent on

[26] Ford, ed., *Journals of Congress*, 6:944–45.

[27] Buel, *Dear Liberty*, pp. 117–18; William Waller Hening, ed., *The Statutes at Large; Being a Collection of All the Laws of Virginia, from the First Session of the Legislature, in the Year 1619*, 13 vols. (Richmond, 1809–23), 9:275–80. Some states came to classing later than others; see Arthur J. Alexander, "How Maryland Tried to Raise Her Continental Quota," *Maryland Historical Magazine* 42 (1947):194; Jonathan Smith, "How Massachusetts Raised Her Troops in the Revolution," Massachusetts Historical Society *Proceedings* 54 (1921–22):354–55.

[28] Buel, *Dear Liberty*, pp. 173, 186–87.

short-term drafts to fill the ranks. All the unfortunate consequences foreseen by Washington and Congress ensued, to an extent that seemed to put the entire war effort in jeopardy by 1780. At the beginning of that year it had become evident to all that the cost of the war had bankrupted Congress.[29] Moreover the terms of roughly half of the "permanent army" recruited in 1777 were about to expire, in addition to which almost all of the Virginia, North Carolina, and South Carolina lines would be lost at the surrender of Charleston.[30] Recognizing the difficulty of reconstituting the army when all it had to offer was payment in a virtually worthless currency, Congress tried to issue a new one in the hope that it would maintain a value commensurate with that of specie. But the new currency depreciated too, often more rapidly than the old.[31] Meanwhile yet another obstacle to recruitment had arisen in that the commissaries and quartermasters, again because of the depreciating currency, which was all that they could offer by way of payment, had begun to experience increasing difficulty in providing for the army. Word that lack of food and inadequate clothing had joined worthless wages as one more hazard facing the Continental soldier spread like wildfire, with predictable results.[32] The states could still find some who would enlist, but only for the short term and at ever-rising rates of compensation. And though they continued to draft, they did so with progressively poorer results.

After 1779, the army suffered a drastic decrease in size. Nor was this the only disadvantage to follow from the depreciation and the shortage of supplies. These factors also restricted the army's movements and hindered the concentration of the remaining troops against key British positions. Though small forces like Greene's in the South or Lafayette's in Vir-

[29] E. James Ferguson, *The Power of the Purse* (Chapel Hill, N.C., 1961), pp. 46–47.

[30] Lesser, ed., *Sinews of Independence*, p. 161; Rankin, *North Carolina Continentals*, p. 232; Ramsay, *Revolution of South-Carolina*, 2:60–61; Buel, *Dear Liberty*, p. 215.

[31] Ford, ed., *Journals of Congress*, 16:262–67.

[32] Ramsay, *Revolution of South-Carolina*, 2:102–3; Buel, *Dear Liberty*, p. 223.

ginia could live off the land to some extent,[33] a military operation on the scale necessary to bring the war to a successful conclusion seemed to lie beyond America's grasp.

We know, of course, that the Revolution did succeed in spite of these difficulties, but the long years during which the war dragged on revealed an unsuspected weakness in the republic. Though the potential to raise and support an adequate army clearly existed,[34] just as clearly the agencies who sought to tap it found that their power to do so seemed to diminish with time. When examined in the light of other modern revolutions, the distinguishing feature of America's experience was her failure to develop mechanisms for effective coercion by the state.[35] The failure stemmed in part from a choice: Americans clung to an ideological preference for the marketplace as an appropriate republican means for achieving the proper republican objective of equalizing the burdens imposed by the war.[36] A promise of equivalent compensation for individuals who provided goods and services certainly appeared fully consistent with republicanism, even though the suppliers did not always agree with the authorities on what constituted an equivalency. The legislatures tried from time to time to remove this difficulty by regulating prices, but that tactic conflicted with the belief that a true equalization

---

[33] Nathanael Greene to Morris, Aug. 18, 1781, Ferguson, ed., *Papers of Morris*, 2:70; Lafayette to Jefferson, Apr. 21, 1781, Boyd, ed., *Papers of Jefferson*, 5:522.

[34] See Morris to Jacques Necker, June 15, 1781, Ferguson, ed., *Papers of Morris*, 1:151; also Morris's Circular to the Governors of the States, July 25, 1781, ibid., p. 382; Washington to Morris and Richard Peters, Aug. 21, 1781, ibid., 2:88.

[35] Theda Skocpol, *States and Social Revolutions: A Comparative Analysis of France, Russia, and China* (Cambridge, 1979), pp. 161–73, 182–83, 186, 188–90, 193–96, 206, 210–20, 225, 232–37, identifies state formation as one of the essential features of modern social revolutions.

[36] The operations of the marketplace were so fundamental to the Revolutionary mobilization that they were taken for granted in the early phase of the war. Only when the marketplace lost most of its usefulness did it come to be seen as peculiarly republican; see Morris's "To the Public," May 28, 1781, Ferguson, ed., *Papers of Morris*, 1:85.

of burdens would emerge only from bargains struck with the consent of all parties. Therefore the attempt usually ended in surrender to the market forces.[37]

Ideological preference, however, offers only a partial explanation for the differences between the American Revolution and other modern revolutions. A time came, as we shall see, when the Revolutionary leaders found themselves driven to attempt using the marketplace as an instrument of coercion. But they avoided it as long as they could because the contrast between the power of local institutions and the weakness of central institutions, a contrast intensified by the general absence of social cleavage at the local level, led them to doubt the feasibility of proceeding in such a way. The dependence of Congress upon the states, both before and after ratification of the Articles of Confederation, has received much attention; not so the dependence of the state governments upon local institutions. Though most of the states possessed judicial systems theoretically able to enforce the orders of the central government, the courts never succeeded in bringing more than an occasional anomalous offender into line.[38] Obviously the work of mobilizing the people for war lay well beyond the capacity of this agency; nothing could be done without the full consent and cooperation of local authorities. The widespread resort to classing shows how well the state governments understood that fact.

The one Revolutionary institution not directly dependent upon local institutions was the army itself. This allowed for greater freedom of action, but even then not for an unrestricted use of its power. The army could not recruit by simply seizing men, for instance: not only would that have alienated the entire society, it would have made the soldiery into slaves who might turn on their enslavers at the first opportunity. Nor could the army employ seizure as its principal method of procuring supplies; a producer who had once lost his labor in that way would not work to produce a surplus again.

[37] See Buel, *Dear Liberty*, pp. 140–52, 168.

[38] See Mary Silliman to Joseph Fish, Apr. 11, 1777, Silliman Family Correspondence, Yale University Library, New Haven; also George Skillern to Jefferson, Apr. 14, 1781, Boyd, ed., *Papers of Jefferson*, 5:449.

Faced with a choice between disbanding the army or seizing supplies, Washington and his fellow commanding officers invariably chose the latter course even though it risked alienating political support for the cause. But the diffuse patterns of settlement in America did not lend themselves to this method of maintaining a large, stationary force like Washington's, which spent the greater part of the war in one place. The gains never provided more than a temporary remedy or offered a means to support the concentration of troops that would be needed in order to expel the British from New York.[39]

If the marketplace was so essential to the cause, why did the Revolutionary leaders not work harder to preserve it? They soon recognized the depreciation of the currency as the principal danger to their success. They discussed it endlessly, and repeatedly vowed to halt its progress,[40] yet their professions always seemed to stand in marked contrast to their actions. At the same time as they lamented the decline in demand for Continental bills of credit, they issued a stream of new paper money that ensured a further decline. Congressional leaders may be partly exonerated from the charge of inconsistency since Congress lacked the power to lay the taxes that many thought would pave the way to recovery. They could have pressured the states to take more effective action, but there were several reasons why they did not.

At the outset they, like everyone else, had expected a quick end to the war. By the time that hope had faded, their prestige had sunk to a point where they feared to put the people's loyalty to any additional test. When the victory at Saratoga briefly improved their popularity, Congress did send its first

---

[39] Washington's Circular to the States, Aug. 27, 1780, Fitzpatrick, ed., *Writings of Washington*, 19:450–51. See also Washington to Gouverneur Morris, Dec. 10, 1780, ibid., 20:458; Donald Jackson et al., eds., *The Diaries of George Washington*, 6 vols. (Charlottesville, Va., 1976–80), 3:356–57; Buel, *Dear Liberty*, pp. 233–34.

[40] John Hancock to the Maryland Assembly, Jan. 14, 1777, and Adams to Joseph Palmer, Feb. 20, Burnett, ed., *Letters*, 2:217, 268. Also Jefferson to Benjamin Franklin, Aug. 13, 1777, William Fleming to Jefferson, May 22, 1779, and Henry to Jefferson, Feb. 15, 1780, Boyd, ed., *Papers of Jefferson*, 2:26, 268; 3:293.

requisition to the states, but on the assumption that the withdrawal of its bills of credit from circulation would appreciate their value and make subscription to patriotic loans an irresistible proposition. As the gap between the high price of commodities and the low value of the currency continued to widen, it soon became evident that this was a serious miscalculation; even so, the revelation came too late. The Franco-American alliance and the burden imposed by the cost of combined operations in 1778 made it impossible for Congress to correct the error. Instead it issued bills and yet more bills in order to meet the accelerating demands of producers for the campaign, though this would inevitably add to the difficulties of procurement in the future. When the dream of an early peace had waned, the monstrous and insurmountable financial problem that Congress had made remained, and it its train brought bankruptcy.[41]

This view of the collapse of Revolutionary finance had the widest currency at the time. Locating the source of their troubles in the quantity of money enabled Revolutionaries to believe they could have prevented the depreciation had they possessed the virtue and the resolution to call in the currency from the start. In its assumption that the power to set the republic on a firm financial footing did rest with her leaders, whether properly exercised or not, it was an optimistic view. But it did not explain why the program of heroic taxation that was finally implemented in 1779 should have failed to reverse the depreciation,[42] nor the lack of uniformity that marked the currency's decline. It has long been recognized that the Continental bills of credit depreciated at different rates in different areas and that Congress employed the fiction of a uniform depreciation as an expedient to permit the equitable liquidation of public debts.[43] Varying rates of de-

[41] This account of the depreciation is the one developed in my "Time: Friend or Foe of the Revolution?" in Don Higginbotham, ed., *Reconsiderations on the Revolutionary War: Selected Essays* (Westport, Conn., 1978), pp. 131–32, 134–38, and *Dear Liberty*, pp. 140–52, 165–72.

[42] See Buel, *Dear Liberty*, pp. 198–205.

[43] Ferguson, *Power of the Purse*, p. 31; Ford, ed., *Journals of Congress*, 17:567–68; 22:83–85.

preciation in different areas can still be squared with the quantity theory by emphasizing the local, or at least the regional, character of the market. The quantity theory, however, would imply uniform price rises in the local market in relation to Continental currency. Instead, the currency depreciated at different rates in relation to different commodities *in the same local market.*

To read the correspondence of commissary agents is to find there radical variations in local markets everywhere,[44] but Philadelphia provides the best example for the purposes of this study because its market has received intensive scrutiny. Against the background of a general depreciation, Philadelphia experienced two prolonged and asymmetrical price rises between 1776 and 1780. The first, which occurred between September 1776 and 1777, affected West India goods as well as, to a lesser extent, tea, coffee, and chocolate. It had two causes: a diminished supply of these articles because the war had hampered foreign commerce, particularly with the islands, and a concommitant increase in demand because many holders of the depreciating money sought to secure their holdings by investing in commodities that appeared likely to appreciate in value.[45] Though the quantity of Continental money had started the general depreciation of the currency, the limited supply of foreign goods had accelerated it since those who desired to buy them were forced to raise the price of their own produce in order to obtain the means.[46]

The second surge, in the price of domestic grain, occurred between September 1778 and the end of 1779. The unfortunate coincidence of a poor harvest with an increase in demand, produced partly by the arrival of a French expeditionary force in the western Atlantic and partly by British

---

[44] See, for instance, Samuel Barrett to Wadsworth, June 9, 1777, Wadsworth Papers, box 124.

[45] Anne Bezanson, "Inflation and Controls, Pennsylvania, 1774–1779," *Journal of Economic History* 8 (1948), supplement:9, 12; idem, *Prices and Inflation during the American Revolution* (Philadelphia, 1951), pp. 14, 16, 321–23.

[46] See Michael Hillegas to Franklin, Mar. 17, 1778, *Pennsylvania Magazine of History and Biography* 29 (1905):234.

abandonment of all responsibility for provisioning the captive Convention army, started the trouble.[47] Even so, the demand hardly exceeded the country's potential for increasing the supply, and therefore the discrepancy should not have continued beyond the next harvest.[48] Military operations had disrupted the sowing of winter wheat in 1777, and the fly had levied a further toll on the diminished harvest that resulted. During the following autumn, however, the farmers in the middle Atlantic states enjoyed a virtually uninterrupted planting season; the threat of the fly waned and the hope for a bumper crop waxed strong.[49] The prospect of a bounteous harvest in 1779 was undoubtedly the reason why, though prices of grain at Philadelphia rose sharply in April and May, they leveled off during the six weeks immediately preceding the harvest. But immediately afterward, prices began to climb again and between the beginning of September and the end of November, at precisely the moment when the new crop should have been coming to market, they almost tripled.[50]

Several reasons for the anomaly were offered at the time. Perhaps the most plausible was that requisitions of flour for the French expeditionary force in the West Indies had depleted the stocks and raised the prices of the grain for sale at home. Rumors of a large French demand were forcing grain prices up as early as May,[51] and later that summer they seemed to receive confirmation from a report that d'Estaing's expeditionary force was momentarily expected to arrive along the

[47] Bezanson, *Prices and Inflation*, p. 20; Buel, *Dear Liberty*, pp. 159–72.

[48] Timothy Pitkin, *A Statistical View of the Commerce of the United States of America* . . . (Hartford, 1817), p. 22, suggests that the colonies were capable of producing a marketable surplus of flour and bread by 1770 sufficient to support a quarter of a million men.

[49] See Chaloner and White to G. Morris, July (?) 1779, Chaloner and White Letter Books (Mar. 15–Sept. 18, 1779), Historical Society of Pennsylvania, Philadelphia.

[50] Bezanson, *Prices and Inflation*, p. 336.

[51] Chaloner and White to the Committee of Congress, May 22, 1779, Chaloner and White Letter Books.

coast. The French agent John Holker tried to avoid fueling any further spurt in prices by keeping as quiet as possible his estimate that the fleet would need 25,000 barrels of flour in order to sustain the next six months of operations. To this end he applied to the government of Pennsylvania for 12,000 barrels, and to Maryland for the remainder.[52] Still, it was widely understood that the arrival of the French would bring a steep increase in demand, and Holker's estimates probably circulated through the rumor mill. In itself, however, this should not have caused the precipitate rise that occurred. Twenty-five thousand barrels, when all is said and done, represented no more than 5 percent of the grain exports for the entire country in 1770, and about 7.5 percent of Philadelphia's exports in 1772.[53] Moreover, only a part of the stated need was ever actually procured, and much of that was subsequently diverted for domestic use. In December, Holker reported that of 1,400 barrels—all he had received from Pennsylvania—942 had been given up to the American commissariat when d'Estaing had failed to appear.[54]

It was, in fact, artificial limitations on the supply of domestic grain—limitations that resulted from producers deliberately withholding it—that had more to do with the rise in prices than the demands of the French fleet. While the prospect of sale to the French encouraged producers to withhold their grain, two other factors were more significant. First, the perception of a shortage of foreign goods available for exchange in the Philadelphia markets discouraged the production and release of surplus food. Michael Hillegas, writing to Benjamin Franklin, pointed out this connection as early as 1778. He attributed the depreciation of Continental currency as much to "a Scarcity of foreign Articles" as to the "Quantity of Money which has been issued with us." Though

---

[52] John Holker to the Board of War, Dec. 20, 1779, Papers of the Continental Congress, Record Group 360, National Archives.

[53] See Pitkin, *Statistical View*, p. 22; Chaloner and White to G. Morris, July (?) 1779, Chaloner and White Letter Books, p. 198.

[54] Holker to the Board of War, Dec. 20, 1779, Papers of the Continental Congress.

he thought that taxation would help raise the value of the currency, he also believed that the key to solving the nation's economic problems lay in increasing foreign trade, for "you & I both know that Taxes repeated year after year without a Trade Foreign as well as Domestic will soon move heavy."[55] His letter implied that if foreign goods were more plentiful, domestic production would increase. The arrival of a sizable quantity of West India goods, for example, would result in lower prices both for them and for the domestic produce that local farmers sent to market in exchange for them. A comment by Philadelphia commissary agents hoping to purchase local whiskey in July 1778 is revealing: "The country is full, and a few West India Men will reduce it [the price of whiskey] where it ought to be."[56]

Unfortunately the remedy thus proposed proved impossible to effect. Local merchants found it difficult to resume overseas exchanges following the British evacuation from the city.[57] In the spring of 1779, when the arrival of a commercial fleet from the West Indies caused a brief resurgence in the supply of foreign goods, the sole result was to raise, not lower, the price of both foreign and domestic commodities.[58] This unexpected development occurred not because there was no connection between foreign and domestic scarcity but because it had taken a different form. The change is clearly apparent in the response of the local market to the French ship *Victorious*. She had arrived with the West India fleet but because of a misunderstanding between the owners and the appointed agent, Robert Morris, she did not unload her goods until the other vessels had disposed of theirs. By that time the price of all goods, domestic as well as imported, had be-

[55] Mar. 17, 1778, *Pennsylvania Magazine of History and Biography* 29 (1905):234. See also "Philodemus," *Pennsylvania Packet*, June 19, 1779.

[56] Chaloner and White to Wadsworth, July 24, 1778, Chaloner and White Letter Books (July 1778–Mar. 17, 1779).

[57] See Report of the Philadelphia Committee, *Pennsylvania Packet*, Sept. 10, 1779.

[58] Chaloner and White to Ephraim Blaine, and to Wadsworth, both Apr. 18, 1779, Chaloner and White Letter Books (Mar. 15–Sept. 18, 1779). See also Daniel Roberdeau's speech in *Pennsylvania Packet*, May 27, 1779.

gun to rise sharply. A popular committee charged with investigating the incident accused Morris of deliberately withholding imports from the market on the assumption that the longer he waited, the higher the price people would be forced to pay for these goods.[59] This charge makes sense only if we assume, first, that Morris had a monopoly of the market because further supplies were not expected, and, second, that foreign goods had become necessities, not in the sense that people could not live without them, but because the farmers would accept almost no other medium in exchange for their produce.

By May the fear that ordinary citizens, lacking foreign goods, might find themselves without means to procure the common necessities of life had led to the formation of popular committees to regulate prices. The same concern drove Congress to adopt a program of heroic taxation intended not only to restore the nation's finances but also to force farmers to resume production and exchange on a scale beyond that of strict necessity for individual survival.[60] Unfortunately, both price regulation and the attempt to compel the production of surpluses through the imposition of higher taxes had as much potential for disheartening producers as did the shortage of desired imports.[61] The surge in domestic grain prices toward the end of 1779 suggests that by then these measures together had done more to induce domestic scarcity than could ever be charged to the shortage of West India goods.[62] When

[59] Hubertis Cummings, "Robert Morris and the Episode of the Poleacre 'Victorious,'" *Pennsylvania Magazine of History and Biography* 70 (1946):241–42; Fleming to Jefferson, May 22, 1779, Boyd, ed., *Papers of Jefferson*, 2:267.

[60] Bezanson, "Inflation and Controls," pp. 15–16; William Whipple to Josiah Bartlett, May 21, 1779, Burnett, ed., *Letters*, 4:223; also Daniel of St. Thomas Jenifer to Thomas Johnson, May 24, ibid., p. 232; G. Morris to Robert R. Livingston, May 30, ibid., p. 238; Carroll to Carmichael, May 31, ibid., pp. 239–40.

[61] See "A Farmer of Virginia," *Pennsylvania Packet*, July 15, 1779; also Buel, *Dear Liberty*, p. 202.

[62] Such, at least, was the opinion of those opposed to price limitations. See Memorial of the Philadelphia Merchants' Committee, *Pennsylvania Packet*, Sept. 10, 1779.

matters had degenerated to this point, the simple repeal of regulations could not remedy the problem even had Congress been willing to debase its authority and further prostrate its credit. A revival of economic activity, if it came at all, would come only if and when the next season's importations inspired the farmers to produce to the limits of their capacity.

The theory that an excessive quantity of money had caused the collapse of the Revolutionary economy is an optimistic theory in that, by asserting the leadership's responsibility for the debacle, it implies that the remedy also lay within their grasp. The foregoing analysis, by contrast, sees the oversupply of money as only a symptom of a larger problem that originated in the disruption of the old colonial patterns of exchange whereby Americans had traded their surpluses for European and West Indian goods. According to this view, the greatest incentive that an American producer could have for the production of a surplus was the opportunity to exchange it for the foreign goods he wanted but could not manufacture for himself. The economic disaster of 1779 proceeded not just from the government's failure to tax but also from a structural imbalance between a limited supply of foreign imports and a rising demand for them. It was this imbalance, caused by the war, that had brought about the depreciation of the currency, the shortage of domestic produce, and all the evils that followed in their train.[63]

The structural analysis of the Revolutionary economy failed to take hold in the public mind at the time because it put the intractability of the nation's dilemma into bold relief, and people do not care to be reminded of their vulnerabilities during a war or immediately afterwards. Today, however, it can give us a new perspective on certain aspects of the Rev-

---

[63] See Henry Laurens to John L. Gervais, Sept. 5, 1777, Burnett, ed., *Letters*, 2:478; also "Agricola," *Virginia Gazette* (Dixon and Nicholson), Nov. 13, 1779; Ramsay, *Revolution of South-Carolina*, 2:82; Silas Deane to R. Morris, June 10, 1781, Ferguson, ed., *Papers of Morris*, 1:138. The linkage between diminished imports and declining productivity has been noted by the leading historian of the Chesapeake region (Jacob M. Price, *France and the Chesapeake*, 2 vols. [Ann Arbor, 1973], 2:715).

olutionary War. In particular it suggests that the best and quickest remedy for the financial ills of the young republic would have been the resumption of international trade on a scale sufficient to have provided opportunities for most of her producers.[64]

International trade never completely ceased, of course, but as time went on the stream of imported goods dwindled to a trickle; Americans began to have to do without certain articles, and the longer they lacked them, the more the demand increased. This fact led a man of substantial capital like Robert Morris to believe that one successful venture in importation could repay the cost of three unsuccessful ones;[65] it led Benjamin Rush to suggest that the best use to which a European loan could be put was the importation of goods,[66] and it led the French government to consider supporting the comte de Rochambeau's expeditionary force with imported dry goods rather than with money.[67] Congress had earlier hoped that, along with other advantages, the Franco-American alliance would bring a resumption of overseas trade on a scale comparable to or even grander than what Americans had enjoyed throughout the Seven Years' War.[68] Alas, neither

[64] See R. Morris to Necker, June 15, 1781, Ferguson, ed., *Papers of Morris*, 1:151; to Washington, July 2, ibid., pp. 214–15. On a more limited scale, Holker to Reed, Sept. 8, 1779, *Pennsylvania Archives*, 1st ser. 7 (1853):687.

[65] See Clarence L. Ver Steeg, *Robert Morris: Revolutionary Financier* (Philadelphia, 1954), p. 16.

[66] "A Speech that Ought to Be Spoken," Butterfield, ed., *Letters of Rush*, 1:234.

[67] Lee Kennett, *The French Forces in America* (Westport, Conn., 1977), p. 65.

[68] Jefferson to Franklin, Aug. 13, 1777, and Richard Henry Lee to Jefferson, Aug. 10, 1778, Boyd, ed., *Papers of Jefferson*, 2:26, 209; Committee of Foreign Affairs to the Commissioners at Paris, Oct. 6, 1777, and R. H. Lee and James Lovell to the Commissioners at Paris, Dec. 2, Francis Wharton, ed., *The Revolutionary Diplomatic Correspondence of the United States*, 6 vols. (Washington, D.C., 1889), 2:400, 439; Virginia Delegates to the Governor of Virginia, May 3, 1778, Burnett, ed., *Letters*, 2:216–17. See also "Americanus," *Pennsylvania Gazette*, Aug. 28, 1779.

France nor her ally Spain proved able to establish the necessary naval supremacy in the North Atlantic.

The failure of the Chesapeake region to reestablish the old patterns of trade exemplifies the difficulties encountered by even the most favored of regional economies during wartime. One might have expected that the rising demand for Chesapeake tobacco in Europe, reflected in steadily rising prices as the war went on, would have led to increased commerce in that commodity.[69] But the shortage of tobacco had resulted from the success of British seapower in restricting American access to the European market, and the consequent rise in its price attracted a swarm of privateers to the Capes, which forced what trade there was either to take huge risks or to pursue long circuitous routes across the Delmarva Peninsula or through the North Carolina sounds. Either course dictated the use of shallow draft, fast-sailing ships, so much so that most of the large shipping indigenous to the Bay converted to privateering. Shipping bulk commodities by vessels of light burden was not, however, the best way in which to exchange American produce for overseas goods, and most of the early ventures went forth on public account for arms and ammunition rather than dealing in articles for private consumption.[70] After the conclusion of the Franco-American alliance, French vessels began appearing in the Bay, but not in such numbers as to suggest a resumption of normal economic activity.[71] Besides, they too usually sailed on public account, sometimes to pick up tobacco and at other

---

[69] Price, *France and the Chesapeake*, 2:683.

[70] Virginia's efforts to resume exporting tobacco are documented in Henry R. McIlwaine, ed., *Official Letters of the Governors of the State of Virginia*, 3 vols. (Richmond, 1926–29). For comments on the success of the enterprise, see R. H. Lee to Jefferson, Aug. 10, 1778, Boyd, ed., *Papers of Jefferson*, 2:209; also Jefferson to Richard Caswell, June 12, 1779, and to John Jay, June 19, ibid., 3:5, 9. See also Ver Steeg, *Robert Morris*, pp. 14–15; Price, *France and the Chesapeake*, 2:703.

[71] Price, *France and the Chesapeake*, 2:715–16. The annual demand of the Farmers-General for tobacco before the outbreak of the war could not be satisfied by less than 90 to 100 shiploads. Entries of French ships announced in the *Virginia Gazette* suggest a drastic reduction in the tobacco trade even after 1778.

times provisions for the French fleet in the West Indies. Either way their activities were not calculated to stimulate a general revival of overseas commerce.

There is one other route by which foreign goods might have reentered the American economic system; that is, by privateering.[72] Unfortunately privateering has yet to receive the scholarly attention it deserves. We know that a lot of it went on, that it was one of the few legitimate economic activities which offered investors the prospect of a high return, and that American privateers seized an enormous number of enemy ships and seamen.[73] We know too that men faced with the alternative of serving as privateersmen or as soldiers preferred privateering, at least if we can credit the complaints of recruiting officers that they could not compete with the attraction represented in the share a privateersman received from all the prizes he had helped to take.[74] But though privateering repaid the lucky ones who engaged or invested in it, many others lost by the activity, and in any case the economic benefits often went to a third party, a foreign ally, or even the enemy itself. The enormous number of captures made by American vessels in European and West Indian waters did not necessarily help the states that had sponsored them to procure what was most needed, unless the proceeds from the venture were reinvested in foreign imports. The one study I know of that addresses the question of privateering's profitability (as yet unpublished) suggests that for Connecticut, at least, its economics resembled those of some gigantic lottery in which the economy of the state ended up the loser though some individuals won.[75] But the question of

---

[72] See Adams to James Warren, Apr. 6, 1777, in William B. Clark, ed., *Naval Documents of the American Revolution*, 8 vols. to date (Washington, D.C., 1964–), 8:282, for the economic potential of privateering.

[73] Reuben E. Stivers, *Privateers and Volunteers, 1766–1866* (Annapolis, 1975), pp. 29–32.

[74] C. Lee to Meshech Weare, Nov. 27, 1776, Clark, ed., *Naval Documents*, 7:307; Stivers, *Privateers*, p. 30; Buel, *Dear Liberty*, p. 223.

[75] Wayne E. Verry, "The Connecticut Privateers and Their Prizes: A Comparative Study," M.A. thesis, Wesleyan University, 1976. See also Oc-

how general an experience this was will have to wait for further studies.[76]

Enough impressionistic evidence exists, however, to suggest that some states did gain from privateering and that Massachusetts in particular reaped a disproportionate share of the rewards. Thanks to an extended coastline filled with eminently eligible refuges, and thanks to the prevailing winds (offshore in fair weather, onshore in foul), the Royal Navy could never effectively blockade the area.[77] And though the absence of rich commercial pickings left the Bay relatively free of privateers, the ports of eastern Massachusetts were sufficiently convenient to the shipping routes between the West Indies and Europe, as well as between Britain and North America, to make them attractive both as bases and as destinations for vessels taken as prizes. In 1779, for instance, three Continental vessels seized eight merchantmen from the Jamaica fleet off Nova Scotia and brought them into Boston.[78] Nevertheless, the majority of the prizes captured in American waters were either privateers or carried goods destined for the British army, often Irish provisions. Furthermore, even if a significant amount of dry goods had found their way into America by this route, the crippling cost that British naval supremacy imposed upon their distribution would have kept the benefits derived from them confined to a very small area. The peculiar advantage enjoyed by Massachusetts did grant her a continuous influx of prize goods together with limited imports from Europe, and the two together probably contributed as much as her policy of taxation toward maintain-

---

tavius T. Howe, "Beverly Privateers in the American Revolution," *Publications of the Colonial Society of Massachusetts* 24 (1920–22):424.

[76] It is to be hoped that answers to questions such as these will emerge from the completion of the splendid *Naval Documents of the American Revolution* series.

[77] Richard Lord Howe to Philip Stephens, Feb. 20, 1777, Clark, ed., *Naval Documents*, 7:1247. See also Hamilton to R. Morris, Apr. 30, 1781, Ferguson, ed., *Papers of Morris*, 1:38 and 185n.

[78] Gardner W. Allen, *A Naval History of the American Revolution* (Boston, 1913), 2:385; Edgar S. Maclay, *A History of American Privateers* (1924; reprint ed., New York, 1968), p. 11.

ing some value to the currency in her jurisdiction. But in this she was unique.[79]

The sum of my conclusions from the evidence presented is that the Revolutionary experience revealed a far more complex range of American vulnerabilities than historians have generally acknowledged. Since the infant United States could not hope to attain the status of a major naval power in the foreseeable future, nor even to build a balanced economy that would offer producers a full array of the commodities for which they would willingly produce a surplus, her options were two. She could ally herself with one or more of the other maritime powers in order to compensate for her own deficiencies at sea, or she could establish public credit. Her experience with the French had shown the pitfalls of foreign alliances, but it had also proved that the proper deployment of specie or its equivalents could result in the stimulation of desired economic activity.[80] Specie allowed the seller to bank the value of what he received in exchange for his produce with reasonable certainty that he would be able to use it at some future date in purchasing the foreign goods he wanted. But so long as America's economy retained its colonial character, she would never accumulate a sufficient quantity of specie to use in this way. That is why the ascription of a specie value to the public debt stood so high on the nation's postwar political agenda, at least in the eyes of those who saw and sought to guard against the weaknesses laid bare by a Revolutionary experience that had left the more perceptive of the nation's leaders shorn of their youthful illusions.

[79] Hamilton to R. Morris, Apr. 30, 1781, Ferguson, ed., *Papers of Morris*, 1:37, 212n; William B. Norton, "Paper Currency in Massachusetts during the Revolution," *New England Quarterly* 7 (1934):59–60; Buel, *Dear Liberty*, p. 244.

[80] See Buel, *Dear Liberty*, pp. 241–44.

IRA D. GRUBER

George III Chooses a Commander in Chief

WELL BEFORE BRITISH TROOPS marched to Lexington and Concord on an April day in 1775, George III had appointed all but one of the general officers who would command his armies during the American War of Independence. He had named three of them years before war threatened the empire: in 1763, Lt. Gen. Thomas Gage as commander in chief in North America, and, in 1766, Major Generals Guy Carleton and Frederick Haldimand as governors of Canada and Florida, respectively. But in February 1775 the king appointed three other major generals—William Howe, Henry Clinton, and John Burgoyne—to assist Gage in sustaining British authority at Boston, to use force if necessary to put down the rebellion that was festering in New England. These six officers, together with Charles Earl Cornwallis who volunteered for service in the colonies in November 1775, would direct British forces in America throughout the war—Gage, Howe, Clinton, and Carleton as successive commanders in chief and Burgoyne, Cornwallis, and Haldimand as commanders of independent armies.

According to Burgoyne, the king not only appointed but personally selected three of these commanders—Howe, Clinton, and Burgoyne. Secretary at War Lord Barrington told Burgoyne "that no person, as he believed, had suggested to the king this nomination; that in all military distinctions he was persuaded his Majesty considered the list of his Generals with no other view than scrupulously to appoint to each particular service the person in his judgment best adapted to it; that his Majesty had expressed himself decisively in regard to Generals Howe, Clinton, and myself [Burgoyne] and he was persuaded the whole Kingdom would applaud his deci-

George III Chooses a Commander

sion."[1] If Burgoyne and Barrington may be trusted, the king alone was responsible for choosing the men who would serve him as commanders in chief from late in 1775 until early 1782, as well as the man who would take the Canadian army to Saratoga in 1777.

But were Burgoyne and Barrington correct? Did the king alone select three of the four most important British generals of the war? If so, what criteria did he use? If not, whom did he consult, what advice did he receive, and to what extent did he follow that advice? This essay attempts to reconstruct the process by which Howe, Clinton, and Burgoyne were chosen and, in so doing, to judge whether British forces were as well led in the American War as they might have been.

Consider first how the king usually filled commands. As captain general of British forces, he had final authority in selecting, appointing, and promoting officers throughout the army. Although he had always been jealous of that authority, he had also been careful to exercise it after consulting with his principal ministers or secretary at war. When appointments had political implications, he sometimes yielded completely to the wishes of a principal minister: he made the marquis of Granby commander in chief in 1766 to favor Chatham, promised Henry Seymour Conway a "lucrative and honorable regiment" a year later to assist Grafton, and awarded colonelcies to Sir Robert Hamilton and Lt. Col. John Burgoyne to please Lord North.[2] But if offended by a politician, if asked to violate seniority or to reward someone who had refused active service, or if filling an important command, the king could—and did—insist on making his own

---

[1] Edward Barrington De Fonblanque, *Political and Military Episodes . . . from the Life and Correspondence of . . . John Burgoyne . . .* (London, 1876), p. 122.

[2] Sir Lewis Namier and John Brooke, *The House of Commons, 1754–1790*, 3 vols. (New York, 1964), 3:104; John Earl Ligonier to William Wildman Viscount Barrington, Aug. 7, 1766, the king to Francis Seymour-Conway, earl of Hertford, July 17, 1767, Barrington to the king, Mar. 19, 1770, the king to Frederick Lord North, July 17, 1773, John W. Fortescue, ed., *The Correspondence of King George the Third from 1760 to December 1783*, 6 vols. (London, 1927–28), 1:387–88, 499–500; 2:135–36; 3:3; *A List of the General and Field-Officers . . . for 1772*, p. 94, confirms Hamilton's appointment.

decisions: he refused to let George Grenville name the commander in chief in 1765 because Grenville sought thereby to dominate the king; he denied Lord Townshend's request for a regiment of guards because favoring Townshend would have displeased other, more senior lieutenant generals; he rejected Gen. Robert Monckton's application for a command in Bengal because Gen. John Clavering was "most fit" for the job; and he subsequently refused a pension for Monckton in part at least because Monckton had declined a command in America.[3] But even when denying his ministers and generals or deciding for himself how to fill an important command, the king sought advice.

This was what he did on the eve of the American Revolution. During the autumn of 1774, Lord North, the head of the ministry, proposed sending a major general to assist and invigorate Gage at Boston. The ministry had not developed a plan for sustaining royal authority in the colonies, but it believed that Gage had been too conciliatory and that relying on him alone would merely encourage rebellion. The king, who was ready to use force to break colonial resistance, welcomed North's proposal and suggested three major generals to sustain Gage—three skilled politicians and staunch supporters of British rule in America, Robert Cuninghame, James Gisborne, and Alexander Mackay. The king did not make a final selection among the three; he merely expressed his preferences and solicited North's opinion on the desirability of sending an officer who had served in the colonies. What North replied is unknown except that he did not presume to make the final choice; on December 17 he pressed the king for a decision. By then events had overtaken the king and North. Addresses, a petition, and a declaration of rights had arrived from the first Continental Congress to challenge British rule throughout North America. The king deferred appointing a major general until the ministry had both drafted a comprehensive plan for dealing with the rebellion and con-

---

[3] Namier and Brooke, *House of Commons*, 3:103; the king to John Perceval, earl of Egmont, [May 23, 1765], the king to North, Mar. 5, June 4, 8, 10, 1773, Fortescue, ed., *Correspondence of George Third*, 1:113–15; 2:465, 494, 496, 499–500.

George III Chooses a Commander

sidered whether Gage should be replaced by a more distinguished and resolute officer—specifically, by Sir Jeffery Amherst who had conquered Canada in 1760 and was clearly the most celebrated surviving commander of the Seven Years' War.[4]

Although Gage was in disfavor and Amherst in high esteem, it was nearly six weeks before the king decided who should command. In the interim he invited the ministry to discuss employing Amherst and even suggested that Amherst be consulted on who might serve under him. But the ministry, preoccupied with developing a plan for ending the rebellion, let weeks go by without recommending whether to replace Gage, and the king seemed willing to postpone a decision. The ministry agreed on January 13 to send reinforcements to Boston and to put punitive restrictions on American trade. It also decided on January 27 to order Gage to use his reinforcements in crushing the rebellion—to arrest leading rebels, seize military stores, and prevent colonial militia from exercising. The ministry may well have hoped that by ordering Gage to be resolute it could avoid, temporarily, recommending whether to replace him. But on January 28 the king refused to delay any longer. He told Lord Dartmouth, the secretary of state for the colonies, that the troops in America and the general officers at home thought Gage unequal to managing a war. He proposed, therefore, to let Gage remain in Massachusetts as royal governor and to ask Amherst to become commander in chief with full power to negotiate a settlement with the colonists. When Amherst promptly but emphatically refused to serve, the king decided on January 31, in his words, to "leave the command to Gage [and] send the best Generals that can be thought of to his assistance."[5]

---

[4] The king to North, Nov. 18, 1774 (two letters), North to the king, Dec. 17, 1774, and the king to North, Dec. 18, 1774, Fortescue, ed., *Correspondence of George Third*, 3:154, 153, 157; Ira D. Gruber, *The Howe Brothers and the American Revolution* (Chapel Hill, N.C., 1974), pp. 3–5.

[5] The king to North, Dec. 18, 1774, William Henry Nassau de Zuylestein, earl of Rochford, to the king, Jan. 24, 1775, Fortescue, ed., *Correspondence of George Third*, 3:157, 168; Gruber, *Howe Brothers*, pp. 13–15; the king to William Legge, earl of Dartmouth, Jan. 28, 31 (quoted), 1775,

ARMS AND INDEPENDENCE

At first glance that decision seems remarkably unsound—an example, perhaps, of giving too much consideration to Gage's feelings. The king and his closest advisors wanted a commander in chief who would deal firmly and successfully with the rebellion in Massachusetts; they knew there was little in Gage's record to suggest he would do either. While saying that he supported the supremacy of Parliament throughout the empire and that he would carry out coercive measures, he had all too often talked of compromise, of avoiding extreme measures. Moreover, his performance in the French and Indian War scarcely encouraged anyone to think he would deal decisively and effectively with the colonists in the event of war: he had served as a subordinate in a succession of disastrous or inconclusive campaigns and, when given an independent command, had shown an exasperating lack of determination. That the king should have kept such a man as commander in chief seems, then, an example of giving undue weight to his personal feelings.[6]

But could the king have found a better officer to replace Gage? He had tried and failed to persuade Sir Jeffery Amherst—a general far more able than Gage—to become commander in chief. Once Amherst declined, were there other better prospects among the remaining twenty-one generals and twenty-four lieutenant generals who were senior to Gage? Was there not someone else who might have served as commander in chief while Gage remained in Massachusetts as royal governor? The answer is that there was not. Among the officers senior to Gage there was not a single one who was preferable to him, unemployed, and willing to serve in the colonies.

Nearly two-thirds of them had not the health or competence to be considered seriously. Five between the ages of sixty-three and eighty-five would die in 1775; eleven more,

---

Historical Manuscripts Commission, ... *The Manuscripts of Rye and Hereford Corporations* (London, 1892), p. 501.

[6] The standard biography is John Richard Alden, *General Gage in America* ... (Baton Rouge, 1948); this interpretation of Gage's qualifications follows my own instincts and those of John Shy, "Thomas Gage: Weak Link of Empire," in George A. Billias, ed., *George Washington's Opponents* ... (New York, 1969), pp. 3–38.

between sixty-five and ninety, were in advanced stages of physical and professional decay; and four suffered from chronic, disabling illnesses.[7] In addition to those twenty, there were another eight who lacked the competence to be a commander in chief. Certainly no one would have been tempted to employ the earl of Harrington, who was known mainly as a libertine, or the duke of Ancaster, whom North called "a very egregious blockhead."[8] Nor were the earl of Loudoun, James Abercromby, or Theodore Dury viable candidates. Loudoun and Abercromby had served as commanders in chief in America during the Seven Years' War, and both had been recalled—Loudoun for failing to attack Louisbourg and Abercromby for attacking Ticonderoga, rashly and disastrously. Dury, for his part, had had the misfortune to command a brigade that was mauled during an unsuccessful attack

[7] Those who died in 1775 were George Boscawen, James Cholmondeley, Charles Colville, Michael O'Brien Dilkes, and William Kerr, marquis of Lothian. See Romney Sedgwick, *The House of Commons, 1714–1754*, 2 vols. (New York, 1970), 1:475; Namier and Brooke, *House of Commons*, 2:103–4; 3:11–12; *London Magazine* 44 (1775):491; *Gentleman's Magazine* 45 (1775):454; Charles Dalton, *George the First's Army, 1714–1727*, 2 vols. (London, 1910–12), 2:373–74; Leslie Stephen and Sidney Lee, eds., *Dictionary of National Biography*, 22 vols. (London, 1949–50), Lothian. Those in advanced stages of decay included Charles Lord Cadogan, Archibald Douglas, Hugh Viscount Falmouth, Studholme Hodgson, John Lambton, Sir John Mordaunt, John Mostyn, James Oglethorpe, William Maule, earl of Panmure, John Parslow, and William Strode. See Sedgwick, *House of Commons*, 1:512, 477; 2:305–6, 248; Namier and Brooke, *House of Commons*, 2:329, 104; 3:18–19, 163–64, 176–78, 120–21; *Dictionary of National Biography*, Hodgson, Lambton, Mordaunt, and Oglethorpe; Dalton, *George the First's Army*, 2:265, 267; *Gentleman's Magazine* 46 (1776):47. Those who were ill were Lord Robert Bertie, Charles Lord Cathcart, Lord Robert Manners, and Sir Charles Montagu. See Namier and Brooke, *House of Commons*, 2:88–89; 3:107; *Dictionary of National Biography*, Cathcart; Sir James Balfour Paul, ed., *The Scots Peerage ...*, 9 vols. (Edinburgh, 1904–14), Cathcart; *Gentleman's Magazine* 47 (1777):404; Richard Arthur Austen-Leigh, *The Eton College Register, 1698–1752* (Eton, 1927), Montagu; Montagu to Horace Walpole, Nov. 12, 1768, W. S. Lewis and Ralph S. Brown, Jr., eds., *Horace Walpole's Correspondence with George Montagu*, 2 vols. (New Haven, 1941), 2:268.

[8] Namier and Brooke, *House of Commons*, 3:467; George Edward Cokayne, *The Complete Peerage of England, Scotland, Ireland ...*, 13 vols., rev. ed. by Vicary Gibbs (London, 1910–59), 1:128.

ARMS AND INDEPENDENCE

on the French coast at St. Cas in 1758.⁹ Although Lord John Murray, Cuthbert Ellison, and John Fitzwilliam were not burdened by failure, none of them was experienced enough to be a commander in chief. Murray, who sought command, had not seen active duty since 1747; Ellison had resigned his commission in 1745 and was on the list of generals merely because he had held a staff appointment at the time of his resignation; and Fitzwilliam is not known to have served after 1747.¹⁰ In short, more than 60 percent of the officers senior to Gage were too infirm, incompetent, or inexperienced to hold a chief command.

Another 29 percent—thirteen generals—either opposed coercive measures or were better suited to employment at home. Four, including Henry Seymour Conway and Sir Griffin Griffin, were members of the House of Commons who regularly voted against using force in the colonies. Although none of them was so obstinate in his opposition as to be absolutely unemployable, none was so distinguished as to be employed in spite of his views.¹¹ Similarly, among the nine senior generals serving at home, only one, George Augustus Elliott, the commander in chief in Ireland, was a truly distinguished commander; and Elliott would soon be reassigned to Gibraltar to replace the ineffectual governor Edward Cornwallis.¹² The rest of the senior generals employed at home

---

⁹ Stanley McCrory Pargellis, *Lord Loudoun in North America* (New Haven, 1933); Allen Johnson and Dumas Malone, eds., *Dictionary of American Biography*, 20 vols. (New York, 1928–36), Abercromby; Dalton, *George the First's Army*, 2:263, 264; Frederick William Hamilton, *The Origin and History of the First or Grenadier Guards*, 3 vols. (London, 1874), 2:161.

¹⁰ Namier and Brooke, *House of Commons*, 3:186–87; 2:437; *Dictionary of National Biography*, Murray; Sedgwick, *House of Commons*, 2:10; James Hayes, "Two Soldier Brothers of the Eighteenth Century," *Journal of the Society for Army Historical Research* 40 (1962):150–56.

¹¹ The four were William A'Court Ashe, Conway, Griffin, and Philip Honywood. See Namier and Brooke, *House of Commons*, 2:5, 244–47, 553–55, 635–36.

¹² *Dictionary of National Biography*, Elliott; Namier and Brooke, *House of Commons*, 2:256–57; Beckles Willson, *The Life and Letters of James Wolfe* (London, 1909), pp. 308–9, 344.

were simply better suited to administrative posts than high command. The duke of Argyll (commander in chief in Scotland), the earl of Sandwich (first lord of the Admiralty), Earl Harcourt (lord lieutenant of Ireland), and Sir Joseph Yorke (ambassador to The Hague) had long since abandoned the army for politics and diplomacy.[13] William Belford and William Skinner, nearing the end of long, distinguished careers in the artillery and engineers, had no expectation of command. Nor did the king's favorite brother, William, duke of Gloucester, whose rank was merely a tribute to his royal birth.[14]

Four senior generals remain to be considered. All were experienced commanders, all had enjoyed successful careers, and at least two—John Earl Waldegrave and Robert Monckton—were better qualified than Gage for the chief command in America. Yet by 1775 none was willing to serve in the colonies. Earl Waldegrave was, next to Amherst, the most celebrated British general living. He had made his reputation in Germany during the Seven Years' War, commanding various divisions of the allied forces and distinguishing himself particularly at Minden and Kloster Kamp. Although he supported the ministry's colonial policies, he was apparently more interested in becoming commander in chief at home than in suppressing rebellion in America.[15] Monckton was by no means as distinguished as Waldegrave; he was, however, a popular, courageous, and competent general who had served in America for more than a decade and who had become famous as second to Wolfe at Quebec in 1759 and as commander of the expeditionary force that captured Martinique in 1762. He, too, supported the ministry's colonial policies. Yet, when in 1773 the king offered to make him commander in chief in America, he declined, and there is no evidence

[13] Namier and Brooke, *House of Commons*, 2:188–90, 580; 3:679–80; *Gentleman's Magazine* 76 (1806):585; George Martelli, *Jemmy Twitcher: A Life of the Fourth Earl of Sandwich, 1718–1792* (London, 1962); *Dictionary of National Biography*, Harcourt.

[14] *Dictionary of National Biography*, Belford, Skinner, and Gloucester.

[15] Namier and Brooke, *House of Commons*, 3:592; *Dictionary of National Biography*.

that the king ever renewed the offer.¹⁶ Unlike Waldegrave and Monckton, Sir George Howard and Edward Sandford were not clearly better qualified than Gage to command in America. Both had served successfully as brigade commanders in Germany, but until 1775 Howard opposed using force against the colonists, and Sandford was by that time preoccupied with Irish politics.¹⁷ There were among all officers senior to Gage, then, only three who were unemployed and clearly preferable to him for the chief command in America; yet none among the three—Amherst, Waldegrave, and Monckton—would willingly have served at Boston in 1775.

It is understandable why the king decided to keep Gage and to "send the best Generals that can be thought of to his assistance." But how did he proceed on January 31 and February 1, 1775, in selecting generals to assist Gage? How did he choose Howe, Clinton, and Burgoyne from among the twenty-seven lieutenant and forty-five major generals junior to Gage for service in America? Did he, as usual, seek advice or, as Burgoyne had it from Barrington, did he make this decision alone? Although it is impossible to be sure, it seems likely that the king followed his usual pattern—he consulted his closest advisors and then made his own selection.

In making a preliminary list of officers to be considered for service under Gage, the king was apparently influenced by those around him. That influence was not great because he had his own strong preferences among his officers and was determined to have men he thought talented and personally acceptable. Thus he included in his list men who had

---

[16] Namier and Brooke, *House of Commons*, 3:149; *Dictionary of National Biography*; J. Clarence Webster, ed., *The Journal of Jeffery Amherst . . . from 1758 to 1763* (Toronto, [1931]), p. 3; the king to North, June 8, 10, 1773, Fortescue, ed., *Correspondence of George Third*, 2:494, 499–500.

[17] Namier and Brooke, *House of Commons*, 2:645–46; *Dictionary of National Biography*, Howard; *The Army List of 1740*, Society for Army Historical Research, special no. 3 (Sheffield, 1931), p. 43; Ligonier to Sandford, June 2, 1758, Ligonier Letter Book, 1758–60, William L. Clements Library, University of Michigan, Ann Arbor; E. A. H. Webb, *History of the 12th (The Suffolk) Regiment, 1685–1913* (London, 1914), p. 113; Edith M. Johnston, *Great Britain and Ireland, 1760–1800: A Study in Political Administration* (Edinburgh, 1963), p. 387; Albert Lee, *The History of the Tenth Foot* (Aldershot, 1911), 1:269.

performed well in combat and on campaign in a variety of wars, who had made imaginative contributions to British military practice, and who were his particular favorites. But he also included men who were neither distinguished nor experienced and who were not even close to him. These few generals were probably nominated by at least one of the king's advisors.

The king may have been particularly receptive to nominations because his choice was limited to the youngest and least experienced of his general officers. The king's list included Gage and thirteen generals junior to him: Sir William Draper, Henry Clinton, Frederick Haldimand, William Howe, John Burgoyne, Richard Pierson, William Augustus Pitt, William Alexander Sorell, Sir Charles Hotham Thompson, John Irwin, Lord Adam Gordon, James Gisborne, and Robert Cuninghame. These fourteen men were not exactly young (the oldest was fifty-seven and the youngest forty-five), yet their average age, forty-nine, was nine years below that of all the general officers, and only four of them had ever held an independent command in wartime.[18]

Some of those on the king's list were included primarily because they were accomplished soldiers. Not that the king disliked or failed to reward Sir William Draper, Henry Clinton, or Frederick Haldimand, but he does not seem to have been personally attached to any of them. Draper, son of a Bristol customs official, had risen in the army on the strength of a good education and a powerful father-in-law as well as an unusual aptitude for leading men in battle. During the Seven Years' War he had raised a regiment and taken it to Madras, served in the attack on Belle-Isle, and returned to the Far East to capture Manila in 1762. Although he retired

---

[18] List of Generals (for commands in America), n.d., Fortescue, ed., *Correspondence of George Third*, 3:162; as neither Alexander Mackay, who was considered for the command at Boston in November 1774, nor Jeffery Amherst, who was considered until January 31, 1775, are on this list, the list may have been drawn up on January 31, 1775; but it is impossible to be sure of the date. Average ages are computed from the ages of all 14 officers on the king's list and from the ages of 116 of 119 generals in *A List of the General and Field-Officers . . . for 1775*, pp. 1–4. Sources of biographical information for all 119 officers are included in notes accompanying the remainder of this essay.

on half pay because of poor health, he was subsequently promoted to major general so that he might, as the king said, do "future Service to his Country."[19] Clinton, the son of an ineffectual admiral, entered the army through the Coldstream Guards and advanced with the help of his uncle and cousin, successively the dukes of Newcastle-under-Lyme, and of the venerable field marshal Lord Ligonier. But his career was not built on patronage alone: he won a reputation for courage while serving in Germany at the close of the Seven Years' War, and he used the ensuing years of peace to make a thorough study of the art of war.[20] Unlike Clinton and Draper, Haldimand had no powerful family to propel him upward. A Swiss mercenary who had begun his career in the Sardinian and Dutch armies, he entered British service in 1756 as a lieutenant colonel and soon distinguished himself in combat—at Ticonderoga (1758) and Oswego (1759). He earned the praise of such diverse personalities as the earl of Loudoun and Lord Barrington and in 1775 was serving as commander in Florida.[21]

There were at least two officers on the king's list who might have been included either for merit or for favor. William Howe, the fourth son of the second Viscount Howe, was at forty-five one of the youngest and most promising of British generals. He had made his reputation not merely as a skilled and courageous regimental commander during the Seven Years' War—at Louisbourg, Quebec, Montreal, Belle-Isle, and

[19] *Dictionary of National Biography*; J. W. Hayes, "Lieutenant-Colonel and Major-Commandants of the Seven Years War," *Journal of the Society for Army Historical Research* 36 (1958):7–8; and quoting Barrington to Draper, May 25, 1772, Barrington Letter Book, Ipswich and East Suffolk Record Office.

[20] William B. Willcox, *Portrait of a General: Sir Henry Clinton in the War of Independence* (New York, 1964), pp. 3–39; Namier and Brooke, *House of Commons*, 2:222–23.

[21] *Dictionary of National Biography*; John Campbell, earl of Loudoun, to William Augustus, duke of Cumberland, Mar. 8, 1757, Stanley McCrory Pargellis, ed., *Military Affairs in North America, 1748–1765: Selected Documents from the Cumberland Papers in Windsor Castle* (New York, 1936), p. 323; Barrington to Gage, Sept. 2, 1772, and Barrington to North, Aug. 27, 1775, Barrington Letter Book.

Havana—but also as an authority on light infantry tactics. By 1775 he was, according to one of the king's closest advisors, just the man "to restore discipline and confidence" at Boston and to make the British army formidable amid the "trees, walls, and Hedges" of New England.[22] Only slightly less celebrated than Howe was John Burgoyne, a bold and ambitious cavalry officer. Although Burgoyne's improvidence had interrupted his career—he had been forced to sell his commission and spend five years on the Continent avoiding his creditors—he had reentered the army in 1756 and risen rapidly with the help of his father-in-law, the earl of Derby. He served as a volunteer at Belle-Isle, distinguished himself as second in command of an international force in Portugal in 1762, and devoted considerable time between the wars to military studies and the improvement of his regiment. Like Howe, Burgoyne had been rewarded with lucrative military sinecures as well as the esteem and affection of the king.[23]

But the king's favor was not always bestowed on men of conspicuous achievement, and there were at least four relatively undistinguished officers on his list in January 1775. To be fair, it should be said that while the four may have been good soldiers, it has been difficult to find evidence that any of them ever distinguished himself. Richard Pierson, an officer of the First Foot Guards, had been captured during a raid on the French coast in 1758 and was repeatedly criticized while serving as supervisor of the commissariat in Germany in 1760–61. He subsequently commanded a brigade of guards with the allied army on the Ohm in September 1762. Like Pierson, William Augustus Pitt, a cavalry officer, also commanded a brigade with the army on the Ohm in September 1762. But nothing is known of Pierson's or Pitt's performance in Germany except that in 1770, when the king

[22] Gruber, *Howe Brothers*, pp. 56–59; Namier and Brooke, *House of Commons*, 2:649–50; James Wolfe to Henry Parr, Dec. 6, 1758, Willson, *Life of Wolfe*, pp. 404–5; and quoting De Fonblanque, *Burgoyne*, p. 126, and Lord George Germain to [Henry Howard, earl of Suffolk, June 16 or 17, 1775], Sackville-Germain Papers, Clements Library.

[23] De Fonblanque, *Burgoyne*, pp. 8–131; George A. Billias, "John Burgoyne: Ambitious General," in Billias, ed., *George Washington's Opponents*, pp. 142–92; Namier and Brooke, *House of Commons*, 2:141–45.

gave Pitt the colonelcy of a regiment of dragoons, he referred to his "meritorious conduct" and said he had "long had reason to expect such a mark of my favor."[24] Nor is anything known about the services of William Alexander Sorell or Sir Charles Hotham Thompson except that both were officers in the foot guards and that Thompson was an adjutant general at St. Malo and in Germany during the Seven Years' War. That there is so little evidence of military distinction for any of these officers suggests that the king may have allowed his personal feelings to influence his preliminary selection. It is clear that Pitt's family had long supported the crown in Parliament and that Thompson, a groom of the bedchamber and a knight of the Bath, was particularly close to the king.[25]

The remaining four generals on the king's list were apparently nominated by Lord George Germain. Germain, reared a soldier but dismissed from the service for disobedience at the Battle of Minden in 1759, was emerging as one of the ministry's principal supporters in the House of Commons and as one of the foremost advocates of using force to sustain British authority in America. If not yet a minister, he was a participant "in all consultations upon American measures," and it is likely that he now recommended four of his Irish and Scottish friends—John Irwin, Lord Adam Gordon, James Gisborne, and Robert Cuninghame—for service in the colonies.[26] The king knew and liked John Irwin, an Irishman who

---

[24] Ligonier to Pierson, Nov. 24, 1758, Ligonier Letter Book; Reginald Savory, *His Britannic Majesty's Army in Germany during the Seven Years War* (Oxford, 1966), pp. 304, 307, 393, 512, 511; Hamilton, *First Guards*, 2:174, 182, 193; Namier and Brooke, *House of Commons*, 3:302; and quoting the king to North, Oct. 21, 1770, Fortescue, ed., *Correspondence of George Third*, 2:165.

[25] Russell Gurney, *History of the Northamptonshire Regiment, 1742–1934* (Aldershot, 1935), pp. 382–83; Namier and Brooke, *House of Commons*, 2:641–43; 3:302, 282–83; A. M. W. Stirling, *The Hothams . . .*, 2 vols. (London, 1918), 2:18–23, 70–71.

[26] Gerald Saxon Brown, *The American Secretary: The Colonial Policy of Lord George Germain, 1775–1778* (Ann Arbor, 1963), pp. 1–26; Namier and Brooke, *House of Commons*, 3:390–96; Jan. 10, 1775, A. Francis Steuart, ed., *The Last Journals of Horace Walpole*, 2 vols. (London, 1910), 1:423–25; and quoting De Fonblanque, *Burgoyne*, p. 126.

had served on the coast of France and in Germany during the Seven Years' War and who regularly supported the North ministry in Parliament. But, as North observed, Irwin was held "in no great estimation as a general." Similarly, Lord Adam Gordon, the son of a Scottish duke, had served at St. Cas in 1758, gone to the West Indies with his regiment in the 1760s, and consistently supported firm measures for America in the House of Commons. Yet he was never thought worthy of a high command even though he would have gone to America or Asia to have had one.[27] James Gisborne and Robert Cuninghame were, like Irwin and Gordon, distinguished more for their political loyalty than military merit. Both had served mainly in Ireland where they were important members of the Irish House of Commons and where they held lucrative military appointments. Yet neither had had much experience in combat, and it seems doubtful that either would have been seriously considered for a command in 1775 without Germain's support.[28]

Here then were the general officers considered for commands in America in January 1775. Although the king apparently had some help in constructing his list of fourteen, he probably made the final selection of Howe, Clinton, and Burgoyne without further consultation. That selection was announced on February 2, only two days after he decided to keep Gage as commander in chief and "send the best Generals that can be thought of to his assistance."[29] In those two days the king chose three of the principal commanders of the American war. Was this a hasty and ill-advised choice? Knowing as we do how the war turned out and how British generals performed, we might be tempted to conclude that

[27] Namier and Brooke, *House of Commons*, 2:667 (quoted), 510–12; and *Dictionary of National Biography* for both.

[28] Neil Bannatyne, *History of the Thirtieth Regiment . . ., 1689–1881* (Liverpool, 1923), pp. 115, 119, 121, 126, 132–33; Johnston, *Great Britain and Ireland*, pp. 23, 224, 242, 381; *Scots Magazine* 40 (1778):111; Namier and Brooke, *House of Commons*, 2:284–85; and E. M. Johnston, "Members of the Irish Parliament, 1784–7," Royal Irish Academy *Proceedings* 71, sec. C, no. 5 (1971), Cuninghame.

[29] Barrington to Gage, Feb. 2, 1775, Gage Papers, English Series XXVII, Clements Library.

this was the case. But how does this selection look from the perspective of January 31, 1775? Were Howe, Clinton, and Burgoyne the best prospects on the king's list? A review of the evidence suggests that they were.

Considering that the king now sought able soldiers to support Gage—that he put more emphasis on military skills than on other qualities—his selection is a plausible one. In November 1774, before the ministry had decided to use force to uphold it authority in Massachusetts, the king had preferred Gisborne and Cuninghame for service under Gage— presumably because they had proved themselves to be firm friends of authority in Ireland and unwilling to temporize with rebels (Gisborne had successfully put down a rebellion in Ulster in 1772).[30] But now that the king sought able commanders, he can scarcely be criticized for rejecting officers who had seen little active service in wartime (especially, Gisborne and Cuninghame) or who had not distinguished themselves (Irwin, Gordon, Pierson, Pitt, Sorell, and Thompson). It is also understandable that he should have preferred Howe, Clinton, and Burgoyne to Draper and Haldimand. All had excellent reputations as commanders. But there were intractable disadvantages to sending Draper, whose wife was an American, or Haldimand, a foreigner. The king could not risk having another general at Boston who was too sympathetic with the colonists or having a foreigner succeed to the command.[31] By contrast, the obstacles to appointing Howe, Clinton, and Burgoyne were surmountable. Although Howe had publicly criticized coercive measures and said he would refuse to command against the colonists, he privately assured Lord North that he would be willing to serve as second to

[30] The king to North, Nov. 18, 1774, Fortescue, ed., *Correspondence of George Third*, 3:153; Johnston, *Great Britain and Ireland*, p. 224.

[31] Even in peacetime the prospect of having Haldimand command in America had created considerable anxiety. As Barrington said, "A foreigner should not have so important a trust, notwithstanding his personal merit." Although Barrington subsequently authorized Haldimand to command in Gage's absence, Haldimand was recalled in 1775 so that Howe would be next in seniority to Gage. Barrington to Gage, Dec. 5, 1768 (quoted), and to Haldimand, June 4, 1773, Barrington Letter Book; De Fonblanque, *Burgoyne*, p. 128.

George III Chooses a Commander

Gage; and although both Clinton and Burgoyne favored a negotiated settlement and expressed a reluctance to serve, both accepted—as did Howe—"in the most becoming manner."[32] The king, then, had selected the most promising of the officers on his list.

But while this selection was a plausible one, we should still ask if there were not other officers, more able than Howe, Clinton, and Burgoyne, who were omitted from the list of fourteen. Had the king given too much weight to his private feelings and the advice of men like Germain in drawing up that list? Had he excluded from serious consideration experienced and distinguished men, men who lacked influence but who might have put down the rebellion in America? This does not appear to have been so. There were twenty-five lieutenant generals and thirty-four major generals junior to Gage in 1775 who were excluded from the list. But when training, health, experience, and reputation, as well as social standing, compatibility with the king and ministry, willingness to serve, and availability are considered, none seems to have been better suited to command in America than Howe, Clinton, or Burgoyne.

About one-third—nineteen of the generals junior to Gage—may be dismissed at once as decrepit, incompetent, or unacceptable. Three, aged sixty-eight, seventy, and seventy-seven, would die in 1775; four, between the ages of sixty-eight and seventy-six, were clearly past their days of active service.[33] Another six simply lacked the stability, competence, or ex-

---

[32] Philip Skene to North, Jan. 23, 1775, and Barrington to Dartmouth, Feb. 3, 1775 (quoted), Historical Manuscripts Commission, *The Manuscripts . . . of the Earl of Dartmouth . . .*, 3 vols. (London, 1887–96), 2:262, 266.

[33] Those who died were William Deane, William Cunningham, earl of Glencairn, and John Owen. See *Gentleman's Magazine* 45 (1775):407, 455; Dalton, *George the First's Army*, 2:313; Paul, ed., *Scots Peerage*, 4:250–51; Sedgwick, *House of Commons*, 2:316. Those who were past their service included John Severn, Benjamin Carpenter, Thomas Erle, and Richard Bendyshe. See *Gentleman's Magazine* 57 (1787):644; *Scots Magazine* 50 (1788):154–55, 39 (1777):111; L. B. Oatts, *Emperor's Chambermaids: The Story of the 14th/20th King's Hussars* (London, 1973), p. 36; Dalton, *George the First's Army*, 2:365, 205; Austen-Leigh, *Eton College Register*, Bendyshe.

perience to undertake a major command overseas. When the earl of Pembroke, who had twice astounded his wife and society by eloping to the Continent, volunteered for service in America, the king dismissed the offer as merely another figment of Pembroke's "lively brain." Nor would the king have been tempted to employ a man like John Scott, who had been recalled from Boston in 1768 to avoid any possibility of his succeeding Gage, or Charles, earl of Drogheda, who had entered the army in 1755 and risen to major general without seeing any active service.[34] Of the experienced officers, some, like Lord Frederick Cavendish, refused to serve against the colonists; others, like the duke of Richmond and the earl of Shelburne, were so obstinate and conspicuous in their opposition to the ministry's American policy that no one would have considered employing them.[35] All told, at least five lieutenant and major generals were disqualified because of their opposition to the American war, and one because he was personally obnoxious to North.[36]

Another twelve—or one-fifth of the generals junior to Gage—probably were not considered because of their particular training or current employment. George Williamson and Thomas Desauliers were respected and experienced officers of artillery who held secondary commands during the Seven Years' War. Yet neither could expect—as artillerists—to be considered for important, independent commands in the American war. Nor could John Salter, who had risen from private to major general in the First Foot Guards through the favor of the duke of Cumberland: however talented, a sixty-six-year-old officer without family could not expect to

---

[34] Tresham Lever, *The Herberts of Wilton* (London, 1967), pp. 160–97; the king to North, Jan. 9, 1778, Fortescue, ed., *Correspondence of George Third*, 4:7–8; Namier and Brooke, *House of Commons*, 3:413–14, 160; Barrington to Gage, Dec. 5, 1768, Barrington Letter Book; *Dictionary of National Biography*, Drogheda.

[35] Namier and Brooke, *House of Commons*, 2:200–201; *Dictionary of National Biography*, Richmond, Shelburne.

[36] In addition to Cavendish, Richmond, and Shelburne, William Keppel and Lord George Lennox opposed the American War; David Graeme was obnoxious. Namier and Brooke, *House of Commons*, 3:11, 35–36, 2:523–25.

be preferred over younger, experienced, and aristocratic officers. Nor could Robert Clerk, a "worthy, intelligent, and skillful officer," who had the misfortune of being an engineer and of having taken part in the disastrous attacks on Rochefort and St. Malo during the Seven Years' War. His training alone would have barred him from command.[37]

Although there were accomplished men among the eight lieutenant and major generals who held commands or ministerial posts in 1775, those with the most ability were needed where they were, and the remainder had not the talent to warrant more demanding assignments in America. James Murray, who had performed with "infinite spirit" at Louisbourg in 1758 and defended Quebec against a superior French force in the spring of 1760, Guy Carleton, "a galant and Sensible Man," according to the king, who had proved himself at Quebec and Havana during the Seven Years' War, and Robert Boyd, who had won a lieutenant colonelcy for his determination and courage during the defense of Minorca in 1756, were the kind of men needed to protect Minorca, Canada, and Gibraltar in 1775.[38] Conversely, Edward Harvey, the adjutant general, and George Viscount Townshend, the master general of ordnance, had too little distinction as soldiers and too much value as politicians to be given active commands; William Haviland and Sir James Adolphus Oughton were well suited to their insignificant posts in England and Scotland; and John Clavering, although esteemed by the king, lacked the talent to justify reassignment from Bengal to Boston.[39]

But what of the remaining twenty-eight lieutenant and

---

[37] Webster, ed., *Journal of Jeffery Amherst*, pp. 51, 232; Cumberland to Loudoun, Mar. 21, 1757, Pargellis, ed., *Military Affairs in North America*, p. 327; *Dictionary of National Biography*, Desaguliers; *Scots Magazine* 49 (1787):413–14; Whitworth Porter, *History of the Corps of Royal Engineers*, 3 vols. (London, 1889–1915), 1:161–64, 182 (quoted)–84.

[38] Wolfe to Lord George Sackville, July 30, 1758 (quoted), Willson, *Life of Wolfe*, p. 388; *Dictionary of National Biography*, Murray and Boyd; the king to Henry Seymour Conway, Apr. 2, 1766 (quoted), Fortescue, ed., *Correspondence of George Third*, 1:292; A. G. Bradley, *Lord Dorchester* (New York, 1926).

[39] Namier and Brooke, *House of Commons*, 2:594–95, 3:548–52; *Dictionary of National Biography*, Haviland, Oughton, and Clavering; the king to

major generals junior to Gage—men who were neither patently unacceptable nor currently employed? Nineteen of them were relatively inexperienced and undistinguished officers. All save one were members of aristocratic families, and all had the wealth and capacity to become generals. Yet few had the desire and fewer still the opportunities and skill needed to distinguish themselves. Only five of the nineteen had been willing to give up the security of established regiments during the Seven Years' War—regiments that would not be disbanded during any postwar reduction of the army—for the chance to command newly created units and to see active service; and none of those five had been fortunate and talented enough to gain the reputation of a Howe, Clinton, or Burgoyne.[40] The other fourteen remained with elite guards regiments, ensuring thereby that they would have secure and, as it turned out, obscure careers. A few of these, James Johnston (d. 1795) and Bernard Hale among them, won reputations for initiative and bravery in minor roles. But service as battalion officers with the guards at home, on the coasts of France, and in Germany offered fewer opportunities for glory than service as regimental or brigade commanders in North America and the West Indies. As a result, then, of various combinations of choice, chance, and capacity, these nineteen officers emerged from the Seven Years' War without distinction; by 1775 most seem to have been more interested in politics and genteel living than in military preferment.[41]

North, June 8, 1773, Fortescue, ed., *Correspondence of George Third*, 2:494–96.

[40] The five who left established regiments were Sir William Boothby, Bigoe Armstrong, John Pomeroy, Sir John Sebright, and Cadwallader Lord Blayney. John Davis, *The History of the Second Queen's Royal Regiment . . .*, 6 vols. (London, 1887–1906), 6:17; *A List of the General and Field-Officers . . . for 1755* (and Lists for 1759, 1761, 1765, 1775); *European Magazine* 11 (1787):374, 26 (1794):158, 17 (1790):480; Barrington to Gage, Dec. 5, 1768, Feb. 2, 1773, and Barrington to Haldimand, June 4, 1773, Barrington Letter Book; *The Army List of 1740*, p. 31; *Alumni Dublinenses . . . 1593–1860*, new ed. (Dublin, 1935), Pomeroy; Johnston, "Members Irish Parliament," p. 198; Namier and Brooke, *House of Commons*, 3:419; Cokayne, *Complete Peerage*, 2:189.

[41] The fourteen officers were Richard, earl of Cavan, John Earl DeLawarr, Robert Dalrymple Horn Elphinstone, William Evelyn, Charles

George III Chooses a Commander

Nine officers junior to Gage remain to be considered. While all were clearly more distinguished than a majority of the generals on the king's list, none was better qualified to command British forces in America than Howe, Clinton, or Burgoyne. Simon Fraser and Alexander Mackay were sons of Scottish noblemen and had made their way in the British army by raising regiments and supporting successive ministries. The king had considered sending Mackay to Boston in November 1774 because Mackay had served in America and favored coercive measures. But neither Mackay (who had last seen active duty in wartime in 1748) nor Fraser (whose service in the British army had been limited to two campaigns in America) had the experience or reputation to match a Clinton or a Burgoyne.[42] Cyrus Trapaud, Francis Grant, and Hunt Walsh had the experience but lacked the distinction, social standing, and youth. Trapaud, the son of a Huguenot refugee, had taken part in the principal battles of the War of the Austrian Succession and Scottish Rebellion, served on the coast of France in 1757, and commanded a brigade at Guadeloupe in 1759. Grant, the third son of a Scottish baronet, and Walsh, a member of the Irish House of Commons, had seen active

---

Fitzroy, Mariscoe Frederick, Bernard Hale, James Johnston (d. 1795), Alexander Maitland, George Lane Parker, Philip Sherrard, Nevil Tatton, John Thomas, and Edward Urmston. See *A List of the General and Field-Officers . . . for 1755* (and *Lists* for 1759, 1761, 1765, 1775); *Army List of 1740*, p. 14; Hamilton, *First Guards*, 2:179, 193, 182; Cokayne, *Complete Peerage*, 3:119; *Gentleman's Magazine* 47 (1777):556, 71 (1801):381, 90 (1820):282; Alan Valentine, *The British Establishment, 1760–1784 . . .*, 2 vols. (Norman, Okla., 1970), 2:921; Paul, ed., *Scots Peerage*, 8:132; Elphinstone to Loudoun, Feb. 17, 1756, Loudoun Papers, Box 19, Henry E. Huntington Library, San Marino, Calif.; Namier and Brooke, *House of Commons*, 2:408, 435, 3:98, 249; W. T. J. Gun, ed., *The Harrow School Register, 1571–1800* (London, 1934), p. 12; Frederick Barton Maurice, *The History of the Scots Guards . . . to the Eve of the Great War*, 2 vols. (London, 1934), 1:158; *Scots Magazine* 57 (1795):750; George Arthur, *The Story of the Household Cavalry*, 2 vols. (London, 1909), 2:453; *The Times* (London), Oct. 2, 1790, Dec.5, 1792; G. F. Russell Barker and Alan H. Stenning, eds., *The Record of Old Westminsters . . .*, 2 vols. (London, 1928), 2:904, 911–12.

[42] Namier and Brooke, *House of Commons*, 2:470–72, 3:83–85; Hayes, "Lieutenant-Colonel . . . Commandants of the Seven Years War," p. 10; the king to North, Nov. 18, 1774, Fortescue, ed., *Correspondence of George Third*, 3:153.

service in the Forty-Five and had risen to command regiments in North America and brigades at Martinique during the Seven Years' War. Yet, for all their experience, the three had never had the kind of military success that would enable them to gain high command without unusual political or family support. At sixty-one, fifty-eight, and fifty-five they were aging, experienced major generals with little prospect of further employment.[43]

There were, however, four of these nine officers who had the youth and distinction as well as the experience to be strong candidates for command and who were better qualified for service at Boston than all except three or four on the king's list. James Johnston (1724–97), the son of a Dublin army agent, and George Preston, a Scot without aristocratic lineage, were dragoons officers who had made their reputations in Germany: Johnston, by capturing a regiment of French cavalry near Warburg in July 1760, commanding a brigade successfully in 1762, and gaining the particular esteem of the allied commander, Prince Ferdinand of Brunswick; Preston, by distinguishing himself repeatedly in battle during the War of the Austrian Succession and the Seven Years' War.[44] Conversely, Henry Fletcher Campbell and John Hale were officers of foot who had distinguished themselves in North America. Campbell, a member of the Scottish gentry, had won unusually rapid promotion for his efforts as a regimental commander at Louisbourg, Quebec, and Martinique. Hale,

---

[43] *Gentleman's Magazine* 71 (1801):483; Richard Cannon, *Historical Record of the Seventieth Regiment . . . of Foot . . .* (London, 1849), p. 16; Namier and Brooke, *House of Commons*, 2:529; Gertrude Kimball, ed., *Correspondence of William Pitt . . . with Colonial Governors and Military and Naval Commanders in America*, 2 vols. (London, 1906), 2:129; *Alumni Dublinenses*, Walsh; Pargellis, ed., *Military Affairs in North America*, p. 450; Richard Cannon, *Historical Record of the Fifty-Sixth or the West Essex Regiment of Foot . . . 1755 . . . to 1844* (London, 1844), p. 56; Johnston, *Great Britain and Ireland*, pp. 346, 245.

[44] *Gentleman's Magazine* 67 (1797):1077, 55 (1785):157; Dalton, *George the First's Army*, 2:365; Barker and Stenning, eds., *Record of Old Westminsters*, 1:521; Charles Philip DeAinslie, *Historical Record of the First or the Royal Regiment of Dragoons* (London, 1887), pp. 92–97; *Army List of 1740*, p. 8; John W. Fortescue, *A History of the 17th Lancers . . .* (London, 1895), pp. 29, 188.

whose father had been a baron of the exchequer and whose brother was a major general, had so impressed his superiors during the campaigns of 1758 and 1759 that he was given the honor of bearing the dispatches that announced Wolfe's victory at Quebec.[45]

Johnston, Preston, Campbell, and Hale were experienced and distinguished officers. But they were not—all considered—better prospects to command a British army than Howe, Clinton, or Burgoyne. Neither Hale nor Johnston seemed eager for further active service: Hale had given up his colonelcy of a regiment for a military sinecure in 1770, and Johnston had accepted and then resigned the governorship of Quebec in the autumn of 1774.[46] Although Preston and Campbell had retained their colonelcies and may have aspired to command, neither had great personal or political standing to complement his military reputation. An officer was not required to be English or to have offices and titles to be eligible for command. Yet, as the officer corps was a complex hierarchy of military reputation, social standing, and political power, it was clearly easier for an Englishman of aristocratic birth and political importance than for a Scot of no prominence to exercise command. It is not, therefore, unfair to say that Preston and Campbell were not so well qualified for command as Howe, Clinton, or Burgoyne—even though all seem to have had comparable military service and reputations.

The king's decisions of 1775—to keep Gage as commander in chief and to send Howe, Clinton, and Burgoyne

---

[45] *Gentleman's Magazine* 73 (1803):292, 76 (1806):295; *Army List of 1740*, p. 71; Richard Trimen, *An Historical Memoir of the 35th Royal Sussex Regiment of Foot* (Southampton, 1873); Fortescue, *History of the 17th Lancers*, pp. 4–29; Charles Townshend, *The Military Life of Field-Marshal George First Marquess Townshend: 1724–1807* ... (London, 1901), pp. 247–48; *Dictionary of National Biography*, Sir Bernard Hale.

[46] Barrington to Hale, Dec. 5, 24, 1770, Apr. 23, 1771, Barrington Letter Book; Robert Beatson, *A Political Index to the Histories of Great Britain and Ireland or A Complete Register of the Hereditary Honours, Public Offices, and Persons in Office from the Earliest Periods to the Present Time* (Edinburgh, 1786), pp. 145–46; Paul David Nelson, *General Horatio Gates: A Biography* (Baton Rouge, 1976), pp. 10, 33–34.

to assist him—were, then, clearly plausible. Those decisions were shaped not just by a system that yielded few senior officers with the competence and desire to be a commander in chief but also by the king's determination to work within that system, to respect the wishes of individual officers, and to adhere to seniority in making appointments. The system itself—a system of promoting, retaining, and employing senior officers—severely limited the king's choices. Because generals did not formally retire and because the king and his ministers deliberately sought to limit the total number of generals, only forty-nine officers had been advanced from colonel to general since 1762.[47] No wonder that in 1775 nearly half of all generals lacked the health or competence for active service and that, allowing for those who were already employed or who were politically or personally undesirable, only about one-third could even be considered for command. Of that one-third perhaps twelve were genuinely well qualified: two generals, one lieutenant general, and nine major generals.

The king's choice among the twelve was further limited by his determination to respect the wishes of each man and to adhere to seniority in his appointments. Had the king been willing to put more pressure on officers senior to Gage or to choose someone junior to him, he might well have found a replacement who had more talent and enthusiasm for crushing the rebellion. But in January 1775 the king was unwilling to jeopardize morale in an effort to get a better commander in chief. He tried to persuade Amherst; and when Amherst refused, he decided at once to keep Gage. There was no other general senior to Gage who was preferable to him, unemployed, and willing to serve; and the most promising generals junior to Gage were very junior indeed. (Howe, who was senior to Clinton and Burgoyne, stood one hundred eleventh among one hundred nineteen generals.)[48] The king was not entirely satisfied with Gage, but he was not ready in early

---

[47] *A List of the General and Field-Officers . . . for 1775* (and *Lists* for 1759, 1768, 1772).

[48] *A List of the General and Field-Officers . . . for 1775* (and *Lists* for 1759, 1768, 1772).

1775 to replace him with an unwilling senior officer or a most junior major general.

Events did not seem to warrant such a departure from his usual way of making appointments. In February of 1775 most Englishmen believed that the colonists would be unable to resist regular troops and that Gage, with reinforcements and the assistance of Howe, Clinton, and Burgoyne, would soon end rebellion in New England and restore order throughout America. Few appreciated the extent of colonial unrest or the difficulties of using force successfully in America. The king would have preferred Amherst as commander in chief, but he assumed that Gage, with his major generals, would be equal to the tasks at Boston. Indeed, it would be some months and several defeats before the king changed his mind—before he was willing to recall Gage and rely primarily on Howe. It would be much longer before he elevated a colonel to an important command in America.[49]

What, then, were the consequences of the king's efforts to find commanders among those few generals who had both the competence and the desire to serve? How did his efforts affect the conduct of the American war? Because there were so few viable prospects for command, it is likely that the king was all too willing to minimize the faults of those under consideration. Gage had been an indecisive commander and now talked of compromise, but Gage was at Boston and he was willing to stay there as commander in chief. Similarly, when Howe, Clinton, and Burgoyne agreed to serve, it was easy to forget that Howe had been publicly critical of coercive measures, that Clinton was comparatively inexperienced as a commander, and that Burgoyne was perhaps too ambitious to be entirely reliable. Beyond that, with such a small number to choose from, it was nearly impossible to consider how individuals might work together.

The king chose men who proved far less effective, individually and collectively, than he expected. Gage's irresolute behavior merely inspired the rebels and encouraged his major generals to develop the pernicious habit of criticizing their chief and each other. Howe, preoccupied with conciliation,

[49] Gruber, *Howe Brothers*, pp. 20–42.

proved incapable of developing a consistent strategy or of cooperating with Burgoyne; Burgoyne, obsessed with fame, destroyed his reputation and his army in a desperate campaign in the hinterlands of New York; and Clinton, incapable of managing authority, could neither work well with others nor act decisively on his own. In short, George III did his best to choose able commanders for the American war without violating the wishes or seniority of his general officers. But a restrictive system of promoting, retaining, and selecting officers yielded men of only ordinary talent for a most extraordinary war.

PIERS MACKESY

What the British Army Learned

ABOUT FIFTEEN YEARS after the close of the War of Independence, a British officer who had served in America put together two volumes of his memoirs and opinions. Col. George Hanger had fallen on hard times. He had seen the inside of a debtors' prison and was now making a living as a coal merchant. But once he had been an officer in the First Regiment of Guards, and in the American War he had served with the crack companies of Hessian riflemen under Col. Ludwig von Wurmb. He claimed to be an even better shot with a rifle than his old companion Maj. Patrick Ferguson, inventor of the Ferguson rifle, who had lost his life at King's Mountain in 1780. Here surely must be a man who could have told one at first hand about the innovations of the American War. The seeker after insight peruses chapter after chapter of scandalous anecdote and eccentric opinions till he comes at length to the moment when George Hanger embarks for America to join the Hessians. At last the reader seems to stand on the verge of illumination. But the author addresses him thus: "Reader, be not alarmed! I am not going to fight over the American War; it is as much forgotten as the Trojan War, and the recital of the one would be full as interesting to the public as the other."[1]

One might excuse Colonel Hanger for his indifference to the lessons of the American War because he was writing in the seventh year of another great struggle that had seen even greater changes in the art of war. Alternatively, however, one could see his words as evidence that the British army never

---

[1] *The Life, Adventures and Opinions of Colonel George Hanger ...*, 2 vols. (London, 1801), 2:351. Much of the work was evidently written before the middle of 1799.

learned from the past, a belief firmly held in recent years by that controversial military polemicist Capt. Basil Liddell Hart. British experience with amphibious warfare at the end of the eighteenth century would seem to support the view. In January 1799 Gen. John Graves Simcoe, a veteran of the American War in which he had commanded the Queen's Rangers, was urging that another American veteran, Sir Charles Stuart, who was commander in the Mediterranean at Minorca, should be given 10,000 troops and a naval squadron with carte blanche to attack the Italian coast. "It is a wrong fashion to decry the American education," he concluded; "the conjunct expedition of army and navy had arrived at great perfection, and this is an invaluable branch of our profession in our present situation."[2] Indeed it was, with Britain excluded from her Continental bridgeheads and reduced to amphibious attacks. Yet when 10,000 troops were landed in Holland later in the year, they were put on to the beaches in indescribable confusion. The experience of organizing the boats for a military landing, gained in America by men like Com. William Hotham, seemed to have been totally forgotten. It was only after a further muddle at Cadiz the following year that the problem was taken in hand by Sir Ralph Abercromby and a drill rehearsed for the Egyptian landing of March 1801. The trouble stemmed from the convention of the day that it was the navy's responsibility to land the troops on the beaches. An experienced commodore was needed who would work closely with the general, and perhaps it was the navy rather than the army that had dissipated its knowledge.

That the army, too, was guilty of forgetting was hinted in 1788 by the distinguished physician Dr. John Hunter, who had been the senior medical officer in Jamaica during the American War. Five years after the end of the war he lamented that the lessons learned about hygiene in the West Indies had been forgotten. "The useful experience of one war has been lost before the commencement of another."[3] Is

---

[2] To Henry Addington (for Pitt), Jan. 29, 1799, Sidmouth Papers, Devon Record Office.

[3] Alan Jamieson, "War in the Leeward Islands, 1775–1783," Ph.D. diss., Oxford University, 1981, p. 95. Hunter had established the damaging ef-

What the British Army Learned

that, after all, the truth? Did the British learn no lessons from the war? In one sense, of course, they could not fail to learn: there is no substitute for active service to teach the soldier. One sees this clearly in the Hessian army, which emerged ten years later at the beginning of the French Revolutionary wars as the crack troops of Germany, whose minor tactics astonished the Prussians and excelled those of the French. But if the Hessians benefited from the practical experience of war, the British army needed that experience even more. At home in peacetime it had scarcely been possible to conduct efficient field training at a level higher than that of the individual soldier. The battalions were broken up and scattered in small parties, perpetually on the move to keep public order in the absence of a police force, or supporting the revenue officers in antismuggling patrols. There were few barracks except in Ireland, so the units were quartered in public houses scattered through the towns. This was burdensome for landlords, and close association with the locals encouraged desertion, so quarters were constantly being changed. If there was a militia muster in the town, or a fair or a race-meeting, the regulars were moved out to make room and avoid fights, and were dispersed still more widely in the surrounding country villages, scarcely under the supervision of their company commander. Tactical training under these conditions was next to impossible; if the company officers attempted to teach the fundamental minor skills of patrolling, ambushes, and outpost duties, they found Farmer John Bull blocking the gateway to every field and wood, proclaiming the rights of property and warning the redcoats off his land.

Once a year the battalion was assembled and trained for ten days for the annual inspection, the only time when it was likely to be seen by a general. But combined training of more than one battalion was almost unheard of. There were no permanent camps in Great Britain with enough room for a brigade exercise, and in Ireland, there was only Phoenix Park

---

fect of drinking rum, having observed the connection between new rum and lead poisoning, but the drinking of the deadly brew continued unabated (Roger N. Buckley, *Slaves in Red Coats: The British West India Regiments, 1795–1815* [New Haven, 1979], pp. 100–101).

in Dublin. In wartime some of the troops were assembled in camps to meet invasion, and generals had an opportunity to command a brigade on field days. But America was an incomparably better training area. Here generals had an opportunity to command brigades in the field; Howe, Clinton, and Cornwallis commanded small armies. Company officers practiced the "little war" of outposts and patrols in real country against a real enemy. They returned from the war as seasoned soldiers, full of the practical knowledge that peacetime England could not provide. Their morale was unimpaired, and men like General Simcoe were to look back on the British army in America as the touchstone by which they measured the quality of their later commands.[4]

Practical experience, then, was the first lesson of the war, and it was an important one for the British army. But surely there were lessons more profound and general? The American theater of war was unique in history. The strategic problems of how to seek a decision were new. The nation-in-arms was seen in embryo for the first time. Guerrilla warfare and the control of an armed and hostile population were problems seen in a new form. There were hints of a new concept of discipline. Open-order tactics and skirmishing were used as never before. Do we not see in these developments the seedbed of the new warfare of the French Revolution and Napoleon?

Before one asks what the British learned, then, one needs to look at the lessons they were offered. In the higher strategy of the campaigns in America there was nothing that foreshadowed the coming developments in Europe. When the great military theorist Karl von Clausewitz looked back on the Napoleonic era, he saw at the heart of the system the search for decision: a decision to be achieved by an overwhelming blow at what he called the enemy's center of gravity, to paralyze the enemy's will and destroy his capacity to

[4] Simcoe to Addington, Feb. 27, 1799, Sidmouth Papers. For the peacetime conditions of the army, I have drawn on J. A. Houlding, *Fit for Service: The Training of the British Army, 1715–1795* (Oxford, 1981). See also Col. David Dundas, *Principles of Military Movements, Chiefly Applied to Infantry* (London, 1788), pp. i–iii, 12, 15, appendix, p. 87.

fight. Such a blow was struck against the Prussian army at Jena in 1806; at Austria's army and Austria's capital city on several occasions. But where was the center of gravity of the American rebellion? This loose confederation had no centralized administration to be overthrown by the occupation of a capital city, no common economic interest whose destruction would bring down the edifice. Was the center of gravity of the rebellion to be found in the Continental army? It was unassailable; for Washington's aim was to avoid or postpone decision, and he could do so by withdrawing into inaccessible country and impregnable positions. Was the center of gravity in the people? Perhaps; and a strategy of counterinsurgency was worked out by the British, with hopes of success that were not wholly irrational. But there were no lessons here that could be applied in the next war in the centralized nation-states of western and central Europe. When the state administrations of Europe capitulated to the victor, the population capitulated too.

There were lessons to be learned about how an occupying force might control hostile insurgents. John Shy has shown how in a sense the Revolutionary War was won before a shot was fired, when the Revolutionary activists secured control of the institutions of authority and coercion.[5] Above all, they secured control of the militias. Thereafter the loyalists stood no chance. They could not organize a counterforce, for they were disarmed, atomized, and terrorized. If the British temporarily returned to an area, the demoralized loyalists were immediately swamped again on their departure. The American militias secured the rear areas of the Continental army in the field, disrupted the British rear areas, and in emergencies joined the Continental forces in battle. This was appreciated by the British government, and in the southern campaigns of 1780–81 a deliberate effort was made to organize a counterforce of loyalist militia. Whether the British linked the events in America to the problem they faced dur-

---

[5]"The American Revolution: The Military Conflict Considered as a Revolutionary War," in Stephen G. Kurtz and James H. Hutson, eds., *Essays on the American Revolution* (Chapel Hill, N.C., 1973), pp. 121–56.

ing the French Revolution is hard to demonstrate. After the British army was excluded from Europe in 1795, the foreign secretary, Lord Grenville, and his colleagues and successors always included the aid of native insurgents as an indispensable element in every invasion plan. They were often disappointed, as the secretary of state for war, Henry Dundas, had foretold: "I cannot forget the American war, where we were so miserably disappointed in the promised and expected cooperation." In Holland in 1799 the peasants "lounged about with their pipes in their mouths, as silent and sullen spectators of an unpleasant disturbance";[6] and in France disconnected risings were put down by republican forces that the British army was incapable of warding off. Nowhere could the British maintain a lodgment or protect a native insurrection against the masses of the French armies until in 1808 they found a secure bridgehead in a remote corner of Europe, in Portugal.

One theater, however, afforded a more direct parallel with the American problem. In Ireland, unlike Continental Europe but like America, insurgents were enemies to be contained, not friends to encourage. Here was a true civil war, and a strong British military presence. Whether the Irish government and commanders consciously applied the lessons of America may be hard to demonstrate, but in the 1790s the Dublin administration made sure that its friends were not disarmed and helpless when the explosion came. Seen as a military problem, there was another parallel with the American War. In America the tension had been acute for the British army between concentration and dispersal: it had to concentrate to fight the Continental army, yet it had to disperse to maintain internal security and protect its friends. The problem was the same in Ireland. The regular forces had to be ready to concentrate to meet a French invasion, but in the words of the duke of Wellington, "Ireland, in a view to military operations, must be considered an enemy's

---

[6] Historical Manuscripts Commission, . . . *Report on the Manuscripts of J. B. Fortescue . . . Preserved at Dropmore . . .*, 10 vols. (London, 1892–1927), 5:215; Sir Henry Bunbury, *Narratives of Some Passages in the Great War with France (1799–1810)* (London, 1927), p. 7.

country."[7] If the army concentrated, it would lose control of the countryside. Anarchy and confusion would ensue, and a hostile Catholic peasantry would terrorize the landlords and Protestants and play havoc on the army's lines of supply. The Irish government's answer was to ensure that its friends were armed when the crisis came. The militia remained under loyalist control, and two years before open rebellion broke out in 1798, the loyalist Irish yeomanry were raised for local service and security duties. "God and the yeomanry saved the capital," the commander in chief declared when the rebellion came. The humane Lord Cornwallis, who came over from England as viceroy to cope with the crisis, described the yeomen as being "in the style of the loyalists in America, only much more numerous and powerful, and a thousand times more ferocious." "These men have saved the country," he admitted reluctantly. However atrocious the yeomanry's conduct may have been—and one must remember Nathanael Greene's dismay at the excesses on both sides in the civil war in the Carolinas—the government in Dublin had not allowed its authority to slide out of its hands for want of determination and force to defend it.[8]

The role of the civil population in the American struggle raises two further considerations: the idea of "the nation-in-arms" and the European intellectuals' search for the "natural man." Both were sought in America, but the British found neither. The nation-in-arms, as it was to emerge in Revolutionary France, required a compound of popular enthusiasm with a very powerful centralized government. The achievement of the Revolutionary government in Paris was to put

---

[7] K. P. Ferguson, "The Army in Ireland from the Restoration to the Act of Union," Ph.D. diss., Dublin University, 1981, p. 123.

[8] Ibid., pp. 157, 161. Ferguson cites an earlier disturbance of 1793 in County Wexford, when the commander of a party of infantry went forward to speak to the mob and was killed with scythe. The soldiers immediately fired and put the mob to flight. A French traveler saw in the incident "a perfect parallel to the revolution in France in its beginnings." If the authorities had temporized or parleyed with the rebels, "instead of 3000 they would have numbered 30,000, and in all probability they would have destroyed the government" (ibid., p. 187).

huge armies in the field; when those armies melted away through battle and privation, they could be replaced by conscription from the vast reservoir of French manpower. No machinery capable of doing this had existed in Europe before this time, and no such machinery was created in America: no Committee of Public Safety, no semaphore telegraph bearing the government's decrees instantly to every headquarters and every provincial authority, and above all, no guillotine. The Continental army was therefore starved of men and resources; it was often barely able to exist, its wastage either not replaced or replaced with the scum and flotsam of the states. There was no image here to suggest to the British imagination a future of vast conscript armies flooding across Europe. The "nation-in-arms" of the French Revolution was national and offensive; service in the American militia was essentially local and defensive.

Nor did the British find the image of the "natural man" in America, though other Europeans may have done so. Military publications in Europe had been obsessed since the middle of the eighteenth century by "the little war," *la petite guerre*: the war of posts and ambushes. But the soldiers suitable for this kind of war must not be the clockwork automata of the mechanically drilled regular forces: they must act naturally and instinctively. "Nature," Peter Paret has observed of these publications, "is the great underlying theme."[9] Like the philosophers, the European military writers feasted their imagination on fantasies of the New World. Here they thought they had found the "natural man" who was to be the ingredient of a new kind of war. The British who actually fought in America, however, did not find it. If they found a model for the light infantryman of the future, it was not the American rifleman but the Hessian Jäger. Light infantry tactics were not for amateurs. They required a higher training and an even truer discipline than the tactics of the line. These qualities were found at their best, not in free Americans, but in the docile subjects of a German despot. In the eyes of a Brit-

---

[9] "Colonial Experience and European Military Reform at the End of the Eighteenth Century," *Bulletin of the Institute of Historical Research* 37 (1964):57–59.

ish officer in 1776, the Hessians provided "riflemen . . . as much superior to those of the rebels as it is possible to imagine."[10]

With the mention of riflemen one is brought down from the commanding heights of the new warfare to the nuts and bolts—from political organization and movements of peoples to the machinery of armies. At this level the essential new ingredients of French Revolutionary warfare were a simplified supply system, self-contained divisions of all arms, and changes in tactics. The new supply system consisted of a shift from dependence on magazines to living off the country by requisitioning. It was not a system that could be applied in America. In the American War both armies requisitioned; but when a British force of any size was on the move, the country it could control did not provide enough for its daily needs, and an army of 20,000 men (tiny by European standards though very large for America) consumed thirty-three tons of food a day. Such a force needed a large wagon train to sustain it; and as each wagon was hauled by two or four horses, the problem was multiplied by the need for forage. Virtually all provisions and forage had to be imported from the British Isles, and the army on campaign could not afford to be more than a few miles from a navigable river to supply its magazines.[11] Provisioning had always been a laborious and methodical business in America, most of all in the northern parts, where Amherst's advance by the Mohawk route to Montreal in 1760 had been more a matter of pushing forward his lines of supply than of fighting. The duke of Wellington was to put the matter succinctly in 1812: "In such countries as America, very extensive, thinly peopled, and producing but little food in proportion to their extent, military operations by large bodies are impracticable, unless the party carrying them on has the uninterrupted use of a navigable river, or very extensive means of land transport, which

---

[10] Rodney Atwood, *The Hessians: Mercenaries from Hessen-Kassel in the American Revolution* (Cambridge, 1980), p. 69.

[11] For British supply problems, see R. Arthur Bowler, *Logistics and the Failure of the British Army in America, 1775–1783* (Princeton, 1975).

such a country can rarely supply." This constraint had no real parallel in the populous agricultural lands of western and central Europe, but there was a parallel in the bleak Iberian Peninsula, where Wellington organized elaborate river lines of supply from his ports to the front. In the winter of 1812 he forced his opponent, Marshal Marmont, to concentrate his forces, with the result that the French troops could not collect their supplies from the scattered and impoverished population and became dependent on the old-fashioned system of supply depots. "Marmont says he can do nothing without magazines," Wellington wrote happily, "which is quite a new era in the modern French military system."[12] It was indeed, and Washington had imposed the same constrictions on the British. It was in a colonial theater that Wellington had learned the rigid control of supplies that enabled him to cope with Spanish conditions. But not in America: it was in India that he had learned, as he said, "to count bags."

America, then, provided no lessons in logistics for the new warfare of western Europe, though it did suggest how, in a primitive country, a hostile population might make the new logistics difficult. Nor did the American War point the way toward the self-sufficient division. The advantages of permanent divisions composed of all arms had been advocated in Europe since the middle of the eighteenth century. Such formations would allow an army to advance on a broad front, using many roads, which simplified supply, speeded movement, and made operations more flexible. Independent divisions did not appear in America, nor, perhaps, would they have been particularly useful on American terrain and on the limited American road system, though mixed tactical units, such as the Queen's Rangers and Tarleton's Legion, were introduced for special operations. So for operational lessons one turns at last to seek them in tactics.

Tactical reform was developing in Europe and in America in two opposite directions. More will be said later of what was

---

[12] Lt. Col. Gurwood, comp., *Selections from the Dispatches and General Orders of Field Marshal the Duke of Wellington*, new ed. (London, 1851), pp. 518, 792.

What the British Army Learned

happening in Europe, but in essence the improved firepower of infantry following the introduction of the late seventeenth-century flintlock had caused armies to deploy in line to maximize firepower, though still closed up tightly to ward off cavalry. What was peculiar to America had already been identified during the French and Indian wars of the middle of the century. Infantry had no cavalry to fear, and the tactics that became characteristic of America developed from what one might call bush fighting, in the dense country of the west and north. In such terrain and against the Indian marksmen, troops fighting shoulder to shoulder in rigid lines and firing volleys at invisible enemies were useless. Amherst and Montcalm trained their men in individual aimed fire instead of unaimed volleys. Light infantry were raised and trained in open-order skirmishing tactics, to prevent ambushes and to cope with the enemy, hidden among the trees, who had destroyed General Braddock's column in 1755. In places where open country allowed more orthodox line formations to be used—such as the Heights of Abraham outside Quebec—the troops fought in two ranks instead of the customary three and in looser order than the arm-to-arm formations of Europe.[13]

From the British performance during the retreat from Concord in 1775, one might suppose that in the interval between the wars all these lessons had been forgotten. That was the impression of the new secretary of state, Lord George Germain, who guessed from reports of the fighting that the troops had repeated Braddock's mistakes, keeping together and firing volleys against an enemy who stayed in cover and refused to stand up and face them in the open.[14] Those troops, however, had been cooped up in a difficult garrison, and one should be cautious of generalizing from their performance. The British remembered the lessons of the earlier war and adapted more rapidly to American conditions than the ac-

---

[13] Peter Paret, *Yorck and the Era of Prussian Reform, 1807–1815* (Princeton, 1966), p. 39; Houlding, *Fit for Service*, p. 373; information from Glenn Steppler.

[14] Historical Manuscripts Commission, *Report on the Manuscripts of Mrs. Stopford-Sackville . . .*, 2 vols. (London, 1904–10), 2:2.

tions of 1775 might suggest. In England a light infantry company had been added to every battalion five years before the outbreak of revolution in America, and some of them were collected together and trained by William Howe, who was to become General Gage's successor as commander in chief in America. Howe was an expert in light infantry and a firm believer in two ranks for colonial warfare. For the landing on Long Island in 1776 he resumed the practice of fighting in two ranks and even imposed it on the Hessians.[15] To the envy of the Hessians, the uniforms of the newly arriving British reinforcements had already been modified to take account of American conditions. The Hessians were skeptical, however, about the loose British line, for which an interval of six inches between the files had been officially prescribed. Though they adopted the two-deep order, the Hessian files remained closed up arm to arm. But they were to be converted by experience. They found that the British in looser order could advance faster and that the closed-up Hessian line fell back thirty paces behind the British in every hundred they advanced. In 1781 the senior Hessian general, Freiherr von Knyphausen, asked his sovereign, the landgraf of Hessen, for permission to open out the line. But his request was refused because, said Landgraf Friedrich II, "the whole force of the infantry and of every attack comes solely from good order with fully closed up ranks and line."[16]

There spoke a European with no experience of American warfare. The disadvantage of this heavy formation was that it was too slow to close with the enemy—an enemy who was totally vulnerable to the bayonet when armed with the rifle and who even when armed with musket and bayonet and drilled conventionally was often too raw and unsteady to stand a charge of veterans.[17] The open line of two ranks was con-

[15] Atwood, *The Hessians*, p. 61.

[16] Ibid., pp. 243–44. Glenn Steppler informs me that the Guards modified their clothing and were issued some special items before they arrived in America in 1776, evidently acting on experience gained in America in the previous wars.

[17] Sergeant Lamb describes a charge at Guilford Courthouse in 1781, "in excellent order, in a smart run, with arms charged" (R. Lamb, *An Orig-*

sidered safe in America because there had always been relatively few enemy regular troops in the theater and, more importantly, very few cavalry. It is true that in a suspect passage of self-justification Banastre Tarleton blamed the open order of the British files for his defeat at Cowpens in 1781; but the imputation was forcefully refuted by another British officer, and the defeat owed more to Tarleton's inexperience in handling a combined force of some size than to his infantry's tactics.[18] British tactical practice in the American War has not yet been thoroughly investigated, and much research in regimental archives would be needed to escape from generalizations based mainly on a few memoirs of the early campaigns. It is clear, however, that the British army retained the tactics of the line, with a looser formation and more use of light infantry.

The American regulars, of course, fought very largely with the same linear tactics as the British. Aided by Baron von Steuben, Washington drilled his army to fight the war in the Middle Colonies in line formations. Perhaps he need not have done so, and Professor Shy has suggested that his choice was made for conservative social reasons.[19] If Charles Lee had had his way, there might have been no drillmaster Steuben, and the war would have been fought in a style that Lee, a former British officer, regarded as peculiarly suited to the American character. The British would have been harassed by guerrilla bands drawn from the militia, and if necessary the Americans would have withdrawn into the rough country west of the Susquehanna, where they would have been inaccessible to British logistics. But the social price of such a protracted civil war would have been too high. Guerrilla bands easily became bandits, recognizing no law but their own survival; and such warfare easily slid into feuding and vendet-

---

inal and Authentic Journal of Occurences during the American War [Dublin, 1809], p. 361).

[18] Roderick Mackenzie, *Strictures on Lt. Col. Tarleton's History of the Campaigns of 1780 and 1781, in the Southern Provinces of North America* (London, 1787), pp. 114–16.

[19] George A. Billias, ed., *George Washington's Generals* (New York, 1964), pp. 41, 47.

tas. It could have torn apart the social fabric of the Middle Colonies and Virginia as it was to do in the Carolinas toward the end of the struggle. Instead, Washington chose to dispute the possession of the cultivated country of the east and observe the laws of war, and that meant using disciplined regular troops trained in the tactics of Europe.

What did the British army learn from all this? The officers who had served in America came home believing firmly in two loose ranks for combining firepower and movement, they were skeptical of the shock produced by a slow-moving deep formation against a mobile enemy skilled in musketry, and they had learned to regard light troops as a vital component of the major battle as well as of the little war of posts.

But this corpus of beliefs was not incorporated into drill manuals and formal doctrine. The army returned to the usual British peacetime administration. The regiments, which had returned with depleted numbers from the western theaters, sank to a low peacetime establishment and became too weak and scattered for effective training.[20] Worse still, perhaps, the post of commander in chief lapsed, as was usual in peacetime, so there was no effective authority to impose a uniform system. The battalions that returned from Canada, New York, the Carolinas, the Caribbean, and India each brought the habits and practices of their own theater and their own experience. Some battalions used the 1778 drill book, others stuck to the 1764 book, and still others used a mixture of the two with individual variations; some commanding officers even used systems of their own invention. "It is our misfortune to have had no line of conduct laid down," Col. David Dundas complained: "The good order of regiments has less depended on the rules of the service, than on the accidental efforts of individuals, and on the fashion of the day."[21]

From this chaos the army was rescued by a Scottish colonel and an English prince. The Scotsman was Col. David Dundas (1735–1820), a veteran of the Seven Years' War who was later to rise to the post of commander in chief. In 1788 Colonel

---

[20] The point is made in J. L. Pimlott, "The Administration of the British Army, 1783–1793," Ph.D. diss., University of Leicester, 1975.

[21] *Principles of Military Movements*, p. 11.

Dundas published his *Principles of Military Movements*, in which he analyzed the defects of the British infantry: the absence of a common set of regulations and the lack of brigade training. Dundas put forward a system whose adoption would, he hoped, "put an end to the uncertain practices of our service; the prevalence of review show; of loose desultory movements, and consequent unconnected support; of want of solidity, etc." Four years later Dundas's system was incorporated by Dundas himself in the *Regulations* of 1792, but some time elapsed before they were enforced. To quote Wellington yet again: "Nobody in the British army ever reads a regulation or an order as if it were to be a guide to his conduct, or in any other manner than as an amusing novel."[22]

What was needed was a commander in chief to enforce the *Regulations*. On the outbreak of war in 1793 Amherst was reappointed commander in chief, but he was too old to tackle the problem, and the army was thrown into confusion by mobilization and the hasty cobbling of battalions strong enough for the field from the understrength peacetime establishment. It was not till Amherst was replaced in 1795 by King George's second son, Frederick, duke of York, that Dundas's *Regulations* were enforced and uniformity began to descend on British tactics.

It was a uniformity that explicitly rejected the American experience. In America the regiments had learned to fight an enemy who had little cavalry, and this, wrote Dundas, had encouraged "the present loose and irregular system of our infantry." A fad for light infantry had come to dominate battalion training and attracted all the notice at reviews; the battalion companies had learned to undervalue themselves and to forget "that light infantry—yagers—marksmen—riflemen, &c. &c. vanish before the solid movements of the line."[23]

To remedy the infantry's "want of solidity," Dundas turned to the Prussians. He had not himself served in America, but he had fought five campaigns in Germany and had attended the peacetime maneuvers of Frederick the Great. Following the Prussian example, Dundas required his battalions to form

---

[22] Ibid., pp. i–iv; Gurwood, comp., *Dispatches of Wellington*, p. 650.

[23] *Principles of Military Movements*, pp. 11–13.

in three ranks, one pace apart, with the files closed up so that each man with shouldered arms could just feel the touch of his neighbor's elbow. In this close formation, movement had to be deliberate to preserve order, and Dundas's standard drill step was a slow seventy-five paces to the minute, little more than two miles an hour. The light companies, when not in the line, were allowed to open their files to six inches, and in open order to two feet, and were to maneuver at a hundred and eight paces to the minute, or three miles an hour.

Dundas's system was designed for a warfare that America had never seen: for the clash of great armies in the plains of northern Europe. These armies had masses of highly drilled cavalry, which Frederick had taught to charge home with speed and density. And the French, the enemy that the British would most likely have to face, had learned from the Prussians. Their cavalry were "now capable of a vigorous and united charge, instead of that *en fourageurs* [i.e., *en fourrageurs*, in dispersed order like foragers]: a term implying the disorder in which they formerly attacked."[24]

To cope with this cavalry, the Prussians emphasized "superior order, regularity and weight of fire." But Frederick's close-order system had a more positive aim than just to ward off cavalry. He had brought the linear tactics of the flintlock and bayonet to a peak. Before his time, large modern armies extended in line had become unmanageable. Their ponderous deployment "in the processional manner" had been slow and inflexible, and once ordered, it could not be changed. Frederick found the remedy in the close column of maneuver. As his advanced guard approached the enemy, the relaxed columns of march of the main body would deploy into the close, silent columns of maneuver: columns whose dispositions could be altered without long, detailed orders, columns which could deploy into line in an instant, and which had advanced so exactly in relation to their neighbors that when the line was formed each battalion locked into the flanks of the next. The whole army could wheel rapidly into an unbroken line with no gaps for alert enemy cavalry to penetrate; brigade upon brigade, division upon division, the lines

[24] Ibid., pp. 5–6.

interrupted only by the pairs of light guns on the flanks of the battalions. The British infantry, unaccustomed even to brigade exercises, had not seen such a maneuver for a quarter of a century and was now incapable of performing it. But trained in Dundas's system, British troops could learn to fight as a coherent army, or slot into the order of battle of an allied force. "Famed as we are for the valour of our soldiers, what might not be expected from the ability and zeal of our generals, if the same means of instruction and conduct, which regulates other services, existed in ours."[25]

These close-order tactics were designed to withstand and deliver shock, and for this Dundas maintained that three ranks were needed. Two ranks were useful against "an irregular enemy who deals only in fire"; but the clash of great armies in battle required weight and the capacity to maneuver masses of men in order to bring superior force against a chosen point. Dundas was rejecting American experience in favor of European war as he had known it:

> The great science and object of movement being to act with superiority on chosen points; it is never the intention of an able commander to have all his men at the same time in action; he means by skill and manoeuvre to attack a partial part; and to bring the many to act against the few; this cannot be accomplished by any body in *open* files, and *two* deep. A line formed in this manner would never be brought to make or to stand an attack with bayonets, nor could it have any prospect of resisting the charge of a determined cavalry. In no service is the fire and consistency of the third rank given up; it serves to fill up the vacancies made in the others in action, without it the battalion would soon be in a single rank.[26]

Was Dundas wrong? Not when measured by the thought of his day; and in a sense not even by the test of later experience, for the Frederickian system he describes is remarkably close to the Napoleonic system. The tactical procedures into which he hoped to reabsorb the British army were not

---

[25] Ibid., p. 16.

[26] *Rules and Regulations for the Formations, Field Exercises and Movements of His Majesty's Forces, 1792*, rev. ed. (Dublin, 1803), pp. 75, 77, 95.

the ossified clockwork that its caricaturists have painted but a living and developing system. Frederick had continually improved it, and new ideas were still being tested and incorporated. Even in the British army there had been considerable developments in linear tactics since the 1750s. The battalion firing system had been simplified, while the introduction of many new maneuvers produced greater flexibility and precision without sacrificing speed. When brigade exercises could be arranged, they became more elaborate, and by the 1770s a greater variety of tactical exercises was being introduced into the annual battalion inspections.[27] Across the Channel in France, controversy and experiment were raging. During the American War, when much of the British army was fighting in loose order beyond the Atlantic, the French army preparing to invade England was fighting the battle between the proponents of line and column, the so-called *l'ordre mince* and *l'ordre profond*. The issue, worked out in a series of large exercises in 1778, was to play as prominent a part in the new warfare as was light infantry drill.[28]

But what of the light troops? There were plenty of them in the European armies but they were irregulars, and in war these pandours, Croats, hussars, and Jäger had been confined to the *petite guerre*, the war of outposts, reconnaissance, raids, and ambushes. After the Seven Years' War, however, there was considerable expansion of light forces within the framework of the regular armies. The French were moving toward the integration of skirmishing with the regular tactics of the line, and besides their battalion skirmishers they now had twelve elite battalions of light infantry, trained for mass skirmishing. The inspiration for that development appears to have come from the Seven Years' War and not from the American War. The military manual published in the 1790s by the future reformer of the Prussian army, Gerhard von Scharnhorst, cites more than sixty examples of outpost warfare from the Seven Years' War, but only four from the American War, all of the American examples taken from the

[27] Houlding, *Fit for Service*, pp. 295–99.

[28] Robert S. Quimby, *The Background of Napoleonic Warfare: The Theory of Military Tactics in Eighteenth-Century France* (New York, 1957), ch. 9.

What the British Army Learned

work of the former Hessian Jäger Johann Ewald, which Scharnhorst described as useful but not new. Nevertheless, there was nothing in any of this to prepare the world for the skirmishers of the 1790s. In the early years of the French Revolutionary War, the French skirmishers became for a time the decisive factor in battle. German light infantry were more systematically trained, but their use was still confined to the war of posts, while the French skirmisher became a major element in the battle.[29]

How did it happen? A favorite explanation is psychological: the citizen soldier fighting for a cause could be trusted not to desert, he was better educated and more alert than the long-service automata of the ancien régime, and his patriotism made him willing to fight without the officer's cane and the sergeant's halberd at his back. There is truth in this, but there were also mechanical causes of the upsurge of skirmishing. The French army's peacetime training had been more flexible than that of the Germans; and in war poor training of French recruits and National Guard battalions caused the conventional formations to break up into loose crowds under fire. Mobility and overwhelming superiority of numbers enabled the French armies to smother their enemies in protracted battles of attrition without formal assaults or close-order fighting.

Where does this leave Dundas and the eighteen prescribed maneuvers of his drill book? Not looking very credible, it might seem. And indeed Dundas omitted two factors from his calculations that were to be crucial for a time in the 1790s. He did not foresee the temporary collapse of the French cavalry in the Revolution, which made his close order less necessary for a time, and he forgot the agricultural revolution. It was Germany that he knew; but in much of Belgium, where the British army was to fight, the open fields had given way to enclosures. Among small fields enclosed by hedges and ditches, checkered with orchards and copses, and traversed by narrow, fenced lanes, infantry could not deploy in regular lines nor cavalry form for the charge. If they tried to form, sharpshooters in the hedges shot them down; if they at-

---

[29] Paret, *Yorck*, pp. 40–42, 72, 77–78.

tacked, the unseen enemy was protected by the hedges and ditches that broke the cohesion of the charge. From the French frontier the allied armies were hustled and harried back to Holland by overwhelming numbers through hedgerows, orchards, and farmyards. In patches of open country their cavalry could still win resounding successes, but these did not avail against the relentless pressure in the hedgerows.

What did the British to do meet the new warfare? In the West Indies two veterans of the American war, Gen. Sir Charles Grey and Col. Eyre Coote, exercised their light infantry for colonial warfare; Coote's instructions specifically alluded to his American experience and the paucity of light infantry drill in Dundas's regulations. In Portugal in 1796–97 another veteran of America, Sir Charles Stuart, formed a battalion of flank companies whose training he supervised in light infantry drill.[30] But in England nothing was done for a long time. Dundas's system prevailed unmodified, and there was no official attempt to recover the experience gained in America. Yet the need for light troops to resist invasion was great. Another American veteran, Cornwallis, mourned the lack of them: "The system of David Dundas and the total want of light infantry sit heavy on my mind."[31] Between the capital and the enemy landing places on the coasts of Kent and Essex, the country was densely enclosed. Light troops would be needed, and the enemy could land few cavalry to trouble them. John Moore, the future general, recently back from the bush warfare of the West Indies and surveying the preparations against invasion in East Anglia in 1797, noted that "to prevent the progress of an enemy marching to Colchester when landed would require a great superiority of

---

[30] J. F. C. Fuller, *Sir John Moore's System of Training* (London, 1925), p. 43; information from Glenn Steppler, derived from the Coote papers, which are no longer accessible. I am very grateful to Mr. Steppler for this and the other information acknowledged here. It is interesting that General Moore and Colonel Manningham (first commanding officer of the experimental rifle corps, later the Ninety-fifth and then the Rifle Brigade) served in the West Indies during the irregular phase of fighting in the 1790s.

[31] Charles Ross, ed., *Correspondence of Charles, First Marquis Cornwallis*, 3 vols. (London, 1859), 2:333.

light troops."[32] But where were such troops? Sir Henry Clinton's son expressed his anxiety to a cabinet minister at "the total want of light infantry." About the same time, in early 1798, Sir William Howe conducted exercises on the Essex coast with an experimental battle group of light troops, consisting of two troops of light horse, thirteen companies of light infantry drawn from the regiments of the line and militia, and a detachment of a new horse artillery. He told the same cabinet minister that much light infantry was needed and that the great difficulty in training them was to teach them to disperse. It is notable that these opinions all come from veterans of America and the Caribbean. Evidently in some minds the lessons of American warfare survived.[33]

In the following year, 1799, the want of light infantry training was sorely felt in the expedition to Holland, when French infantry disrupted General Moore's advance through the sand dunes to Egmond aan Zee. The British infantry, wrote a Highland officer, were "perfectly unacquainted with the system of sharp-shooting (and it is impossible not to lament the want of that species of warfare in our army)."[34] Shades of Simcoe and his Queen's Rangers!—that green-clad loyalist regiment in America, which had learned to aim its

---

[32] J. F. Maurice, ed., *The Diary of Sir John Moore*, 2 vols. (London, 1904), 1:267. Moore, soon to be one of the best younger generals in the British army, is remembered as the man who trained the first British light infantry brigade in 1803–4, and commanded the retreat to Corunna in 1808, where he was killed.

[33] Mrs. H. Baring, ed., *Diary of the Rt. Hon. William Windham* (London, 1866), pp. 386, 392, 395. General Money, who wrote an often quoted pamphlet at the same time (see, for example, J. F. C. Fuller, *British Light Infantry in the Eighteenth Century* [London, 1925], pp. 200–204), argued that both cavalry and conventional infantry would be helpless in defending the enclosed approaches to London: "Is there between London and Harwich, or Ipswich, any ground on which three squadrons of horse can form, without being in reach of musketry from the hedgerows on their front and flanks?" Nor, he wrote, could infantry form up in such country in the presence of advancing enemies: "meet them as you ought with men armed and trained, to dispute hedgerow after hedgerow."

[34] Piers Mackesy, *Statesmen at War: The Strategy of Overthrow, 1798–1799* (London, 1974), p. 290n.

fire, to disperse and rally, and never to march in slow time. No wonder Simcoe himself was critical of the system imposed by Dundas's drill book. "The German system," he wrote to the future prime minister Henry Addington in 1799, "was always said by the French theorists to be erroneous, and they have proved it so in practice. An *English* officer [was this a jibe at the Scottish Dundas?] would select what he thought useful in the Frederickian code, but he would not despise that of Marlborough and Wolfe, diametrically opposed in its tendency to our present mechanical system."[35]

It would be quite wrong to conclude, however, that the collapse of light infantry training was due simply to Dundas; still more that his system was a disaster. His *Regulations* of 1792 had included about ten pages on light infantry drill— not enough, in the eyes of Cornwallis and Coote—but like the rest of the book its enforcement had to wait for the duke of York's appointment as commander in chief three years later in 1795. True, the duke had studied in Germany and had attended Prussian maneuvers, but he was not unconscious of the importance of light infantry: he scarcely could be after fighting the French in Flanders in 1793–94. Not long after his appointment as commander in chief, he began to place more emphasis on light infantry. In 1797 the brief light infantry section of the *Regulations* was printed as a separate pamphlet and distributed to all regiments; in 1798, the year of Howe's exercises with his experimental force in Essex, a full drill book was issued, *Regulations for the Exercise of Riflemen and Light Infantry*. The duke recommended it particularly to officers who had not had practical experience of war, experience that their seniors had gathered in America and the West Indies. It contained, said the preface, "much useful instruction to young officers, not familiarised by practice to the arduous duties to be performed in the face of an enterprising enemy."[36] These regulations, practiced at first by companies, became the model for General Moore's famous

[35] Jan. 29, 1799, Sidmouth Papers.

[36] *Regulations for the Exercise of Riflemen and Light Infantry* (London, 1799), p. iii.

battalion and brigade training with the original Light Brigade at Shorncliffe in 1803–4.[37]

The inspiration for this impressive drill book was German rather than American. It was, in fact, a translation from the German of the manual of Colonel de Rottenburg, who himself had formed the first of the British army's permanent rifle battalions, the green-clad fifth battalion of the Sixtieth Regiment. The duke of York followed up these innovations in the winter after the Dutch expedition by forming an experimental battalion of riflemen under Col. Coote Manningham, who had commanded light infantry under Grey in the West Indies, forging a link between the American experience and the light division that was to make so great a reputation in Wellington's Peninsular army. As often happens when reforms are in the air, there was little dispute about the need but more about the method. One school of thought held that there was no need for specialist battalions of sharpshooters on the French model and that the need for more light troops could be met by expanding light infantry training in the battalions of the line. This was the view of Lord Cornwallis, who scorned the rifle corps, which he called "a very amusing plaything." The muzzle-loading rifle had a slow rate of fire, and Cornwallis recalled that the Hessian Jäger in America had asked for a large proportion of their men to be rearmed with the conventional smooth-bore musket.[38]

So with some dissent the British rifle and light infantry regiments were born as the new century dawned, and went on to form the Light Division of Wellington's Peninsular army. The partnership of the duke of York with David Dundas had thus contained some seeds from which a new British light infantry could develop. But Dundas's contribution to the British army was more solid than that. He gave it the regulations it needed for a type of warfare very different from what it had faced in America. The Hessian Jäger and military writer Adam von Ochs drew the distinction: "Nowadays we would call all the battles fought in America only serious

[37] Richard Glover, *Peninsular Preparation: The Reform of the British Army, 1795–1809* (Cambridge, 1963), p. 129.

[38] Ross, ed., *Correspondence of Cornwallis*, 3:168, 177, 296.

ARMS AND INDEPENDENCE

skirmishing, for we fought battles there in the same manner as we skirmished in Germany."[39]

The contrast between the two styles of warfare is well marked by a glimpse of the Twenty-third Welch Fusiliers in action in 1799. The regiment had served with distinction throughout the American War. In Holland in 1799 a composite battalion of young light infantrymen enlisted from the militia had been driven back for several miles in increasing disorder by French skirmishers when they saw some veteran regiments advancing to their support. Among them were the Welch Fusiliers, and it was not their loose order and flexibility which young Private Surtees of the militia was to recall in later years, but their close unshakeable front. "Nothing could surpass the steadiness and fine appearance of the Twenty-third on entering into action. . . . When the Twenty-third had given them a volley or two, the French gave way and retreated with as great precipitation as they had advanced."[40] The incident gives force to Dundas's words, "that light infantry . . . vanish before the solid movements of the line."

Eighteen months later the British army won its first major victory against Revolutionary France, in open country in Egypt, and won it with the qualities that Private Surtees had seen in the advancing Fusiliers. Col. Edward Paget watched the infantry beating off a large cavalry force that tried to break their line. They showed, he said, "a degree of system and regularity . . . far beyond belief," and added the significant words: "*the system and regularity of a Berlin review*."[41] Here was a testimonial to Dundas, to Frederick the Great, and to Frederick's drillmaster, Friedrich von Saldern.

In the combination of linear tactics and skirmishing with which the British army went forward into the Napoleonic wars, one unique feature not seen in other armies was developed, and it seems to have been a lesson retained from the American War: the infantry fought in two ranks instead of

---

[39] Atwood, *The Hessians*, p. 235.

[40] *Twenty-five Years in the Rifle Brigade* (London, 1833), pp. 25–27.

[41] Eden Paget, ed., *Letters and Memorials of General the Hon. Sir Edward Paget* (London, 1898), p. 60 (my italics).

What the British Army Learned

three. Though three ranks remained official doctrine until 1824, Sir Arthur Wellesley ordered his force to fight two deep from the moment it landed in Portugal in 1808. Yet all other European armies fought three deep. "What European army (except the English) could be trusted in line only two deep?" asked the distinguished soldier and student of war Antoine Henri Jomini.[42] The "thin red line" had been first adopted in America. Wellesley probably saw it for the first time in India, but it may have been imported there by the veterans of America who won the wars in India of that epoch: by Cornwallis, Lake, Medows, Harris, and Sir Robert Abercromby.

Perhaps this is a tenuous link to trace between the tactics of the American War and those of the long struggle against Revolutionary and Napoleonic France. That it is tenuous is not strange, for Napoleon himself once asserted that one should change one's tactics every ten years. What can one say with absolute certainty that the British army learned in America about warfare? Two things: a corpus of experience of the "little war" that it passed on to its successors and an enthusiasm for light infantry that surfaced again when it was needed. One thing it certainly learned a great deal about was how to fight the American War of Independence. But, fortunately, not quite enough.

---

[42] E. M. Lloyd, *A Review of the History of Infantry* (London, 1908), pp. 217, 232.

THEODORE ROPP

The General Military Significance of the American Revolution

By the rude bridge that arched the flood,
Their flag to April's breeze unfurled,
Here once the embattled farmers stood,
And fired the shot heard round the world.
                                             Emerson

BY APRIL 19, 1836, sixty years after the birth of the nation that Alexis de Tocqueville was using as his model democracy, the political and military significance of the American Revolution was already partly mythological. For the generation of Ralph Waldo Emerson, Tocqueville, and the historian George Bancroft, all born between 1800 and 1805, the political mythology had become enmeshed with the military mythology of the republican soldier.[1] In general military terms, the

---

I would like to acknowledge the help given on the first draft of this essay by Ronald Hoffman, Richard Kohn, and John Shy, among the symposium's participants, and by Donald M. Schurman of the Royal Military College of Canada, Geoffrey Smith of Queens University, Frank Cooling of the United States Army Military Historical Research Collection, and Theodore H. Conway of Duke University.

[1] By the time of his *Address at the Dedication of the Soldiers' Monument in Concord, April 19, 1867*, Emerson was blaming Bull Run on the West Point generals and seeing the New England volunteers as carrying "a higher civilization" to the South. George Bancroft's *History of the United States of America from the Discovery of the American Continent* (Boston: 1834–75) devoted half the story to the American Revolution, but was less explicit about the relative efficiency of volunteer and professional military forces.

Military Significance of the Revolution

American Revolution was of limited significance by 1836. For those other than Americans, its relevance to the mainstream of modern Western military thought and action was already marginal. To mainstream soldiers, the American Revolution was militarily significant or practical only for some two decades after 1775, and again, the years after 1960.

The mainstreams of modern military thought and action were Western European from the late Renaissance to 1945. For a variety of reasons, the most important of which were the development of the nation-in-arms and its reinforcement by the military technologies of the Industrial Revolution, the American military experience was only briefly relevant to soldiers of those great powers which, jostling for position on the European peninsula, increasingly dominated the world before 1914 and seemed to dominate it until 1945. Before 1914 a few British soldiers had looked at the American Civil War for lessons about Anglo-American citizen soldiers. But British military thought was almost as extraneous to and derived from that of the European Continental powers as our own, and Continental European soldiers took our Civil War seriously only after the failure of their historically based science of war in 1914. The first brief connection of American and mainstream military experience—the American Revolution—only reinforced the lessons of earlier colonial wars. For this reason it, too, remained irrelevant, except for colonial wars, until the 1960s, when the Western powers began a frantic search for new precedents for colonial pacification. Much of the resulting work on the Revolution has greatly illuminated its history, expecially its southern phase. But the bulk of this scholarship has been of little relevance to areas that are now two centuries removed in time, place, and cultural, political, and military circumstances.

Determining "military significance" is a task of policy scientists. Candor requires us to admit—as Michael Howard did before the Royal United Service Institute in 1961—that soldiers may not learn much from history because history does not repeat itself.[2] But the status and jobs of some historians

[2] Half of *Parameters* 11 (1981) is devoted to strategy and a reprint of Michael Howard's classic warning "The Use and Abuse of Military His-

depend on their supplying policy scientists with usable data. Walter E. Kaegi, Jr.'s "Crisis in Military Historiography" is a plea for just such relevant data, but its generation, he admits, is made more difficult because both our methodologies and our explanations are mixed with "broader problems of the viability and relative importance of evenemential history, the individual in history, and historical contingencies."[3] For the last factor Polybius, Napoleon, or Karl von Clausewitz would substitute Fortune or chance. Rather than finding that thought "disturbing," Clausewitz would suggest that any science of war that left nothing to chance would founder as the "individual in history" made the decisions that are the stuff of "evenemential," or narrative, military history, of the action-reaction phenomena of organized social violence.

The seriousness of this problem—the lack of information usable to policy scientists—is suggested by the fact that data on almost every one of the fifteen topics that Professor Kaegi feels have been neglected by military historians could be gleaned from the American Revolution. Yet the difficulties of avoiding false analogies in just three of them—"(2) the relative efficiency of mercenaries, citizen-soldiers, and farmer-soldiers, (3) the relative efficiency of military discipline, ... [and] (4) the influence and perhaps tyranny of Graeco-Roman precedents and precepts on ... [modern Western] ideas and practices"[4]—are so obvious that historians can only remind policy scientists that it is now nearly two centuries since the death of Frederick the Great, the last Great Captain of the Old Regime, and our own recognition as an independent republic.

It is not too helpful for C. Vann Woodward to begin a review on one of our own Great Captains, Ulysses S. Grant, by noting that "biography is one thing, history another."[5] This

---

tory," which first appeared in the *Royal United Service Institute Journal* 107(1962):4–8.

[3] Walter E. Kaegi, Jr., "The Crisis in Military Historiography," *Armed Forces and Society* 7 (1980–81):209–316.

[4] Ibid., pp. 311–12.

[5] C. Vann Woodward, "The Enigma of U.S. Grant," *New York Review of Books*, Mar. 19, 1981, pp. 3–6.

statement is true, but it can be easily misunderstood by readers when psychobiographical techniques are being applied to leaders ranging from Alexander the Great to Lyndon B. Johnson, and even to the prosopography of military incompetence.[6] Samuel Kinser's comments on "The Geohistorical Structuralism of Fernand Braudel" show another great historian facing the problems of leadership in history, but far less directly than they were faced by the military historical novelist Leo Tolstoy.[7] And Marcus Cunliffe's *Soldiers and Civilians* goes backwards from Bull Run to explain "The Confused Heritage" of Lexington and Concord. He remarks that, "until recently, American military history has tended to be narrative or antiquarian." The association is not deliberately pejorative, but it may suggest that some military historians have forgotten why narratives that "sing of arms and the man"—of Great Captains, decisions, and battles—are both traditional and necessary to understanding this form of epic and often mutually escalating political violence.[8]

In any case, a "viable," or "usable" past is a policy scientist's, not a historian's, objective. But even from the former's standpoint, the American Revolution was more significant politically than militarily because of the political-military wisdom of such leaders as George Washington. Their decisions may have been most relevant to Latin American revolutionary leaders. But since the latter's revolutions were also colonial ones, occurring during or after the French Revolutionary and Napoleonic wars, mainstream European military and political scientists found it even easier to dismiss them than the American Revolution. Twentieth-century students of militarism, Fascism, and the corporate state eventually came to consider them relevant, but under conditions in which these events were treated in a wildly anachronistic fashion. And though sea power was more frequently recognized to have been a military factor in these Latin American revolutions—

[6] Norman E. Dixon, *On the Psychology of Military Incompetence* (New York, 1976).

[7] *American Historical Review* 86 (1981):63–105.

[8] Marcus Cunliffe, *Soldiers and Civilians: The Martial Spirit in America, 1775–1865* (Boston, 1968), p. 441.

in which the creoles and their European friends commanded local waters more often than had been the case during the American Revolution—the narrow standards of military relevance that still separated military from maritime history reinforced the perception that they had little military significance. Professor Kaegi's deference to "more competent" naval historical specialists may have kept him from seeing this traditional separation as a factor in both past and present "crises" in military historiography.[9]

While some military "lessons" were overlooked because of narrow views of military history, others were soon obscured by the national myths of the era of Emerson, Bancroft, Andrew Jackson, and Tocqueville. Cunliffe defines our "military" myths as those of the Rifleman, the Chevalier, and the practical Quaker. The first two were related to the military-political experiences of the Revolutionary militia and the Continental army. In considering "Why Democratic Nations Naturally Desire Peace, and Democratic Armies, War," Tocqueville suggested that our professional officers would be far less warlike than our noncommissioned officers or Riflemen, like Jackson, a man who had parlayed very modest— by Bonaparte's standards—victories into high political office.[10] Neither Tocqueville nor Cunliffe remarked on our privateering tradition, nor on the Jeffersonians' unsuccessful naval and coast defense militia, the field to which Yankee ingenuity—or the practical Quaker—was now turning attention. Tocqueville used Robert Fulton as an example of the very limited opportunities for an inventor in Jacksonian America. He could have used David Bushnell's *American Turtle*, the Revolutionary War prototype of Fulton's *Nautilus*.[11]

But the myth of American technological ingenuity was just beginning to appear. Its chief example during the American Revolution may have been the great chain across the Hudson

---

[9] Kaegi, "Crisis in Military Historiography," p. 316.

[10] Alexis de Tocqueville, *Democracy in America*, ed. Philipps Bradley, tr. Henry Reeve, 2 vols. (New York, 1945), 2:286–302.

[11] Alex Roland, *Underwater Warfare in the Age of Sail* (Bloomington, Ind., 1978).

at West Point.[12] The American frontiersman's rifle was not a decisive weapon in the Revolutionary War. Its slow rate of fire and lack of a bayonet made it inferior to the musket for close order fighting, and to the German Jäger's bayoneted rifle for skirmishers. But we still link it with the Revolution, as we link the tomahawk with the Indians, or the sawed-off shotgun, superior to both for trench fighting in 1918, with mobsters. More important, insofar as Yankee ingenuity is concerned, even the French could not arm their new mass armies with new, technologically advanced weapons. So Washington had to make do with old militia muskets, a few hunting rifles, and all the regular arms he could get from our overseas supporters. His military conservatism was related to the technological, as well as to the political, facts of eighteenth-century warfare.

Europeans saw the Revolution's military lessons as reinforcing those of the first four rounds of the second Hundred Years War, 1689–1815, between France and Britain, lessons that were to be reinforced again by those of the climactic sixth and seventh rounds. Colonial expansion was to continue during the general peace of 1815–1914, but by 1896, when Charles E. Callwell compiled his famous casebook *Small Wars*, the American Revolution was too remote—technologically and politically—to be relevant.

The American Revolution's immediate military significance to outsiders was, thus, confined to the two decades after Lexington and Concord. One of the best general guides to what Europeans of this era were looking for is Robert R. Palmer. His essay "Frederick the Great, Guibert, Bülow" deals with the theories along which the "Twelve Who Ruled," the French Committee of Public Safety, constructed the revolutionary military system that so quickly overshadowed our own. That study paved the way for his classic survey of the whole era in his *Age of the Democratic Revolution: A Political History of Europe and America, 1760–1800*. However our Revolution failed to live up to our radicals' expectations, Palmer's sum-

---

[12] Dave R. Palmer, *The River and the Rock: The History of Fortress West Point, 1775–1783* (New York, 1969), pp. 147–53.

mary of the "imponderable but very great" European "effects of the American Revolution, as a revolution" remains sound. "It inspired the sense of a new era. It added a new content to the conception of progress, . . . a whole new dimension to ideas of liberty and equality made familiar by the Enlightenment, . . . dethroned England, and set up America, as a model for those seeking a better world."[13]

Palmer deals less directly with the American Revolution's general military "lessons." Since these were primarily maritime and colonial, the war was militarily insignificant for those who compartmentalized mainstream military and maritime affairs. More important, the French revolutionaries had "dethroned" Prussia and reestablished France as a European military model only a decade after the Treaty of Paris in 1783. By 1795, when the five Directors replaced the Committee of Public Safety, all that had to be done was to correct what Karl von Clausewitz later called some "technical imperfections" before this new republican "juggernaut of war, based on the strength of the entire people, began its pulverizing course through Europe."[14] Once the Anglo-American-French wars had ended in 1815, American professional soldiers were more influenced by French and then German ideas than by those of that British army on which they had modeled our Continentals. And British military thought, except in constitutional, maritime, and colonial matters, was almost equally derivative during the next Anglo-American century of "splendid isolation" and "free security."

The American Revolution's immediate military influence was thus confined to some bush-fighting innovations and some possible contributions to the development of what Palmer describes as "the first mass or 'democratic' army, . . . [with] a modern kind of national spirit, with its morale heightened

[13] "Frederick the Great, Guibert, Bülow: From Dynastic to National War," in Edward Meade Earle, ed., *Makers of Modern Strategy: Military Thought from Machiavelli to Hitler* (Princeton, 1943), pp. 49–74; idem, *Twelve Who Ruled: The Committee of Public Safety during the Terror* (Princeton, 1941); idem, *The Age of the Democratic Revolution: A Political History of Europe and America, 1760–1800. The Challenge* (Princeton, 1959), p. 282.

[14] Karl von Clausewitz, *On War*, ed. and tr. Michael Howard and Peter Paret (Princeton, 1976), p. 592.

by political attitudes in the common soldiers, its higher ranks filled with men promoted from the ranks on grounds of 'merit,' and prepared to act, by its training, equipment, and discipline, in a great war among the old military powers of Europe."[15] That it took nationalistic American military historians some time to realize how tenuous were the connections between the American and French revolutionary armies was partly due to the fact that some of the makers of Europe's new armies had participated in an American War that was much more recent in 1792 than the Great War of 1914–18 was to be to the Second World War of 1939–45.

The American Revolution had a limited impact on European military affairs. The comte de Rochambeau and the marquis de Lafayette successively commanded the French Army of the North in 1792, but while Lafayette's memoirs mention skirmishers, it is not in relation to his American experiences. When the later Prussian reformer, Neithardt von Gneisenau, who had gone to Canada with a German rifle battalion, applied for a Prussian commission, Frederick remarked that he would have to learn war all over. Neither he nor his later colleague Clausewitz mentioned this brief American experience as a factor in Prussian military reform. Clausewitz's chapter on defense—the longest in *On War*—repeatedly mentions militia, guerrillas, and partisans in Spain and Russia without referring to America. For the development of the nation-in-arms, Clausewitz saw the French as the major innovators, partly because the effects of France's revolutionary innovations "did not become evident . . . or fully felt until the end of the [French] revolutionary wars."[16] And while Thaddeus Kosciusko, the chief constructor of West Point, was to lead the Polish national uprising of 1794, the rhetoric and military content of that rising was French rather than American.

The Anglo-Americans' nations-in-arms were not fully de-

[15] Robert R. Palmer, *The Age of the Democratic Revolution: A Political History of Europe and America, 1760–1800. The Struggle* (Princeton, 1964), p. 113.

[16] Clausewitz, *On War*, p. 592. On the problem of light infantry tactics and the Prussian reformers, see Peter Paret, *Yorck and the Era of Prussian Reform, 1807–1815* (Princeton, 1966), pp. 40–43.

veloped until the great wars of the twentieth century. Even there any claim that "the American Revolution began the 'democratization of war'" that eventually led "to national conscription and a new concept of total war for total victory"[17] largely depends on legal precedents. Europe's Old Regimes—as André Corvisier's authoritative *Armies and Societies in Europe, 1494–1789*, suggests[18]—already had plenty of precedents for compulsory military service. Frederick and Adam Smith knew that militia could not stand up to "Prussian troops" in the open, but the American and French revolutions did show that "several successive campaigns in the field" could make citizen militia or volunteers "in every respect a standing army."[19] Nevertheless, our Continental army had been too small and ill-supported to make many Continental Europeans see this, especially after the comte de Guibert had repudiated in 1779 many of the lucky prophecies of his famous *Essai général de tactique*, published in 1772. Moreover, while the American War's best-known soldier of fortune, Baron von Steuben, had humanized the old armies' disciplinary system, other armies had also been tending in that direction.

Except for such legal precedents, even nineteenth-century American military historians found few examples of the general military significance of the American Revolution. The three best known, Emory Upton, Alfred Thayer Mahan, and Theodore A. Dodge—born between 1839 and 1842—were all veterans of a Civil War between two American nations-in-arms, partly directed by professional soldiers. Dodge devoted four volumes to a study of the French Revolution and Napoleon. Yet only one of the work's references to "Americans, teach lessons in war," comes from the American Revolution. "At Concord and Lexington," he wrote, "we proved the superiority of good marksmen in open order, each one

[17] Maurice Matloff, ed., *American Military History* (Washington, D.C., 1959), p. 100.

[18] Tr. Abigail T. Siddall (Bloomington, Ind., 1979).

[19] Adam Smith, *An Inquiry into the Nature and Causes of the Wealth of Nations* (Chicago, 1952), p. 305.

taking advantage ... of the ground, over seasoned regulars who fought elbow to elbow."[20] This is straight out of Emerson or Bancroft. In 1925 Oliver L. Spaulding, Jr., Hoffman Nickerson, and John W. Wright's semiofficial text *Warfare* added "the organization of permanent divisions" and the development of skirmishers "into a serious fighting element," while noting the need to trace "the whole development of the American art of war ... and the reciprocal influence of American and foreign systems."[21] Russell F. Weigley and others have now told the American side of that story.[22] Though the foreign side may be largely negative, explaining the reasons for this may shake the idea that our Chevaliers' only contributions to the art of war were the Rifleman's shooting savages with the ever more ingenious devices of Cunliffe's pacific Quakers.

By 1881, when Upton summed up the Chevaliers' case in his unfinished *Military Policy of the United States*, it was as little related to what had happened during the American Revolution as was John A. Logan's unfinished *Volunteer Soldier in America* (1887). Both cases rested on the experiences of our Civil War, a conflict between nations-in-arms directed militarily by a small corps of regular officers. Upton even claimed that the Revolution had cost each person $123, as against a more professional Civil War at $96. His fifteen "lessons of the Revolution" all dealt with organizing volunteers and militia around regulars, with as little political interference as possible. His Revolutionary military heroes were the officers, "great as was the devotion of the private [Continental] soldier." For example, Upton laid the largely negative "Results of the Campaign" of 1775 to an American army of 37,623 men which "for the most part, ... from want of supplies, organization, and discipline, was maintained at public ex-

---

[20] Theodore A. Dodge, *Napoleon: A History of the Art of War, from the Beginning of the French Revolution*, 4 vols. (Boston, 1904–7), 1:24–25.

[21] *Warfare: A Study of Military Methods from the Earliest Times* (New York, 1925), p. 572.

[22] Russell F. Weigley, *Towards an American Army: Military Thought from Washington to Marshall* (New York, 1962), p. 8.

pense in a state of demoralizing inactivity." By 1881 this kind of analysis was, however, of no interest to other soldiers or to anyone who saw the German nation-in-arms—in Upton's *Armies of Asia and Europe* (1878)—as too influenced by Otto von Bismarck's Bonapartist combination of national success and benevolent despotism. "Had Germany been a republic," Upton wrote, Bismarck and Helmuth von Moltke "would have risen to the chief magistracy of the state, but under a monarchy they had to content themselves with fame, titles, and estates, and the patronizing favor of a kind-hearted Emperor."[23]

American historians' traditionally narrow definition of military history limited their perceptions of the military significance of the American Revolution. Far superior was Mahan's "Critical Discussion of the Maritime War of 1778" in his *Influence of Sea Power upon History* (1890). "The history of sea power," Mahan claimed, "is largely a military history; and it is in this aspect that it will be mainly, though not exclusively, regarded."[24] Military historians of the Revolution gradually became as aware as Washington had been of the difficulties of defeating an enemy who stayed "close to the waterways, . . . [and] never got many miles away from the seashore and the main river valleys."[25] This comment and the account of Yorktown in Matthew Forney Steele's *American Campaigns* (1909) also suggest the growing sophistication of American military historians after their subject began to be formally studied in American service schools and war colleges.

Mahan's "Critical Discussion" showed how the command of the sea evolved in a "game of hide-and-seek" along a "chain of naval stations covering one of the shores of the Atlantic,

---

[23] Emory Upton, *The Military Policy of the United States* (1904; reprint ed., New York, 1968),pp. ix, 9, 59–67. Born in 1826, a major general, senator from Illinois, and Blaine's running mate in 1884, Logan was both the highest ranking and the oldest of the four military historians. Upton was born in 1839, Mahan in 1840, and Dodge in 1842.

[24] Alfred Thayer Mahan, *The Influence of Sea Power upon History, 1660–1783* (Boston, 1890), ch. 14, p. 1.

[25] Matthew Forney Steele, *American Campaigns*, 2 vols. (1909; reprint ed., Washington, D.C., 1943), 1:26, 51–55.

Military Significance of the Revolution

linking Canada and Halifax with the West Indies." But his military and literary commitments were to allow him to elaborate only on the "Military History of the Royal Navy, 1763–1792: Major Operations" in William Laird Clowes's seven-volume history of the Royal Navy (1898). Here Mahan saw the war as one in which "control of the water, both ocean and inland" had "a preponderant effect." The minor operations of privateering were left to another author and volume, and Mahan treated the war in the Indian Ocean in a separate section. Thus, American military historians did not study the Revolution from the standpoint of a colonial system that could lose some unprofitable entrepots or for light on our current problems of securing resources too distant and vulnerable to be defended by a general command of the sea.[26] And renewed attention to an enlightened view of the costs of the military and social control of the British Isles and a few posts overseas, compared with those of an expanding, profitable empire, might illuminate the links that whig historians found between the three Anglo-American revolutions and the democratic one that Emerson, Bancroft, and Montesquieu's successor Tocqueville so celebrated.[27]

By the time John Shy and Peter Paret published *Guerrillas in the 1960's* (1962), time and technology had so eroded our Revolution's relevance that such works did more to illuminate the militia's role and the Revolution in the South than current imperial problems.[28] Here again, the Old Regimes had lacked institutions to sort out significant experiences. Only

---

[26] Alfred Thayer Mahan, "Major Operations of the Royal Navy, 1762–1783," in William Laird Clowes, *A History of the Royal Navy*, 7 vols. (London, 1897–1903), 3:353. This was reprinted unchanged just before Mahan's death as *The Major Operations of the Navies in the War of American Independence* (Boston, 1913). Though there has been a great deal of research on privateers and privateering, Richard Buel, Jr., is correct in suggesting that very little has been done on the exact effects of the naval "militia" on the American perceptions of what happened, especially after the failure of Jeffersonian ideas of a naval militia in the War of 1812. There, of course, the naval militia were to be used for coast defense.

[27] See especially the essays in J. G. A. Pocock, ed., *Three British Revolutions: 1641, 1688, 1776* (Princeton, 1980).

[28] (Princeton, 1962).

the great trading companies, some bankers, and a few physiocrats were interested in those balance sheets that now cost out so many military and social ventures. My use of their perceptions of military, maritime, and political significance has been a major factor in my finding so little general military significance in American Revolutionary historiography.

"The American Revolution," one critic wrote, "showed, for the first time, that a small, militarily inferior colonial power could confront and successfully overthrow a militarily stronger mother country. This set the stage for all of the successful colonial revolutions that followed, down to and including the Vietnamese."[29] "Overthrow" still reflects American military historians' views of maritime empires, which can shuck off some entrepots whenever they become too costly, and wait for more politically acceptable arrangements. Readers who welcomed Mahan's and Theodore Roosevelt's historical ideas as those of "true and loyal friend[s] to Britain and her Navy"[30] were as unlikely to find flaws in them as to see the strength of an American anticolonialism that would cause a deep sense of betrayal when it was turned against our allies after World War II.

The basic weakness of any separation of the Revolution's military and political significance is its artificiality. "The colonists won a 'political' victory and not a military one, but as Clausewitz reminded us, this is only quibbling over the means and not the ends."[31] Both victories were limited. Perhaps our lack of national political and military fervor gave our leaders enough control of the people who threw out the royalists in 1775 and those who, at Newburgh in 1783, felt that their heroism had not been appreciated, to accomplish their immediate political goal of legitimacy with the people who then counted most, the English whigs and their Continental admirers. Without the passions that fueled those "real" revolutions and wars beginning in 1789, our rebels' achievements looked increasingly modest. But when the ends and means

---

[29] Theodore H. Conway to author, Feb. 11, 1981.

[30] Clowes, *Royal Navy*, 3:v–vi.

[31] Conway to author.

of the conflict were so limited, both the rebels and a government that hoped for compromise had to follow rules that did not see property confiscations, the use of mercenaries, or deaths in prison hulks as atrocious. Our atrocities could be blamed on mobs and partisans. Great Britain's only deliberate atrocity, raising the Indians, hardened American opposition. But the idea that the rebels deliberately fitted their conservative military means to their ultimate political ends—independence, international recognition, and as much of the West as possible—is fatuous.

Clausewitz saw modern war's action-reaction phenomena as a mechanism pushing it toward totality. Our own need for mythically "Founding a Nation in Blood" may be related to a Revolutionary war which—for various geopolitical reasons—was so geographically and personally limited. Yet its concentration of sacrifice and suffering may have been why—except in our relations with Canada—it left so few scars in comparison with the wars of the French Revolution and Napoleon. One result—in the era of Tocqueville and Thomas Carlyle's *Heroes and Hero-Worship* (1840)—was that Andrew Jackson became a folk hero by "a very ordinary achievement . . . which could only be remembered in a country where battles are rare."[32] This attitude—during two centuries in which only the South suffered greatly from war and social change—was not really shaken until the overthrow of a government that, in Vietnam, had not fitted its military means to its political ends. And before the Civil War, Tocqueville could not have seen that American generals would seldom lose their commands by being too careful of their men, however unNapoleonic their victories.

In eras that increasingly measure social and political progress by their costs in violence and sacrifice, it becomes ever harder for some American historians to appreciate their political and military Founding Fathers. The French historian Elie Halévy related nineteenth-century British social and political progress to its lack of violence, but this did not bolster whig views of our Revolution. So, to paraphrase Wilfred Owen, "This conference is not about heroes. American history has

---

[32] Tocqueville, *Democracy in America*, 1:299.

sometimes become less fit to speak of those of the American Revolution."[33] We still have difficulty in connecting its great political and minor military significance. That the ideas which so successfully related the Revolution's great political ends to its minor military means had so little relation to actual Roman military and political practices is a curious example of what Professor Kaegi calls "the influence and perhaps tyranny of Graeco-Roman precedents and precepts on European and American ideas and practices in the art of war."[34] In the Age of Reason's revolutions Cincinnatus and Caesar loomed larger than life. The republican restraints of one and violence of the other generated new myths. Jacobins' and Jacksonians' "confused" and often contradictory ideas of ends and means in war and politics were among the most significant results of the military and political Age of the Democratic Revolution.

[33] Wilfred Owen, *Collected Poems*, Preface, ed. C. Day Lewis (New York, 1964), p. 31. The passage reads, "This book is not about heroes. English poetry is not yet fit to speak of them."

[34] Kaegi, "Crisis in Military Historiography," p. 310.

Contributors
Index

Contributors

RICHARD BUEL, JR., teaches history at Wesleyan University and is associate editor of *History and Theory*. He received his education at Amherst College and Harvard University. He is the author of several articles and books including *Securing the Revolution: Ideology in American Politics, 1789–1815* (1972); *Dear Liberty: Connecticut's Mobilization for the Revolutionary War* (1980), which received the award of the American Revolution Round Table in 1981; and, with Joy D. Buel, *The Way of Duty: A Woman and Her Family in Revolutionary America* (1984).

IRA D. GRUBER is professor of history at Rice University. His publications include *The Howe Brothers and the American Revolution* (1974) and a number of articles dealing with the theory and practice of warfare in the eighteenth century. He is at present studying the education of British officers in the age of the American Revolution.

DON HIGGINBOTHAM is professor of history and chairman of the department at the University of North Carolina at Chapel Hill, where he has taught since 1967. He has written *Daniel Morgan: Revolutionary Rifleman* (1961), *The War of American Independence: Military Attitudes, Policies, and Practice, 1763–1789* (1971), and the text for the *Atlas of the American Revolution* (1974). He has edited *Reconsiderations on the Revolutionary War: Selected Essays* (1978) and the *Papers of James Iredell*, 2 vols. (1976). He is currently engaged in studies of civil-military relations during the War of Independence and of George Washington as a revolutionary leader.

PIERS MACKESY was born in Scotland and served in the Second World War in northwest Europe in the Royal Scots Greys. Since 1954 he has been a Fellow of Pembroke College, Oxford, and in 1978 was awarded the degree of Doctor of Letters by Oxford University. He is the author of *The War in the Mediterranean, 1803–1810* (1957), *The War for America, 1775–1783* (1964), *Statesmen at War: The Strategy of Overthrow, 1798–1799* (1974), *The Coward of Min-*

CONTRIBUTORS

den: *The Affair of Lord George Sackville* (1979), and *War without Victory: The Downfall of Pitt, 1799–1802* (in press).

JAMES KIRBY MARTIN is professor of history at the University of Houston, University Park. A specialist in the social, political, and military aspects of early American history, Martin received his Ph.D. from the University of Wisconsin, where he studied with the late Merrill Jensen. His writings include *Men in Rebellion: Higher Governmental Leaders and the Coming of the American Revolution* (1973), *In the Course of Human Events: An Interpretive Exploration of the American Revolution* (1979), and *A Respectable Army: The Military Origins of the Republic, 1763–1789* (with Mark E. Lender, 1982). He has also coedited *Citizen-Soldier: The Revolutionary War Journal of Joseph Bloomfield* (with Mark E. Lender, 1982), and he is currently completing biographies of Benedict Arnold and his second wife, Margaret Shippen Arnold.

THEODORE ROPP, A.B., Oberlin College, A.M., Ph.D., Harvard, has taught European, maritime, military, and technological history at Duke University since 1938. He became Professor Emeritus in 1981. He has also taught at Harvard University, the University of Singapore, the University of New South Wales, San Diego State College, the U.S. Naval War College, the U.S. Army War College, and the U.S. Military Academy. He is a past president of the American Military Institute, past chairman of the Board of the Historical Research and Evaluation Organization, and current member of the National Armed Forces Museum Board. His best known work is *War in the Modern World* (1959). He is currently working on a history of modern strategic thought.

STEVEN ROSSWURM received his Ph.D. from Northern Illinois University in 1979 and is an assistant professor of history at Lake Forest College. He contributed an essay to a recent collection of papers entitled *The Origins of Anglo-American Radicalism* and held a postdoctoral fellowship at the University of Pennsylvania's Philadelphia Center for Early American Studies where he completed a manuscript on the Philadelphia militia and laboring poor during the American Revolution. He is currently working on the life histories of the Philadelphia Committee of Privates and the implications of those lives for an understanding of the American Revolution.

CHARLES ROYSTER is associate professor of history at Louisiana State University, Baton Rouge. He is the author of *A Revolutionary People at War: The Continental Army and American Character, 1775–1783* (1979) and *Light-Horse Harry Lee and the Legacy of the American Revolution* (1981). He is now doing research for a book in the Civil War era.

ROBERT K. WRIGHT, JR., received a B.A. degree in history from the College of the Holy Cross in 1968 and M.A. and Ph.D. degrees in early American history from the College of William and Mary in 1971 and 1980, respectively. He served as an enlisted member of a military history detachment in Vietnam in 1969 and 1970, and currently is a captain in the Virginia Army National Guard commanding a military history detachment. He has been a historian with the U.S. Army Center of Military History's Organizational History Branch since 1974. He is the author of *The Continental Army*, a volume in the Army Lineage Series, and a number of articles on unit history and the War of American Independence in service publications and military history journals. His current research interests include early American military organization and tactics, and the social composition of regular and militia units in the seventeenth and eighteenth centuries.

Index

Abercromby, Gen. James, 171
Abercromby, Sir Ralph, 192
Adams, Samuel, 30–31
Addington, Henry, 212
Advance-Guard, *see* Committee of Privates
Age of the Democratic Revolution (Palmer), 221
Allen, James, 100
American Campaigns (Steele), 226
American flag, 42
American Revolution: as an analog of political partisanship, 38–41; in the South, 17–24; irregular warfare in the, 4–8, 15–17; military significance of, 216–17, 220–28, 230; military significance of, for British army, 192–94, 204, 211, 214–15; and modern guerrilla warfare, 2–3, 7–8; parallels with the Vietnam War, 13–15, 18–19; political significance of, 219, 228, 230
Amherst, Sir Jeffery, 4, 169–70, 174, 188–89, 201, 205
American Turtle, 220
Ancaster, duke of, 171
Arendt, Hannah, 11
Argyll, duke of, 173
Armand-Tuffin, Charles (marquis de La Rouerie), 62
Armies and Societies in Europe, 1494–1789 (Corvisier), 224
Armies of Asia and Europe (Upton), 226
Artillery Artificer Regiment, 63
Artillery, 57
Associators, *see* Philadelphia militia
Assunpunk Bridge, 98

Badge of Military Merit, 72
Bancroft, George, 216, 225
Barrington, Lord, 166, 176
Battalion, 51

Becker, Carl, 1
Becker, John P., 48–49
Belford, Gen. William, 173
Berrian, Samuel, 42, 48
Bland, Humphrey, 4, 65
Board of War, 54, 59, 70
Bounties, 148–49
Bouquet, Henri, 67
Boyd, Capt. Alexander, 99
Boyd, Gen. Robert, 183
Braddock, General, 4, 201
Brigade, 51; in the Continental army, 56–57
British army: field training of, 193–94; military significance of the American Revolution for, 192–94, 204, 211, 214–15
Brown, Richard M., 20
Burgoyne, Lt. Col. John, 167
Burgoyne, Maj. Gen. John, 17, 58, 166, 175, 177, 181, 189–90
Bushnell, David, 220

Cadwalader, Gen. John, 97–98
Callwell, Charles E., 221
Camden, Battle of, 23
Campbell, Gen. Henry Fletcher, 186–87
Cannon, James, 88, 90
Carleton, Maj. Gen. Guy, 166, 183
Cavalry, 206
Cavan, earl of, 66
Cavendish, Lord Frederick, 182
Chalmers, James, 46
Charles, earl of Drogheda, 182
Chastellux, marquis de, 9
Church, Benjamin, 68
Church, Thomas, 68
City Light Horse (Philadelphia), 109, 111–12
Clairac, chevalier de, 66
Classing, 101, 149
Clausewitz, Karl von, 194, 218, 222–23, 228–29
Clavering, Gen. John, 168, 183
Clerk, Gen. Robert, 183

237

INDEX

Clinton, Sir Henry, 18, 20, 134, 166, 175–76, 181, 189–90
Clowes, William Laird, 227
"Come on Coolly" (broadside), 104
"Come on Warmly" (broadside), 108
Commentaires sur les mémoires de Montecuccoli (Turpin de Crissé), 67
Committee of Conference, 59–60
Committee of Inspection, 84
Committee of Privates, 76, 108; and articles of association, 82–86; composition of, 81–82; and internal revolution, 88–91; meetings of, 81; role of, 82
Committee of Public Safety, 221–22
Committee of Safety, 86, 95–96, 100; and articles of association, 82–84
Company, 51
Connecticut Line, discontent in, 133
Constitutional Society, 104
Continental army, 12, 152–53, 198, 224; composition of, 122–26; discontent in, 121–22, 126–32, 137–39; in 1775, 53; in 1776, 53–55; in 1777, 56–58; in 1778, 60–63; in 1781, 63–64, 72; and militia, 145–48; raising troops for, 145–51; unit cohesion in, 127–28
Continental Congress, 119–20, 152–54, 159
Continental currency, depreciation of, 150, 153–55
Conway, Gen. Henry Seymour, 167, 172
Conway, Maj. Gen. Thomas, 59, 71
Coote, Col. Eyre, 210, 212
Cornwallis, Charles Earl, 21–24, 166, 197, 210, 212–13
Cornwallis, Edward, 172
Corps of Invalids, 63
Corvisier, André, 224
Counterinsurgency, 196–97; in American Revolution, 195
Cowpens, Battle of, 21, 23

"Crisis in Military Historiography" (Kaegi), 218
"Critical Discussion of the Maritime War of 1778" (Mahan), 226–27
Cumberland, duke of, 65, 182
Cuninghame, Maj. Gen. Robert, 168, 175, 178–80
Cunliffe, Marcus, 219–20

Daggett, David, 32
Dalrymple, Campbell, 65
Dartmouth, Lord, 169
Davis, Thomas, 67
Deane, Silas, 106
Derby, earl of, 177
Desaguliers, Gen. Thomas, 182
Directory, 222
Division, 51, 200
Dodge, Theodore A., 224–25
Drafting, 146, 149–50
Dragoons, in Continental army, 61
Draper, Sir William, 175–76, 180
Drill manuals, 66–67
Dundas, Col. David, 204–7, 209–10, 212–13
Dundas, Henry, 196
Duportail, Louis, 61–62
Dury, Gen. Theodore, 171–72

Ellison, Gen. Cuthbert, 172
Elliott, Gen. George Augustus, 172
Emerson, Ralph Waldo, 216, 225
Engineers, in Continental army, 61–62
Erskine, Robert, 62
Essai général de tactique (Guibert), 65, 224
Essay on Field Fortifications (Pleydell), 66
Estaing, Admiral d', 156
Ewald, Capt. Johann, 73, 209

Fairbairn, Geoffrey, 13
Fanning, David, 22
Ferdinand, Prince, of Brunswick, 186
Ferguson, Maj. Patrick, 20, 191
Field Engineer (Clairac), 66
Fitzwilliam, Gen. John, 172
Flying Camp, 92, 94

238

Index

Folard, Jean-Charles de, 65
Forbes, Gen. John, 4, 67
"Fort Wilson Riot," 76, 109–11
'45, the, 3
Four Letters (Cannon?), 90
Franco-American alliance, 154, 161
Franklin, Benjamin, 69, 157
Fraser, Gen. Simon, 185
Frederick, duke of York, 205, 212–13
Frederick the Great, 64, 68, 205–6, 208, 224
"Frederick the Great, Guibert, Bülow" (Palmer), 221
Friedrich II, landgraf of Hessen, 202
From Resistance to Revolution (Maier), 5–6
Fulton, Robert, 220

Gage, Lt. Gen. Thomas, 166, 168–70, 188–89
Gates, Horatio, 9, 23, 58–59
General Committee of Associators, *see* Committee of Privates
"Geohistorical Structuralism of Fernand Braudel, The" (Kinser), 219
George III: and selection of commanders in America, 166–70, 174–75, 179–81, 187–90; and selection of officers, 167–68
Germain, Lord George, 18, 178, 201
Giap, Gen. Vo Nguyen, 15, 17
Gipson, Lawrence H., 5
Gisborne, Maj. Gen. James, 168, 175, 178–80
Gleason, Benjamin, 47
Gneisenau, Neithardt von, 223
Gordon, Lord Adam, 175, 178–80
Grafton, 167
Grain, price of, 155–57, 159
Granby, marquis of, 167
Grant, Gen. Francis, 185–86
Greene, Gen. Nathanael, 21, 23–24, 72, 197
Grenville, George, 168
Grenville, Lord William, 196

Grey, Gen. Sir Charles, 210
Griffin, Sir Griffin, 172
Guerrillas in the 1960's (Shy and Paret), 227
Guerrilla warfare, modern: American Revolution and, 2–3, 7–8
Guibert, comte de, 51, 65, 224
Guilford Courthouse, Battle of, 24

Haldimand, Maj. Gen. Frederick, 166, 175–76, 180
Hale, Gen. Bernard, 184
Hale, Gen. John, 186–87
Halévy, Elie, 229
Hamilton, Alexander, 142–43
Hamilton, Sir Robert, 167
Hanger, Col. George, 191
Hanson, Thomas, 67
Harcourt, Earl, 173
Harrington, earl of, 171
Harvey, Edward, 65, 183
Hart, Capt. Basil Liddell, 192
Haviland, Gen. William, 183
Heer, Capt. Bartholomew von, 63
Heinrichs, Capt. Johann, 58
Heroes and Hero-Worship (Carlyle), 229
Heroic antecedents, as a basis of American nationality, 36–38
Hessians, 198–99, 202
Higginbotham, Don, 77
Hillegas, Michael, 157–58
History of the Revolution of South-Carolina (Ramsay), 31
Holker, John, 157
Hotham, Com. William, 192
Howard, Sir George, 174
Howard, Michael, 217
Howe, Gen. Robert, 136
Howe, Viscount, 176
Howe, Maj. Gen. William, 58, 166, 175–77, 180, 188–90, 202, 211
Hunter, Dr. John, 192

Imported goods, 157–63
Influence of Sea Power upon History (Mahan), 226
Ingenieurs Géographes, 62
Inspector general, 71

INDEX

Instructions for His Generals (Frederick the Great), 64–65
Instructions to Young Officers (Wolfe), 65–66
Ireland, 10, 196–97
Irregular warfare, 68, 198, 208; eighteenth-century experience with, 3–5; in the American Revolution, 4–8, 15–17, 194; in the South, 21–24
Irwin, Gen. John, 175, 178–80

Jackson, Andrew, 220, 229
Jackson, Henry, 68
Jay Treaty, 32
Jefferson, Thomas, 8, 39
Johnston, Gen. James (d. 1795), 184
Johnston, Gen. James (d. 1797), 186–87
Jomini, Antoine Henri, 215

Kaegi, Walter E., Jr., 218, 220, 230
Key, Francis Scott, 42
King's Mountain, Battle of, 21
Kinser, Samuel, 219
Knox, Henry, 57, 140
Knyphausen, Freiherr von, 202
Kohn, Richard, 12
Komer Report, 18
Kosciusko, Thaddeus, 223

Lafayette, marquis de, 59, 223
Lee, Gen. Charles, 9, 142, 203
Lee, Henry, 62
Lender, Mark Edward, 130
Lewy, Guenter, 19
Light Brigade, 213
Light infantry, 202–3, 205, 208–14
Ligonier, Lord, 65, 176
Lincoln, Abraham, 26–27, 48
Livingston, Robert R., 32
Locke, John, 20
Logan, John A., 225
Logistics, 199–200
Lossberg, Friedrich von, 17
Loudoun, earl of, 171, 176
Loyalists, 195

McCrea, Jane, 17

McDougall, Brig. Gen. Alexander, 67
Mackay, Maj. Gen. Alexander, 168, 185
McKean, Col. Thomas, 92
Mackesy, Piers, 13
Madison, James, 28
Mahan, Alfred Thayer, 224, 226–28
Maier, Pauline, 5–7, 10–11
Maizeroy, Joly de, 65
Manningham, Col. Coote, 213
Mao Tse-tung, 23
Marechausee Corps, 63
Maria Theresa, 3
Marion, Francis, 21
Marketplace, 151–53
Marmont, Marshal, 200
Martin, Pvt. Joseph Plumb, 126, 132–34
Matlack, Timothy, 109–10
Mercer, Gen. Hugh, 92
Mesnil-Durand, François-Jean de, 65
Mes reveries (Saxe), 67
Mifflin, Thomas, 59, 95–96, 101
Military conflict, as a basis of American nationality, 26–27, 30–36
Military Essay (Dalrymple), 65–66
Military Guide for Young Officers, The (Simes), 65–66
"Military History of the Royal Navy, 1763–1792" (Mahan), 227
Military Instructions for . . . Carrying on the Petit Guerre (Stevenson), 68
Military organization, in eighteenth century, 51
Military Policy of the United States (Upton), 225
Military significance, 217–19
Military thought, mainstream, 217
Militia, 52–53, 195
Monckton, Gen. Robert, 168, 173–74
Montcalm, General, 201
Montgomery, General, 9, 147
Moore, Gen. John, 210–12
Morgan, Gen. Daniel, 2, 23

Index

Morris, Robert, 114, 158–59, 161
Moulder, Capt. Joseph, 98
Muller, John, 57, 66
Murray, Gen. James, 183
Murray, Lord John, 172
Musket, 51; "Charleville," 56

Nagel, Paul C., 45
Napoleon, 218
National myths, 220–21
Nation-in-arms, 197–98, 223–24
Natural man, 198
Nautilus, 220
Nelson, George, 113
Newcastle-under-Lyme, dukes of, 176
New Jersey assembly, 119–21
New Jersey Line, 130; mutiny of, 135–37
New Jersey officers, petitions of, 119–21
New Model, 76–77
New Orleans, Battle of, 42–43
New System of Military Discipline (Cavan, earl of), 66
Nickerson, Hoffman, 225
Nicola, Col. Lewis, 63, 67
Norfolk Discipline (Windham and Townshend), 65–66
North, Lord, 167–68, 171, 179

Ochs, Adam von, 213–14
On War (Clausewitz), 223
Ordre mince, l', 64, 208
Ordre mixte, l', 65
Ordre profond, l', 65, 208
Oughton, Sir James Adolphus, 183
Overseas trade, disruption of: impact on American economy, 158, 160–63
Owen, Wilfred, 229

Paget, Col. Edward, 214
Palmer, Robert R., 221–23
Paret, Peter, 15, 198, 227
Parsons, Brig. Gen. Samuel, 67
Partisan, The (Jenny), 68
Paterson, Gen. John, 126
Peale, Charles Willson, 108
Pembroke, earl of, 182

Pennsylvania assembly, and articles of association, 84, 86–87
Pennsylvania Constitutional Convention (1776), 90
Pennsylvania Line, mutiny of, 134–35
Pennsylvania militia law, of 1777, 100–101, 107; of 1780, 112
Pennsylvania Provincial Conference (1776), 89
Petite guerre, 68, 198, 208
Petite guerre, La (Grandmaison), 68
Philadelphia, price fluctuations in, 155–59
Philadelphia militia: active duty experience, 91–102, 113; and articles of association, 76–77, 79–85; and internal revolution, 87–91; and radicalism in Philadelphia, 103–11; composition of, 78–79; creation of, 77–78; in Revolution, 76–77, 115–18
Philadelphia price-fixing committee, 105–6
Philadelphia town meetings: May 1776, 88; May 1779, 104–5; July 1779, 105–6
Phoenix Park, 193
Pickens, Andrew, 21
Pickering, Timothy, 67
Pierson, Gen. Richard, 175, 177, 180
Pitt, William, earl of Chatham, 9, 24, 167
Pitt, Gen. William Augustus, 175, 177–78, 180
Platoon, 51
Plessis, Mauduit du, 69
Pleydell, J. C., 66
Polybius, 218
Preston, Gen. George, 186–87
Pretender, the (Prince Charles), 3
Princeton, Battle of, 98
Principles of Military Movements (Dundas), 205
Privateering, 163–64
Provincial forces, 52
Pulaski, Casimir, 61–62

Quaker Meeting, 84

INDEX

Quartermaster Artificer Regiment, 63
Queen's Rangers, 192, 211–12

Ramsay, David, 31–32
Randolph, John, 41
Rawdon, Lord, 20
Reed, Joseph, 101, 109, 113–14
Regiment, 51; in British army, 54; in Continental army, 54, 61, 63
Regulations (Dundas), 205, 212
Regulations for the Exercise of Riflemen and Light Infantry, 212–13
Regulations for the Order and Discipline of the Troops of the United States, Part I (Steuben), 15, 70
Reid, John P., 11
Republic at war, American preconceptions about, 142–43; revision of, 145, 151
Richmond, duke of, 182
Roberdeau, Gen. Daniel, 92, 94, 105
Robson, Eric, 14
Rochambeau, comte de, 223
Rogers, Col. Robert, 4
Roosevelt, Theodore, 228
Rottenburg, Colonel de, 213
Royal United Service Institute, 217
Royster, Charles, 12, 143–44
Rush, Benjamin, 161

St. Clair, General, 9
Saint-Germain, comte de, 61
Saldern, Friedrich von, 214
Salter, Gen. John, 182–83
Sandford, Gen. Edward, 174
Sandwich, earl of, 173
Saxe, comte de, 4, 51, 67
Scharnhorst, Gerhard von, 208–9
Scott, Gen. John, 182
Seven Years' War, 4
Shelburne, earl of, 182
Shy, John, 19, 77, 195, 203, 227
Silesia, 3
Simcoe, Gen. John Graves, 192, 194, 212
Simes, Thomas, 65
Simpson, Samuel, 81
Sixtieth Regiment, 213
"'64, The" (Harvey), 65, 67

Skinner, Gen. William, 173
Skirmishing, 208–9
"Slow & Sure" (broadside), 112–13
Small Wars (Callwell), 221
Smith, Adam, 224
Smith, Paul, 19
Soldiers and Civilians (Cunliffe), 219
Sorell, Gen. William Alexander, 175, 178, 180
South, irregular warfare in the, 21–24
Spaulding, Oliver L., Jr., 225
Steele, Matthew Forney, 226
Steuben, Baron von, 15, 69–71, 203, 224
Stevenson, Roger, 68
Strategy, in American Revolution, 194–95
Stuart, Sir Charles, 192, 210
Sullivan, John, 120
Sumter, Thomas, 21
Supreme Executive Council, 103, 110
Surtees, Private, 214

Tactics, military, 64–65, 67–68, 205–15; in America, 198–204; mixed, 65; of the column, 65; of the line, 64, 203, 205–8
Tarleton, Banastre, 20, 203
Tate, Thad W., 130
Taylor, John, 39
Thompson, Sir Charles Hotham, 175, 178, 180
Tobacco, 162
Tocqueville, Alexis de, 216, 220, 229
Tolstoy, Leo, 219
Townshend, George Viscount, 65, 168, 183
Trapaud, Gen. Cyrus, 185–86
Treatise of Artillery (Muller), 57
Treatise of Military Discipline (Bland), 65–66
Trumbull, John, 37
Turpin de Crissé, comte, 67
Twenty-third Welch Fusiliers, 214

Upton, Emory, 224–26

Victorious, 158

Index

Vietnam War, parallels with the American Revolution, 13–15, 18–19
Voluntarism, as a basis of American nationality, 27–29
Volunteer Soldier in America (Logan), 225

Waldegrave, John Earl, 173–74
Walsh, Gen. Hunt, 185–86
Warfare (Spaulding, Nickerson, and Wright), 225
War of 1812, 41–43
War of the Austrian Succession, 3
War of the Bavarian Succession, 15
Warren, James, 128
Washington, George, 9, 60, 72, 200, 221; and bounty jumping, 131; and discontent in Continental army, 120, 133, 136; and military discipline, 138; and military tactics, 66–70, 203–4; and plundering, 131–32; and the organization of Continental army, 55–58, 61–63; and the Philadelphia militia, 92, 97–99, 101; as commander of Continental army, 53, 59, 71
Wayne, Gen. Anthony, 134
Weaponry, innovations in, 50–51
Weigley, Russell F., 225
Wellesley, Sir Arthur, 215
Wellington, duke of, 196–97, 199–200, 205
West Point, 62, 223
West, Samuel, 31
William, duke of Gloucester, 173
Williamson, Gen. George, 182
Wilson, James, 109
Windham, William, 65
Wolfe, Gen. James, 4, 65
Woodward, C. Vann, 218
Wright, John W., 225
Wurmb, Col. Ludwig von, 191

Yorke, Sir Joseph, 173
Yorktown, Battle of, 22
Young, William, 65

LIBRARY OF DAVIDSON COLLEGE

Books